# Fast Forward, Play, and Rewind

# Fast Forward, Play, and Rewind

## Michael Oberman

Backbeat
Books

*Guilford, Connecticut*

Backbeat Books
An imprint of The Rowman & Littlefield Publishing Group, Inc.
4501 Forbes Blvd., Ste. 200
Lanham, MD 20706
www.rowman.com

Distributed by NATIONAL BOOK NETWORK

British Library Cataloguing in Publication Information available

**Library of Congress Cataloging-in-Publication Data available**

ISBN 978-1-4930-5092-5 (paperback)
ISBN 978-1-4930-5093-2 (e-book)

♾️™ The paper used in this publication meets the minimum requirements of American National Standard for Information Sciences—Permanence of Paper for Printed Library Materials, ANSI/NISO Z39.48-1992.

*This book is for my brother, Ron*
*8/28/1943 to 11/21/2019*

# Contents

# PREFACE

As I finish writing this book, I am sad to say that my brother, Ron, passed away on November 21, 2019, after a ten-year struggle with fronto-temporal dementia.

Growing up, Ron was my big brother. He is three years and five months older than me, and I wish this book were a collaboration with him. That is what it started out to be. Ron wrote the weekly "Top Tunes" interview column in the *Evening Star* newspaper in Washington, D.C. (hereinafter "D.C."), from 1964 until February 1967. In February 1967, Ron left music journalism for a job at Mercury Records in Chicago. I took over the "Top Tunes" column (later renamed "Music Makers") when Ron left and continued writing the weekly column from February 1967 until March 1973.

Between us, we wrote approximately 450 interview columns (Ron 150 and me 300), interviewing a who's who of rock-and-roll stardom, with an occasional country, pop, jazz, or bluegrass artist thrown into the mix.

If not for Ron, I would not have entered the world of journalism and eventually the world of the music business. More about that later in this book.

Ron's career path took him from Mercury Records to Columbia Records to MCA Records. When he left Mercury, he was the national director of publicity. His career at Columbia took him from the marketing department to the A & R (artist and repertoire) department, where he became vice president. He left Columbia for a job at MCA as senior vice president of A & R and retired from MCA as executive vice president of A & R.

During Ron's time at those three labels, he played a major part in the careers of David Bowie, Bruce Springsteen, Warrant, the Bangles, Toad the Wet Sprocket, and too many others to name here.

When Ron left the music industry, he became a serious poker player. Like most other things in life, he did very well at the poker tables.

In 2009, Ron and I decided to write a book together. The working title at the time was "Backstage Pass." Ron was living in Los Angeles, and I was in Columbia, Maryland. Since there were more opportunities to find a literary agent in Los Angeles than in Columbia, Ron took on that task. Within a week, we had an agent. While the main idea for the book was to publish one hundred or more of our columns and write some remembrances of writing for a newspaper, meet and interview incredible musicians, and paint a picture of the music culture starting with the Beatles' first U.S. concert in D.C., the beginning of Ron's dementia brought the project to a halt.

Before he was diagnosed with his illness, Ron and I would send each other chapters we had written. I immediately noticed that Ron's writing had "no life" to it. Ron was planning a trip back to Maryland for our mother's ninetieth birthday, so I decided to wait to speak to him in person. When he came back to Maryland, I noticed a distinct change in his personality. I asked him what was going on. He told me he had been diagnosed with clinical depression. He also mentioned that he was separated from his wife. I suggested that we hold off writing the book until he felt up to the task. At that time, I had no idea that my brother had been misdiagnosed. Our mother also noticed the change in Ron's personality. I told her that Ron was going through some marital difficulties and that he would be okay.

When Ron returned to Los Angeles, I called our literary agent and told her we were putting the book project on hold. She wanted out of the project anyway because she felt that Ron had some mental problems. Shortly after that, the results of a PET scan showed that Ron had "frontal lobe atrophy" (the beginning of frontotemporal dementia).

Ron's diagnosis was devastating but explained his personality changes and his inability to write anything but simple sentences. Our dream of coauthoring a book was over. Additionally, I became primary caregiver for our mother and decided that authoring a book myself would be too difficult.

Things changed when our mother passed away. I began writing again. Caregiving for my mother had drained me, though I am glad I did it. One of the obstacles that we had to overcome back in 2009 was getting permission to use our music columns that had been published in the *Evening Star*, later renamed the *Washington Star*. The *Star* had been in business from 1852 until it closed in 1981. All editions of the newspaper had been preserved on microfilm and microfiche and were stored in the "Washingtonia" collection at the Martin Luther King Library in D.C.

I spent several days at the library making copies of all of our columns. The *Washington Post* now owned the copyright to all 129 years of the *Evening Star*. I found out that the *Post* was having all of the editions of the *Star* digitized. We were granted permission to use our columns in a book as long as we transcribed them and didn't just put out a book with photocopies of our columns.

I know that Ron would be happy if he knew that I had taken on this project. I only wish that he was part of it more than just in spirit.

Our interview columns were short form, usually 400 to 600 words. I consider them small time capsules of (to me) one of the most important eras in rock 'n' roll, spanning the Motown era and the British invasion and folk, psychedelic, and other styles of music that defined the times.

It wasn't easy for me to pick which of my 300-plus columns to include in this book. I chose a number of well-known artists, such as Joni Mitchell, David Bowie, the Doors, and James Brown. I also have included some one-hit wonders and a few lesser-known groups whose music still holds up today.

What is missing from the book are my brother's columns. Perhaps one day I'll write another book and include his columns. For now, to give you an idea of the range and importance of Ron's interviews, a chronological list of his columns will have to suffice:

**1964**

The Marketts
The Beatles
James Brown
The Four Seasons
The Beach Boys
Diane Renay
Elvis Presley
Betty Everett
Marvin Gaye
Terry Stafford
The Reflections
Peter and Gordon
Mary Wells
The Dave Clark Five
The Dixie Cups

Patty and the Emblems
Chuck Berry
Millie Small
The Kingston Trio
The Carltons
The Chartbusters
The Supremes
Roger Miller
Johnny Mathis
The Animals
Ronny and the Daytonas
The Beatles
The Four Tops
On Tour with the Beatles
The Beach Boys
The Delights

Gale Garnett
Martha and the Vandellas
The Mugwumps
J. Frank Wilson
The Impressions
Jay and the Americans
Sonny James
The Hullabaloos
The Shangri-Las
The Detergents
The Drifters Joe Tex

**1965**
The Righteous Brothers
The Hangmen
Shirley Ellis
Mary Wells
Gary Lewis and the Playboys
The Newbeats
Gerry and the Pacemakers
Little Anthony and the Imperials
Junior Walker
The Trade Winds
The Kingsmen
Bobby Goldsboro
Jewel Akens
Sylvie Vartan
The Reekers and the Nightcaps
Tony Clarke
The Beach Boys
Herman's Hermits
The Rolling Stones
Gerry and the Pacemakers
Sam the Sham and the Pharaohs
Ian and the Zodiacs
Herman's Hermits

Paul Anka
The Kinks
The Dave Clark Five
Roger Miller
Billy Stewart
The Newports
Wayne Fontana and the Mindbenders
James Brown
Sonny and Cher
The Royalettes
Patty Duke
The Beatles in Los Angeles
Smokey Robinson and the Miracles
The Supremes
The Four Tops
The Mad Lads
The Temptations
The Chartbusters
The Toys
The Walker Brothers
Fontella Bass
The Lovin' Spoonful
The Rolling Stones
Marvin Gaye
Ramsey Lewis Trio
Wilson Pickett
The Shangri-Las
Jay and the Americans

**1966**
The Yardbirds
Stevie Wonder
The Hangmen
The Marvelettes
Otis Redding
Ronnie Dove

Motown
S. Sgt. Barry Sadler
Deon Jackson
The Isley Brothers
Barbara Mason
Dino, Desi and Billy
The Four Seasons
The Epsilons
Dionne Warwick
Peter and Gordon
Dallas Frazier
The Outsiders
Chad and Jeremy
Nina Simone
Percy Sledge
Shorty Long
The Swinging Medallions
Robert Parker
The Standells
Walter Jackson and Fangette Enzel
The Byrds
Tommy James and the Shondells
The Mothers of Invention
Roscoe Robinson
Bobby Hebb
The Cyrkle
The Beatles

Darrell Banks
Brian Hyland
The Capitols
The Happenings
The Yardbirds
The Vontastics
Jimmy Ruffin
Mitch Ryder and the Detroit Wheels
The Mamas and Papas
Petula Clark
The Righteous Brothers
The Elgins
The New Vaudeville Band
The Temptations
The Spellbinders
Donovan
The Young Rascals
The Royal Guardsmen
Spyder Turner

**1967**
The Blues Magoos
Tommy Hunt
Young-Holt Trio
The Left Banke
Aaron Neville
Joe Cuba

## -30-

-30- has been traditionally used by journalists in North America to indicate the end of a story. Here, I am just using it to signify the end of my brother's journalism career. When that career ended, Ron went on to become an important figure in the music industry. I am thankful that I had the opportunity to continue the "Top Tunes" column and to witness Ron's many accomplishments in his post-journalism career.

Ron Oberman Interviewing Mama Cass of the Mamas and Papa

PHOTO BY MIKE KLAVANS

# Acknowledgments

ACKNOWLEDGMENTS AND SINCERE THANKS TO MARIJANE MONCK, PATrick Clancy, Brian Clancy, Mike Klavans, Bill Perry, Richard Harrington, Jeff Krulick, Gene Wishnia, Geoffrey Edwards, my former colleagues at the *Evening Star*, the musicians who allowed me to interview them, A&R personnel at record companies who actually listened, music journalists around the world, recording engineers and producers, managers, agents, publicists, disc jockeys, and anyone and everyone who has ever created music or brought that music to all of us.

# Introduction: In the Beginning

IN THE BEGINNING, THERE WAS THE PITCH PIPE. I WAS SIX YEARS OLD when my father was transferred from the National Brewing Company's Baltimore office to D.C., where he would take over as branch manager. We moved to Silver Spring, Maryland (a suburb of D.C.). My father kept his position as baritone in a choir in Baltimore. For my mother, my brother, and me, that meant a forty-five-minute drive from our new home to the synagogue in Baltimore where my father sang. The first few minutes of the drive were usually okay, but then my father would take his pitch pipe out of his pocket and blow into it so he could sing the musical scales at the correct pitch. Ouch! My brother Ron and I would look at each other, grimace, and hope the (what to us was) musical torture would be over quickly.

The National Brewing Company's main beer was National Bohemian, a beer that was also known as Natty Boh. The company's mascot, the one-eyed, handlebar-mustachioed Mr. Boh, has been a recognizable icon since his introduction in 1936. "Oh boy, what a beer!" was Natty Boh's slogan along with "Brewed on the Shores of the Chesapeake Bay."

One of the major benefits of my father's job was season tickets to the Washington Senators baseball team and the Washington Redskins football team. National Bohemian sponsored both teams. When we would go to the Senators' games, we knew we were getting close to Griffith Stadium when we smelled the aroma of bread baking, wafting from the nearby Wonder Bread factory.

In 1955, my father surprised the family with the announcement, "We're going to the World Series!" Ron and I were joyous. We already knew that the World Series would pit the New York Yankees (Mickey Mantle, Yogi Berra, Whitey Ford, etc.) against the Brooklyn Dodgers (Duke Snider, Roy Campanella, Don Newcombe, etc.). My father had been named "Branch Manager of the Year" by the brewery, and the reward was tickets to three

World Series games, four nights in a New York City hotel, and a round-trip flight from Baltimore to New York on National Bohemian's private plane.

The excitement was too much. I couldn't sleep that night thinking about telling my friends at school the good news. This upcoming trip to New York would be my first time flying and my first time in New York. Our tickets were for games 2, 3, and 4, which ensured that we would see three games in two stadiums. Game 2 was at Yankee Stadium, and games 3 and 4 were at Ebbets Field in Brooklyn.

When we arrived in New York, the first game had already been played and won by the Yankees. Walking into Yankee Stadium for game 2 was the height of excitement in my life up to that point, with more than 60,000 frenzied fans of both teams excited over this local/national rivalry.

We had lower-tier box seats on the third-base line between home plate and third base. After the usher showed us to our seats and we settled in, my mother tapped me on the shoulder and whispered to me, "Do you know who that is sitting in front of you and Ron?" I had no idea. She said, "That's Humphrey Bogart and Lauren Bacall. Get their autographs."

Ron and I stood up and walked down the aisle one row. Humphrey Bogart turned to us and smiled. We handed him our ticket stubs and the pencil we had with us to fill out our scorecards. Bogart and Bacall obliged us, and each of them signed our tickets. The home team Yankees won that game and were up over Brooklyn two games to none.

The next two games were in Brooklyn and won by the Brooklyn Dodgers. The series was tied, and we were going home the next day. That night, we went to dinner at Jack Dempsey's Broadway Restaurant. (Known popularly as Jack Dempsey's, this restaurant was located in the Brill Building on Broadway between 49th and 50th streets in Manhattan, New York. Owned by world heavyweight boxing champion Jack Dempsey, it was considered by many to be an American institution.) I didn't realize at that time (there was no reason for me to realize) the place in music history the Brill Building would garner. Hundreds of hit songs written there, with offices of music publishers, songwriters, and producers occupying the building above Jack Dempsey's Broadway Restaurant.

I was a young practical joker. At dinner that night, I reached into my pocket and pulled out what looked like a pack of Wrigley's Spearmint gum. A man at the next table had just finished his dinner, saw me with the gum, and asked if he could have a piece. I handed him the pack, and when he pulled the gum out of the package, "SNAP," on his thumb, like a mouse-trap—totally harmless, but it took him by surprise. "You gotta do that to Jack," he said with a heavy New York accent. "Jack is a good friend of mine."

Well, Jack was Jack Dempsey. The guy I had played the trick on got up and brought Jack Dempsey over to the table. "Mr. Dempsey," I said, "would you like a piece of gum?" I handed him the pack, and "SNAP," on his thumb. Dempsey laughed. He chatted with our parents for a minute. The restaurant had a photographer on staff, and Jack called him over. Jack took a seat by the restaurant's front window and asked Ron and I each to sit on one of his knees. A photo was taken, and the finished print was signed by Dempsey and handed to us before we left the restaurant. I guess there was a darkroom somewhere near the kitchen.

Ron and Michael Oberman in 1955 on the Knees of Former Heavyweight Boxing Champion Jack Dempsey
OBERMAN FAMILY ARCHIVES

There were so many benefits of having a father who worked at the National Brewing Company. In 1956, I decided that for my third-grade show-and-tell presentation, I would show the ingredients that went into brewing beer and tell how beer was brewed. My father obliged and brought home hops, malt, and other ingredients and helped me summarize the brewing process. I think my teacher was somewhat aghast when I started my presentation by saying, "I'm going to explain how to make beer" and I began laying out the ingredients on her desk at the front of the classroom. The presentation went well, and I can only hope that decades later some of my classmates might have become "home brewers" because of my show-and-tell.

Minnesota Fats Shooting Pool With Marty Oberman (Author's Father)
OBERMAN FAMILY ARCHIVES

Later in 1956, there was a musical awakening in our house. My father, Marty, brought home the first Elvis Presley album on RCA Records. Rock 'n' roll had entered my young body and soul and changed my life forever. Elvis was the beginning, but that same year, there were so many new sounds, and I gravitated to them more than riding my bike or playing touch football in the backyard. While my parents were listening to Pat Boone, Gogi Grant, and Doris Day, I was listening to "Blue Suede Shoes" by Carl Perkins, "Honky Tonk" by Bill Doggett, "Be-Bop-A-Lula" by Gene Vincent, "Blueberry Hill" by Fats Domino, and "Long Tall Sally" by Little Richard. While my father opened the door a crack with Elvis, it was my older brother, Ron, who opened the door all the way by building a transistor radio and letting me listen to it.

Ron was thirteen, and I was nine. Record stores had listening stations with turntables and earphones where we would go to listen to new releases by the artists we were listening to on the radio. I was lucky my brother would let me tag along. Ron was in junior high, and I was in elementary school. At that time, our parents gave each of us a weekly allowance: Ron fifty cents and me twenty-five cents. If we pooled our money, we could buy two 45-rpm singles. Usually, we didn't pool our money, and Ron would buy the record of his choice.

Music and sports stayed a constant in our lives. By the time I entered junior high, Ron was in high school and became interested in journalism. He merged his interest and knowledge of sports and his newfound interest in writing and became sports editor of his high school newspaper. Ron was also into hot rods. He bought his first car in high school, a 1956 Chevy convertible. The first thing he did with the car was have it painted midnight (metallic) blue. The second thing he did was get some hot rod friends together and further customize his car by "lowering" it and taking the horizontal chrome bars out of the grill, leaving the vertical bars in and giving the car a more menacing look.

Even though Ron and his friends were into customized cars, I leaned toward wanting a sports car, though I was a few years away from getting my driver's license. Ron's hot rod days seemed to end when he was eighteen. His best friend, Carl Bernstein, helped Ron get a part-time job as a copyboy at the *Evening Star* newspaper in D.C. Carl was already working at the paper.

I'm going to digress here and rewind a year or two to muse about "Carl Bernstein and the Halloween Raid." Seeing Carl as a "talking head" on CNN brings back memories of the night six teenagers were arrested in Silver Spring (two of them being Carl and yours truly, plus my brother Ron and a friend named Louie Singer; the other two will remain unnamed). I was only thirteen, Ron and Carl were seventeen, and Louie was sixteen (much more about Louie later).

Ron and I lived with our parents on Admiralty Drive. Carl lived (I think) on Harvey Road. Louie lived somewhere in Silver Spring. Ron and Carl were best friends. They played poker together and hung out at the Silver Spring Pool Hall and a small convenience store on Eastern Avenue called Mousie's (Mousie's draw was its pinball machines).

Anyway, on to the Halloween night raid. I still am ashamed of what we did but not totally unhappy about it. One street over from Admiralty Drive was Saxony Road. We had friends on Saxony: the Greenstones and the Fleishmans. We also had enemies: elderly Mrs. Nehus and her even more elderly mother. Mother and daughter hated Jews (probably hated others too). When Ron and I would ride our bikes or walk by the Nehuses' house, mother and daughter would come out their front door and call us "dirty kykes" or "g-d damned Jews" and sometimes squirt us with their front-yard hose.

Carl and Louie were also harassed by both women when they walked or rode with us. So, that fateful Halloween night when I was thirteen years old, six of us got together and decided we had had enough of the Nehuses' anti-Semitism. Three of us got in one car and pulled up in front of the Nehuses' house with headlights turned off. The other three drove two blocks over to Dameron Drive and left their car, went through some backyards, and threw small stones on the metal roof of the Nehuses' back porch to draw the two women out their back door. When the Nehuses went out back, the pebble throwers yelled, signaling the three who were in the car in front of the house,. and those three threw rocks (not pebbles), smashing all the windows in the front of the house. Then both parties got into their cars and sped off down Forest Glen Road.

I didn't realize that the driver of the car I was in had covered his front and rear license plates with hand towels. Before we made it six blocks, we were pulled over by Montgomery County police for obscuring the license plates. Police had already been called by the Nehuses, so the police put it all together and realized we were the vandals. After being taken to the Silver Spring police station and lectured by Detective Pey, we were released to our parents. The police were well aware of the Nehuses' bigotry. Our parents had to pay for the damage to the windows, and none of us ended up in court.

Carl, my brother, and I all went on to write for newspapers, with Carl becoming ultra-famous for his and Bob Woodward's Watergate coverage. Carl was later portrayed by Dustin Hoffman in the film *All the President's Men* and Jack Nicholson in *Heartburn*, Nora Ephron's book turned into a movie about her marriage to and divorce from Carl.

Earlier I said there would be more about Louie Singer. Louie was a total goof-off. He worked at his uncle's liquor store, Circle Liquors, on Pennsylvania Avenue in D.C. Finally, his uncle became fed up with Louie and fired him. A few weeks later, Louie bought an Afro wig, painted his hands and face black, and held up an employee of the liquor store as he was making a night deposit of that day's cash receipts. Wielding a .38-caliber revolver, Louie was tackled by a passerby and arrested.

Fast-forward a year. I was in Georgetown (a neighborhood of D.C.) and had witnessed a purse snatching. The police asked if I would come to the Volta Street police station and look at mug shots. The purse snatcher happened to be African American, and the mug shots were in two different books, one labeled "white males" and the other labeled "colored males." The police handed me the colored male book. Leafing through it, there was a photo of Louie Singer in blackface and Afro wig. I stuttered, "Hey, that's Louie Singer. He's a white guy." At first, the police didn't believe me. Then laughter rang out through the mug shot room. Louie was eventually killed when he wrapped his speeding car around a telephone pole.

Rewinding to 1963, a big year for me: getting my driver's license and getting my first real part-time job as a copyboy at the *Evening Star* newspaper in D.C.

I was a sophomore at Northwood High School in Silver Spring when I turned 16. I wasn't happy about going to Northwood. When new school boundary lines were drawn after the Washington Beltway was built, only seven of my classmates from junior high school would be going to Northwood. Almost everyone else from Montgomery Hills Junior High would be going to Montgomery Blair High School. Blair was where most of my friends were going. Blair is where my brother went.

It wasn't that Northwood was a bad school, it was just that I felt that Blair was a better school academically, in sports, and in terms of my friends going there. There were some positive things about Northwood, in particular, two of my teachers. My tenth-grade English teacher, Mr. Teunis, graduated from Harvard and was what I would call at the time kind of a beatnik. He had a full beard, which was unusual for a teacher in those days, and occasionally he was barefoot in class. Instead of the normal tenth-grade English class curriculum, Mr. Teunis turned things topsy-turvy when he told us at the beginning of the school year that we were going to study mainly William Shakespeare's play *Richard III*. What great memories I have of memorizing stanzas from the play and at the end of the school year acting the entire play out in costume.

The other teacher who influenced me greatly was my art teacher, Frances Davila. She taught me in the eleventh and twelfth grades, and she seemed like the oldest teacher I'd ever had (she died at age 100 in 2007). She was quirky in a good way. She once was married to the president of Chile. She was a very wise woman with a good sense of humor and loved music. We had a record player in the classroom, and she allowed us to bring into class whatever albums we'd like to play while we were doing the artwork that she taught us so well. In my senior year, in her class was a girl named Anna-Lou Lebovitz. I don't think she was at Northwood very long, but I remember her well. If I fast-forward now to 1970, she started her career as a staff photographer, working for *Rolling Stone* magazine. She was better known then, and is still better known, as Annie Leibovitz.

In 1963, my brother, Ron, was going to journalism school at the University of Maryland and had moved from copyboy status at the *Star* to become a dictationist. You have to understand that the bottom layer of the totem pole at a newspaper, at least in the newsroom, is copyboy. The next step up is dictationist. Dictationists sat at a long desk with headphones on and a typewriter in front of them, and when a reporter called in a story, they typed the story and, when finished, yelled "Copy," and a copyboy would scurry over, grab the story, and take it to the appropriate editor.

I asked Ron if he could get me a job as a copyboy. He did. During the school year, I would work every Saturday as a copyboy. Over the summer school break, I would work full-time, with the exception of two weeks when I would go to the beach. A copyboy's day could start at 6 a.m., 9 a.m., 10 a.m., 1 p.m., or 2 p.m.; in the worst-case scenario, you could pull the 6 p.m. to 2 a.m. shift. The exception was that if you were under eighteen years of age in the District of Columbia, you couldn't work past 10 p.m. The first two years as a copyboy, I never had to work past 10 p.m.

It was really, really a cool job for a sixteen-year-old. I was in the newsroom. The pace could be frenetic with small periods of calm. You were never bored for long. One day you might be working in the wire room. Another day you could be working on the copy desk. Another day you could be driving to the White House, the U.S. Capitol, or elsewhere to pick up press releases or a story written by a White House correspondent. Copyboys liked to get out of the building and drive anywhere they were sent. The newspaper allowed us to charge cab fare for driving to any of those places and then back to the *Star*. D.C. was split into cab zones, and the newspaper office was in a part of town where you knew that wherever you were driving, you would cross several zones and be able to put in an expense report for anywhere from $5 to $15. That was great because our salary was $1.65 an hour. A short drive got us out of the building and could bring us $10 or more.

On Friday, November 22, 1963, I was in my high school metal shop class when an announcement came over the public address system that President Kennedy had been shot. There was utter silence in that classroom except for some sobbing. We didn't know the president had been killed, only that he had been shot. I think that if the school could have, they would have let everyone go home, but school buses were on schedules, parents weren't expecting children home, and so on. At the end of the day, I went home. When John Kennedy was elected, I did a pencil sketch of him that hung in the family recreation room. I took it off the wall and back upstairs to a television in our den. By that time, my father had come home from work, and my parents, my brother, and I were glued to the television news. I think that up to that point in my life, I had never experienced the sadness that I experienced when we learned that the president was dead.

The next day was a Saturday, and I had to be at the newspaper. Chaotic does not describe the scene in the newsroom on that Saturday. It was orderly chaos mixed with total sadness and a lot of overtime hours put in. Vice President Lyndon Johnson was sworn in as president on the plane ride back from Dallas, where Kennedy had been assassinated. Johnson's official inauguration was in January 1965. The day of his inaugural parade is another day that I'll never forget. I was asked to drive two or three reporters on the parade route (actually, in the parade) with a pass on my windshield allowing me to be there. As a copyboy, I had been to the White House many times, and it was always interesting to see the tourists staring at me and my little Alfa Romeo convertible riding through the White House gates. The day of the parade was totally different. I knew I was going to be driving reporters, so I left my two-seater sports car at home and took my mother's car into work. That car held four or five people. There were more than 5,400 police and soldiers guarding President Johnson during his inauguration and the parade. There I was, only seventeen years old and still grieving over the loss of President Kennedy, but now I was driving in the new president's inaugural parade.

On April 6, 1965, I turned eighteen. That meant several things: I would be graduating from high school and preparing to go to the University of Maryland, I could work past 10 p.m. at the newspaper, and, saving the best for last, I could legally drink beer and wine in D.C. If you lived in Maryland (as I did) or Northern Virginia, simply driving across the district line into D.C. meant that you no longer had to be twenty-one to drink or get into establishments that required you to be of drinking age to enter. Many of those establishments had live music.

The D.C. music scene was thriving. My favorite band was the British Walkers, and my favorite club was the Roundtable in Georgetown (where the British Walkers was the de facto house band). My brother had started writing the weekly "Top Tunes" column in the *Evening Star* newspaper in 1964. He turned me on to the British Walkers.

Rewinding to 1964 for a moment. The Beatles came to town on February 11, 1964, to play at the old Washington Coliseum, their first U.S. show ever. I was at that debut, thanks to my brother getting me tickets. The same time as the Beatles concert, Washington's top forty AM radio stations were still blaring such hits as Lesley Gore's "You Don't Own Me" on WEAM, Diane Renay's "Navy Blue" on WEEL, Andy Williams's "A Fool Never Learns" on WPGC, the Rip Chords' "Hey Little Cobra" on WWDC, and Dionne Warwick's "Anyone Who Had a Heart" on WINX.

At the same time, "She Loves You" and "I Want to Hold Your Hand" had already begun making inroads into radio stations throughout the metropolitan area. Before that first Beatles concert, the Fab Four held a press conference, sitting inside of a boxing ring in the Washington Coliseum.

My brother had a several-minute conversation with John Lennon. He asked him how he and Paul McCartney wrote the group's songs. "Generally, we like off-tempo, happy songs," he said, little anticipating the sophistication and universal appeal of so many of their more mature later efforts. "We just sit down, bang them out, and hum the tunes."

Ron also asked George Harrison, "Do you currently have a girlfriend?" His reply? "Yes, love, you."

Later in 1964, prior to the Beatles concert at the Baltimore Civic Center on September 13, Ron waited for an hour outside their rooms at the Holiday Inn with Carroll James, the late WWDC disc jockey who was the first to play the Beatles' music in Washington. Eventually, all four came out and schmoozed with them and posed for pictures for several minutes.

Getting back to 1965 and drinking beer and seeing a lot of great bands in D.C., I often thought about how lucky my brother was, writing the weekly music interview column and meeting a lot of beautiful members of the opposite sex. Yes, interviewing acts like the Beatles, the Dave Clark Five, and the Mamas and the Papas had the effect of drawing young women to my brother. Some became girlfriends, while others just wanted to hang out with Ron on the off chance that he would get them into a concert or take them backstage to meet an act.

My mind wandered to my someday writing the "Top Tunes" column and getting the perks that came with the territory. In 1967, my dreams turned into reality. My brother was offered a job as assistant director of publicity at Mercury Records in Chicago. Ron had been in contact with many record companies when he wrote his column. It was usually the publicity department of those companies that arranged for Ron to have access to their artists. Now, Ron was getting the opportunity to work for a major record company. He accepted the job.

I would miss my brother, but I also realized I needed to act quickly and try to grab the golden ticket. The day after Ron gave his notice to the *Evening Star*, I went to the editor of the "Teen" section of the paper, Fifi Gorska, and said, "I want to write the column." Fifi reminded me that I was only nineteen and still in college. I reminded her that my brother was only twenty and still in college when he began writing the "Top Tunes" column.

Fifi said, "Mike, write three columns and I'll make a decision." I thanked her and went to my brother and said, "Help!" Ron responded, "It will be a piece of cake for you. Start at the Howard Theater. Everyone there already knows you."

Ron was right. I had gone with him to the Howard to see James Brown, Martha Reeves & the Vandellas, Marvin Gaye, Mary Wells, the Supremes, Stevie Wonder, and many other R & B artists. Often, I would go to their dressing rooms with Ron when Ron would interview the groups.

I listened to my brother, conducted three interviews at the Howard, handed them in to Fifi, and waited. A week later, she said, "Good job. The column is yours."

# THE *EVENING STAR* INTERVIEWS

# Musings . . . Phi Zappa Krappa

"Phi Zappa Krappa and the University of Maryland." It seems like such a long time ago, and it was. I was a sophomore (1967) at the University of Maryland. I was studying journalism and was also on the concert committee on the Student Union Board. One of the concerts we booked was Frank Zappa. Now, a little of the backstory. None of the toilet stalls in the men's rooms at the Student Union had doors on them. There were no dressing rooms for acts that played the Student Union Ballroom, so the artists had to use the public restrooms. Picture the night of the concert: much excitement, lights in the ballroom dimmed, and Zappa walks to the center of the stage (spotlight on him) and says, "I just took a crap in front of a bunch of students. The first time I've ever sat on a toilet in a public bathroom and there was no door on the stall. Thanks a lot University of Maryland!" Several months after that, the "Phi Zappa Krappa" poster and T-shirts were in stores.

When the Mothers of Invention's first album, *Freak Out!*, was released in 1966, my brother, Ron, received a call from Sol Handwerger. Sol was an "old-school" record company publicist. He worked for MGM Records, and the Mothers were signed to Verve (a subsidiary of MGM). For several weeks, Ron had received an envelope in the mail from Verve Records. Each envelope contained one piece of a jigsaw puzzle. When the final envelope arrived, all of the pieces came together as the cover of *Freak Out!* Now, Sol was calling to say the real album was on its way. He hoped Ron would interview the group, and the group would be in D.C. to do some promotion in a couple of weeks. Sol was hoping that Ron would show them around town.

*Freak Out!* was released on June 27, 1966, on Verve Records. Often cited as one of rock music's first concept albums, the album is a satirical expression of Frank Zappa's perception of American pop culture and the nascent freak scene of Los Angeles. It was also one of the earliest double albums in rock music and the first two-record debut album.

The album was produced by Tom Wilson, who signed the Mothers, formerly a bar band called the Soul Giants. Zappa said many years later that Wilson signed the group to a record deal under the impression that they were a white blues band. The album featured Zappa on vocals and guitar, along with lead vocalist/tambourine player Ray Collins, bass player/vocalist Roy Estrada, drummer/vocalist Jimmy Carl Black, and guitar player Elliot Ingber (later of Captain Beefheart's Magic Band, performing there under the pseudonym "Winged Eel Fingerling").

Ron took Sol up on the invitation. That led to Ron interviewing Zappa for his column that appeared in the *Evening Star* on July 16, 1966. In that interview, Zappa said the main problem with youth on the West Coast was drugs. "I don't use any and I've never encouraged it," Zappa said. "Anyone who takes acid [LSD] is taking his mind in his own hands.

"The same state of psychedelic happiness can be induced through dancing, listening to music, holding your breath and spinning around, and any number of the old, easy to perform and 100 percent legal means—all of which I endorse."

The evening of the interview, Ron took the Mothers of Invention to Georgetown to "check out the scene" and drop into the Roundtable nightclub. I don't know if the British Walkers were playing at the club that night. I hope they were. One of the best bands in D.C., the British Walkers featured guitar legend Roy Buchanan for a time. Roy's guitar prowess drew many musicians to his gigs, where all they could do was sit in awe. Rumor has it that the Rolling Stones asked Roy to join the band after the death of Brian Jones.

After their night in Georgetown, I asked Ron how it went. "The interview was great," Ron said. "Our jaunt to Georgetown wasn't so good. Seems like not even the hippies in Georgetown could make heads or tails out of the Mothers. We weren't really welcomed there."

In 1999, *Freak Out!* was honored with the Grammy Hall of Fame Award, and in 2003, *Rolling Stone* ranked it among the "500 Greatest Albums of All Time." In 2006, the MOFO Project/Object, an audio documentary on the making of the album, was released in honor of its fortieth anniversary.

# 1967

THERE WERE THREE DIFFERENT WAYS THAT I COULD ACCOMPLISH WRITING a weekly interview column. The first was to sit down with the artist or group I was interviewing—in a dressing room, at a hotel, at a press conference, or wherever the act felt most comfortable. Often, the interviews were done at venues like the Howard Theater, the Cellar Door nightclub, or local concert halls like the Alexandria Roller Rink. Occasionally, when an act was playing in town for a few days, the interview would take place at my home. Face-to-face interviews were always what I aimed for.

The second way was a phone interview. Often, concert promoters wanted an act they were presenting in concert to do an interview with me before the act came to the D.C. area. Preconcert publicity saved promoters advertising dollars. These were the days before the concert industry was monopolized by companies like Live Nation. I had a very good rapport with a number of independent concert promoters like Durwood Settles (the Doors at the Washington Hilton Ballroom, Cream at the Baltimore Civic Center) and Mike Schreibman (the Who at Georgetown University, Led Zeppelin and the Who at Merriweather Post Pavilion). While I always liked to help out promoters like Durwood and Mike, I had a way of giving them preconcert publicity and interviewing the acts the night of their performances. The last few paragraphs of my column were subtitled "Notes and Halfnotes" and talked about upcoming concerts in the area. That gave the promoters some free publicity and kept open the opportunity to interview the acts in person.

The third (and my least favorite) way to get an interview was from press kits that record companies sent out. In a pinch, I could pull quotes from an artist's bio or other promotional material contained in a press kit.

For the purposes of this book, I am omitting the "Notes and Halfnotes" portion of my columns. It's probably of little interest to most readers that DJ

Jack will be bringing Jay and the Techniques to T. C. Williams High School on January 28, 1968.

I tried to choose certain interviews and exclude others for this book for a variety of reasons. Those reasons probably only make sense to me, so I'll leave it at that.

My interviews were "short form," ranging from 400 to 700 words with few exceptions. They are a time capsule of the years 1967 to 1973. Since I also managed artists, worked for record companies, and had and have a life outside of music, this book fast-forwards and rewinds to my life before and after writing my column. The "play" part of this book is my columns. Each one will be a fast read.

# Freddie Scott

## *February 18, 1967*

With such friends as Sammy Davis Junior, Lou Rawls, Gene Chandler, and James Brown, why should Freddie Scott choose to sing about loneliness?

Whatever the reason, there's no doubt that Freddie has come up with what probably is the biggest hit of his career, "Are You Lonely for Me?"

Asked why he had not had a hit since his first smash, "Hey Girl," four years ago, the singer, who recently appeared at the Howard Theatre, replied, "There was a difference of opinion between me and the record company and I left the company with no hard feelings." Then, Freddie said he worked with another record company but was not successful until he joined his present label, Shout.

Freddie recently sang on a stage show with the Monkees and he was quick to point out what he says is the truth about the talents of the foursome. The rumor that the Monkees can't sing or play their instruments isn't true, he said. The boys are talented musicians and great guys.

It doesn't matter to Freddie what type of crowd he sings for, as long as he's well-received. "English people are beautiful," he said. "They appreciate an artist for what he does and they don't follow trends. They have respect for everyone." He believes his type of music, rhythm and blues, will last forever. He figures that as long as there is music people will ask for soul, and there will always be a legitimate rhythm and blues singer to supply it.

The sudden rise of Latin American rhythm and blues, with such artists as Joe Cuba, Hector Rivera, and Jimmy Castor, excites Freddie. As he puts it, the public is no longer one-sided. There's now room for everyone. Washington, D.C., and Memphis, Tennessee, are two of his favorite cities, although

Freddy attributes much of the success of "Are You Lonely for Me" to the city of Charlotte, North Carolina. It was there that the record broke big, thanks to the help of a female disc jockey, Chatty Hattie.

Freddy was born in Providence, Rhode Island, and now lives in New York City. It was in Augusta, Georgia, where Freddy lived most of his life, that he met and worked with James Brown in various talent shows. Freddy hopes there won't be another long break between hit records. Whether or not there is, he nevertheless plans to tape a future *Ed Sullivan Show* and put together a lively nightclub act.

# Gene Chandler

## *March 4, 1967*

UNLIKE MOST SINGERS WHO MUST WORK HARD TO ACHIEVE SUCCESS, GENE Chandler had it comparatively easy.

The singer, who recently appeared at the Howard Theatre, explained how his big break came about.

"I'd been singing with a group of guys at clubs and parties in the Chicago area, but I never had any desire to record or go solo," he said. "This lady came to us with some songs, and within a matter of months she had us recording.

"A production company leased our first record, 'Nightowl.' Another company had publishing rights to our songs. This company, Vee Jay, decided to record one of our songs."

Vee Jay decided that the song, "The Duke of Earl," should be recorded by a solo artist. After thinking it over, Gene broke with his group and made the record. His decision was wise, for the "Duke of Earl" became his first hit.

Although he's away from his home in Chicago most of the year, Gene doesn't mind traveling. He says that as long as the money is right and the audiences are appreciative he is willing to do road shows.

When asked what type of crowd he prefers singing for, Gene replied: "I can adapt myself to any type of crowd, adults in a club or kids at a concert. But if I appeared in a whole lot of clubs, I'd probably get tired of it."

Gene said that his type of music, rhythm-and-blues, will continue forever.

"Every now and then, the charts get flooded with British music, but rhythm-and-blues always makes its way back to the top of the charts," he added.

Although he doesn't particularly care for the British music scene, Gene admits that the Beatles have influenced American music quite a bit.

"Any spark to the industry means a lot," he said. "The Beatles and other English groups brought a lot of people back into the record shops. And besides being just a general spark to the industry, the Beatles have produced some standards like 'Michelle' and 'Yesterday.'"

Twenty-six-year-old Chandler has had many hits. Currently under contract to two labels, his last hit was "I Fooled You This Time," on Chess, and his new release is "The Girl Don't Care," on Brunswick.

Explaining why he is on two labels, Gene said that his most recent contract is with Brunswick, but under his old contract with Chess he's required to record a few more songs.

If he ever gets tired of singing, Gene will always have something to fall back on. Not only does he own a publishing company and real estate in Chicago, but he also recently opened his own nightclub, the Algiers Lounge, in the same city.

# The Five Americans

## *March 11, 1967*

THE DAYS OF PEANUT BUTTER AND JELLY SANDWICHES ARE OVER FOR THE Five Americans.

When the boys moved to Dallas, looking for rock 'n' roll rainbows, they were likely candidates for the President's poverty program. Deep in financial trouble, all five crowded into a tiny apartment and tried desperately to make ends meet.

They had already signed a contract with Abnak record company. When John Abdnor Jr., son of the owner of the company, came to their apartment to talk business, he discovered the mess they were in.

The first thing John Jr. did was move the group into a decent apartment and see that they had enough money to take them off their diet of peanut butter and jelly sandwiches.

It's been a few years since the Five Americans were just another group trying to make it big and starving in the meantime.

Now they have three hits under their belts. Their latest is "Western Union Man," which was preceded by "Evol Not Love" and their first smash, "I See the Light."

Norman Ezell, rhythm guitar player for the group, explained during a telephone interview from Dallas how they came up with "Western Union Man."

"Mike Raybon, our lead guitar player, was just fooling around with his guitar when he came up with a unique sound," Norman said. "It sort of reminded us of a telegraph key. That's when we decided to write 'Western Union Man.'"

Besides Norman and Mike, who are twenty-three, the group consists of John Durill, organist, twenty-two; bass player Jim Grant, twenty-one; and drummer Jimmy Wright, nineteen. All the boys except Jimmy, who is still in high school, met while attending Southeastern State College in Oklahoma.

John, Mike, and Norman do all the writing for the group. When asked what it takes to have a hit record, John replied, "The main ingredient for a hit record is a love for the art of pop music. Just like anyone who aspires to be successful, you have to love what you're doing.

"Another thing is that we never argue," he added. "You can't expect to put out hit records if the guys in the group don't get along. We are the same guys who came out of Oklahoma and will always be the same."

The Five Americans have already played concert dates with Herman's Hermits and other big-name acts. They hope to do more of the same in the future. To ensure bookings on the East Coast, they recently signed with Paramount Artists of Washington, D.C., who will handle their bookings in the East.

# Keith

## *March 18, 1967*

IT WOULD BE A SAD DAY FOR THE WORLD OF POP MUSIC IF JAMES BARRY Keefer, better known as just plain "Keith," had decided to carry out his plans to become a commercial art teacher.

At one time, Philadelphia born Keith was a serious student of commercial art at the Kutztown (PA) State Teacher's College. He had always been interested in music, and suddenly chose to give up his pursuit of an art education to try his hand at singing and songwriting.

His choice was a good one, for the first two songs he wrote and recorded became hits. The first of his two hits was "Ain't Gonna Lie," which was followed recently by the even more successful "98.6." After "98.6," Keith decided he wanted to change his style.

"After all, you can't go on with the same shuffle all your life, even if it is an individual style," he said.

His latest release, "Tell Me to My Face," a likely candidate for the top of the charts, shows a definite change in style. Written by the team of Nash, Clarke, and Hicks, of the Hollies, the song has an up-tempo, relentless beat and Eastern flavor, unlike Keith's previous two records, which were soft and gentle.

Until recently, twenty-year-old Keith, whose records bear the Mercury label, was a loner. While he was on the road, he would travel with and pay the expenses for one or two of his close friends.

Then, in January of this year, while on a cross-country tour, he came upon a new group, the Wild Kingdom, whose sound fascinated him. He immediately signed the boys as his backing group.

The Wild Kingdom consists of Ray Witham, twenty-one, electric bass; Mike Johnstowne, nineteen, lead guitar; Steve Swenson, nineteen, drums; and Tom Moore, nineteen, rhythm guitar. Besides singing with the group, Keith plays the harmonica and shakes his tambourine.

"I'm hardly Junior Parker or Little Walter when it comes to harmonica playing, but I enjoy it and I'm listening to harmonica records and practicing," says Keith.

The singer invested some of the royalties from his records in an apartment on the Upper East Side of Manhattan. "I had to move to New York for business reasons," he said. "My mentor, Jerry Ross, the Philadelphia artist-and-repertoire man who discovered me and gave me my first chance, advised me to try to reside in New York City."

Keith is now in the Midwest with the Beach Boys' tour. When that tour ends, he'll keep himself busy, joining the Caravan of Stars, Dick Clark's nationwide tour.

# Jerry Butler

## *March 25, 1967*

IF JERRY BUTLER HAD NOT ATTENDED THE TRAVELLING SOULS SPIRITUAL-ist Church in Chicago, he might not have become the success he is today.

It was in that church's choir that Jerry began singing a year after he got out of high school. Also, in the choir with young Butler were Curtis Mayfield and Sam Gooden. After choir rehearsals, Butler, Mayfield, and Gooden would practice pop singing at one of their homes.

Shortly thereafter, the trio became known as "Jerry Butler and the Impressions." Their first hit on the Vee Jay label was "For Your Precious Love," which was written by Butler.

In 1958, Butler split with the Impressions, and Fred Cash took his place (Mayfield, Gooden, and Cash are the current members of the group).

Jerry recorded other hits, such as "Let It Be Me" and "Moon River"—before Vee Jay ran into financial difficulties.

"I was going to leave Vee Jay in October of 1965," he said. "I knew they were having financial difficulties, but they asked me to try and stick out another six months with them.

"I signed another six-month contract and shortly afterward they went bankrupt," Jerry said. "For six months I couldn't record, but after my contract ran out I signed with Mercury, which is my present label."

Jerry feels very strongly about the future longevity of rhythm-and-blues, which he sings. As he puts it: "Rhythm-and-blues will go on and get bigger. The gap between r & b and pop music will get smaller—to the point of non-existence."

When asked whether the British sounds have influenced him, Jerry replied: "I don't think there's such an animal as English music. Groups like the Beatles, Stones and Kinks copied us.

"American artists like John Lee Hooker and Lightnin' Hopkins were always big in England—but they couldn't draw crowds in America," he said. "Then English groups started copying them, and not only did the English groups make it big, but they helped bring Negro artists like Hooker and Hopkins into the spotlight back here in the States."

Twenty-seven-year-old Butler is married and admits that constantly being on the road, away from his home in Chicago, gets him down.

"Travelling is a drag, but it's a hazard of the business," he says. "Every business gets to be a bang-up after a while."

Jerry, who recently appeared at the Howard Theater, plans to follow up his current hit, "I Dig You Baby," with more records, songwriting, and publishing. And, of course, he would like to do more concert dates, especially on the college and nightclub circuits.

# The Impressions

## *April 1, 1967*

IF THE IMPRESSIONS SHOULD EVER DECIDE TO GIVE UP SINGING, THEY HAVE their "ace in the hole" in the business world.

Twenty-four-year-old Curtis Mayfield, one of the Impressions, owns two record companies, Windy Sea and Mayfield Records, and three music publishing companies. The two other members of the group, Sam Gooden, thirty-two, and Fred Cash, twenty-seven, recruit much of the talent for Mayfield's companies.

The Impressions have been singing together since 1959. Over the years, they have produced such hits as "People Get Ready," "Amen," "I've Been Tryin,'" "I'm So Proud," and many more.

Their latest release, "You Always Hurt Me," was written by multi-talented Curtis Mayfield, who writes all the material for the Impressions. Besides writing for his own group, Curtis has written for Major Lance, Walter Jackson, Gene Chandler, and Jerry Butler.

During an interview at the Howard Theater, Sam Gooden told of the group's plans for the future. "In June, we are going to Canada, and then in August we're going to London, Paris, Switzerland and North Africa," he said.

Constant traveling doesn't bother the group anymore. As Sam put it: "We've cut down a lot on traveling. We schedule our dates to be off three or four days a month."

Their road manager, Eddie Suiter, quickly added that the Impressions are only on the road seven months of the year. The rest of the year they spend with their families and recording in Chicago, where they all live.

"Rock 'n' roll and rhythm and blues will be around forever," says Sam. "More artists are beginning to sing rock 'n' roll and more people want to hear it.

"Even pop singers like Perry Como have gotten the beat," Sam said. "They realize that to really entertain you have to have something to clap to."

Sam's two favorite singers are Sammy Davis Jr. and Nat King Cole. "You could never find another act as great as Nat Cole's, he was smooth as silk," Sam said. "And Sammy Davis is just an all-around great entertainer."

When asked what type audience the Impressions prefer singing for, Sam replied, "All of them! As long as they enjoy music, we enjoy singing for them. All of them have been nice to us, so we love them all."

The Impressions, along with their bass guitarist, Lenny Brown, and drummer, Billy Griffin, have been doing a lot of college concerts recently. "College kids buy a lot of our records," said Sam. "We've been very successful at all the colleges we've played, and we hope to play for a lot more."

The Impressions plan to put out many more records for the ABC label. Their next release will be titled "Running."

# James Brown

## *April 15, 1967*

IF IT WEREN'T FOR A SEVERE LEG INJURY, JAMES BROWN MIGHT BE PLAYING "pro" baseball today—instead of singing rhythm-and-blues.

Actually, the James Brown story started long before the up-and-coming young athlete got the injury that forced him to give up his job as a pitcher for a professional club at the peak of his baseball career.

James was born into a poverty-stricken family in Augusta, Georgia.

"My family was so poor," he says, "that you wouldn't even believe it. My father greased and washed cars in a filling station. Sometimes I worked with him. Other times I picked cotton, worked on a farm, worked in a coal yard. I had to walk home along the railroad tracks and pick up pieces of coke left over from the trains. I'd take that home and we'd use it to keep warm."

The ambition that makes James strive for even higher heights grew from those days of poverty. "I always wanted to show that any man, regardless of race, color, or creed could be something if he tried."

James says of his childhood, "I was a good dancer, the best in my crowd. Even when I was little, the other kids would pay me a dime to dance for them.

"Near Augusta, there was a big Army training center and the soldiers would get me up on a little stand when I was ten years old and I'd sing and dance for them. And they'd throw pennies, nickels, dimes—sometimes even quarters—at me."

As he grew older, James became interested in all kinds of sports. Boxing was one of James's earliest sporting interests. A former boxing great, "Beau Jack," took an interest in James because of the youngster's boxing skill and fast footwork.

"Before that, I had played football at school, first in the line, then as a halfback, finally as a quarterback. I was pretty small for the game, but I liked it," James says.

After winning sixteen out of seventeen fights as a bantamweight, James decided to try his hand at baseball. Forced out of baseball by a leg injury, James formed a gospel singing group called "The Famous Flames."

In January 1956, "The Famous Flames" gathered together what little money they could and cut a record. The record, "Please, Please, Please," had no musical accompaniment, but one of James's disc jockey friends decided to give it one play.

The radio station was swamped with requests for the song. Soon "Please, Please, Please" was rerecorded, this time with musical accompaniment. The song was the first in a long line of hits for James which include "Lost Someone," "Try Me," "Prisoner of Love," "Papa's Got a Brand New Bag," and many more.

# Musings . . . James Brown, 1963–2005 . . .
# The Years I Knew Him

I was sixteen years old. James Brown was thirty when I first met him in his dressing room at the Howard Theater in D.C. What was a white boy with peroxide in his hair and a Beach Boys shirt doing backstage with the Godfather of Soul?

My brother, Ron, did a lot of interviews backstage at the Howard. If you wanted to see, hear, and possibly write a story on a rhythm-and-blues artist, the Howard Theater (D.C.'s equivalent of the Apollo Theater in New York City) was the place to be. I often tagged along with my brother and would sit in the audience while Ron was backstage interviewing musicians. One day, Ron said to me, "Why don't you come backstage with me? It's an interesting scene back there." I jumped at the chance, especially since we were going to see James Brown.

We entered the theater through the stage door, putting us directly behind the stage and in line with the dressing rooms. Ron had interviewed James before and had been to the Howard so many times that the stage-hands knew him by name. James had a dressing room separate from his band. Ron knocked on the dressing room door, and James opened it and greeted Ron like he was James's brother. Ron then introduced me to James. I may have stammered, "Mr. Brown, you're the best," or something just as trite.

James was shirtless and had the physique of the boxer he once was. Around his neck, on a silver chain, was a mezuzah: decorative silver case that contained a piece of parchment inscribed with Hebrew verses from the Torah. James saw me staring at it. He said, "It's a mezuzah, a gift from my manager, Ben Bart. You know, it's a Jewish thing . . . and it brings me luck." I had a Kodak Instamatic camera with me and asked James if my brother could take a photo of me and James. He agreed, and my first real memento of meeting a superstar would soon be developed, framed, and placed on my bedside table.

Little did I know that four years later, in 1967, I would write my first story on James Brown for my weekly music column. A few months earlier, before Ron left journalism for a career in the music industry, Ron took James to the White House to meet Vice President Hubert Humphrey.

James had just released a single, "Don't Be a Dropout." One of Hubert Humphrey's programs as vice president was to keep kids from dropping out of school. It seemed like a match made in heaven, and it was. "Don't Be a Dropout" became a hit record, and James would promote the vice president's pet program while touring in support of the song.

I saw and spoke to James a number of times over the years. He was always gracious and took the time to speak with me, whether I was interviewing him or just saying hello. The last time I saw him was at the House of Blues in Los Angeles in 2005. By then, his show was more Vegas than soul—dancing girls in bikinis onstage, glitz, and glimmer. I longed for the young James who could drop down on his knees and plead, "Please, please, please," have a cape draped over his shoulder, and start to walk offstage, only to throw the cape off, walk back to the center of stage, and continue singing, "Please, please, please." The next year, James was dead.

# The Casinos

## *April 29, 1967*

"They're all in their twenties, they're neat and typically clean-cut and Middle Western, the nine young guys making up the Casinos, out of Cincinnati, are the most enthusiastically accepted new group in the country today."

The above quote comes from the liner notes written by syndicated columnist Earl Wilson on the Casinos' new album on the Fraternity label. Wilson met the group at a kickoff party in New York, was immediately impressed by them, and consented to write the liner notes for their album.

Right now, the Casinos are down to eight members, and they are Gene Hughes, lead singer; Glen Hughes, trumpet and vocals; Pete Bolton, vocals; Ray White, bass and vocals; Joe Patterson, sax; Bob Armstrong, organ; Mike Denton, guitar; and Tom Matthews, drums.

Gene, spokesman for the group, explained how they got started: "Ray, Pete, Joe, my brother Glen, and I started out as a vocal group nine years ago. As time went on, we added our own instruments.

"A disc jockey friend of mine had just come back from Las Vegas," Gene said. "Jokingly, he suggested we call ourselves the casinos, and the name stuck with us."

The group's first single release, "Then You Can Tell Me Goodbye," became their first hit. Their current single is "It's All Over," and from all indications it looks as if they might have another hit.

The Casinos recently completed two tours with the Beach Boys. "Originally, the Beach Boys heard our record and booked us for an eight-day tour," Jean said. "When that tour was finished the Beach Boys liked our act and booked us again."

They have a repertoire of 500 songs, including rock 'n' roll, rhythm and blues, folk, and many other types. As Gene put it, "We play everything." 'Then You Can Tell Me Goodbye' was a combination of soul and good music but we don't limit ourselves to any one type of song."

Their great versatility can be seen by looking at some of the cuts from their album: "What Kind of Fool Am I," "Gee Whiz," " Hold on I'm Coming," and "Rag Doll," to name a few.

They were offered an appearance on the *Ed Sullivan Show*, but their agency felt they shouldn't take it because they would be allowed to do only one number. But they're hoping they'll get the offer again and will be allowed to do several.

In the future, the group primarily wants to build a better nightclub act. Club work in Vegas is their ultimate goal.

# Joe Tex

## *May 20, 1967*

THE TITLE OF JOE TEX'S FIRST SONG, "HOLD ON TO WHAT YOU'VE GOT," sums up the thirty-year-old singer's feelings on life.

Joe, who recently appeared at the Howard Theater, said, "A depression will come again and I want to be ready for it. Those screams and hollers I hear while I'm on stage aren't going to last forever.

"My name in lights doesn't mean anything," he said. "All I want to do is make enough money and quit."

By quitting, Joe doesn't mean retiring and living in a mansion with servants waiting on him. In fact, when Joe leaves show business, he hopes to have accumulated enough money to buy a farm and raise a sizable crop of beans.

Joe once worked as a bean picker on a farm, and he says that when he has his own farm, he wants to pick the beans and have his grandmother preserve them.

It will probably be quite a while before Joe stops belting out rhythm-and-blues tunes because, as he puts it, "It took me ten years to get where I am now, and although I should be resting, I've got to keep on making it while I'm hot."

Joe's last two records, "Poppa Was Too" and "Show Me" were easy to dance to, so they appealed mainly to teenagers. But Joe feels that most of the other songs he sings are "too deep" for teenagers.

"My songs are very deep," he said. "Kids don't want to have to think, they want to dance. That's why my things sell mainly to adults."

Right now, traveling is the biggest hang-up in Joe's life. He only gets home to Baton Rouge, Louisiana, one week out of every month. "I would like to spend more time with my wife and son," Joe said.

"I was on the road when my son was born," he said. "He knows who his daddy is, but he never sees him. My wife and mother-in-law always play my records for him. I even bought a horse for him. But that doesn't make up for my being away from home so much."

Joe attributes much of the success of R & B to increasing white audiences. "A lot of the white teenage kids are just beginning to find out who some of the Negro artists are," Joe said. "For a while, all anyone saw on television or heard on the radio was English groups.

"Now pop radio stations are playing R & B records and cats like James Brown are making appearances on television. It's a new bag for white kids and they're going to keep R & B alive for a long time to come."

# Jimmy Castor

## *May 27, 1967*

PEOPLE IN SHOW BUSINESS OFTEN SAY THAT IN ORDER TO BECOME A SUC-cess, you must "pay your dues." Jimmy Castor is no exception to that rule.

Jimmy has spent most of his twenty-five years paying those dues. Now that he's made it to the top, he's proud to talk about the years of hard work and many hours of practice that are now behind him.

During a recent interview at the Howard Theater, Jimmy said, "I started playing the sax in junior high school, and then went on to piano, theory, arranging, and many other aspects of music."

Actually, it was in grade school that Jimmy developed an interest in music. It was his last year of grade school, in the Bronx, when he took a music exam which won him a place in New York's High School of Music and Art.

Besides learning many different instruments in the school, Jimmy sang, danced, and studied acting. He also began writing songs, which included "I Promise to Remember," recorded by Frankie Lymon and the Teenagers.

After graduating from City College of New York, Jimmy went on to play club dates all over New York. He soon came to the attention of Finis Henderson, personal representative in New York for Sammy Davis, Jr. Jimmy worked with the inimitable Sammy, and some of Sammy's perform-ing magic rubbed off onto him.

Jimmy recorded several unsuccessful records on various labels before he landed a contract with Smash Records. His first record on Smash, "Hey, Leroy," became his first hit.

"Hey, Leroy," was one of the most successful records in the "Latin-Rock" genre. The term "Latin-Rock" was coined to describe highly danceable records with a Latin beat and instrumentation.

Describing Latin-Rock, Jimmy said, "I think it's just a soulful thing. You can really groove to it."

Jimmy, who is five feet, ten inches tall and weighs 150 pounds, enjoys buying clothes. He has conservative taste and prefers soft-textured sport coats and casual sweater-shirts.

When asked about his future plans, Jimmy replied: "I enjoy what I'm doing now. I'm thankful to everyone who made my success possible.

"I would never want to give up music, but I would like to go into acting," he said. "Of all the places I play, nightclubs and theaters are my favorites. I'd like to do more of those kind of dates."

# Spanky and Our Gang

## *June 3, 1967*

NOT MANY ROCK 'N' ROLL GROUPS CAN CLAIM HAVING MET AND FORMED IN a chicken coop during a hurricane, but that's how Elaine "Spanky" McFarlane met Nigel Pickering and Oz Bach and set the stage for the formation of Spanky and Our Gang.

Spanky had been renting a one-room converted chicken coop near Miami, FL, when Nigel and Oz showed up during a hurricane to take refuge in her "far from lavish" quarters.

Waiting for the hurricane to subside, they passed the time by singing. Before they flew the coop, Oz and Nigel told Spanky how much they would like to form a singing group with her. "I told them that I might leave Miami soon and if they ever got to Chicago to look me up," said Spanky.

Four months later, Spanky did leave Miami, and shortly thereafter, Nigel and Oz sought and found her. They formed a trio, Spanky and Our Gang, until they acquired a fourth member, Malcolm Hale.

Since they became a foursome, Spanky and Our Gang has rapidly advanced into the top ranks of recording artists. One reason for this is the phenomenal success of their first record on the Mercury label, "Sunday Will Never Be the Same."

In one week, the record moved from number 98 to number 49 on *Billboard* magazine's national record chart.

Each member of the group had some musical experience before that eventful night in the chicken coop. Spanky was born in Peoria, Illinois, where she began singing at the age of three. Later she sang with a Dixieland band, and before she met Nigel and Oz, she sang with the New Wine Singers.

Nigel, born in Pontiac, Michigan, did a lot of singing, mainly in the country-and-western bag, before he joined Spanky.

Oz comes from West Virginia, and at one time he was a well-known performer in Miami coffeehouses. How did Oz get his first big break in the business? As he tells it, "I was sweeping the stage once in a coffeehouse and I knocked over a guitar rack. It got applause, so I decided to come back the next night and do it again."

Malcolm is known as the "baby brother" of the group. He was born in Cleveland, where he began his musical career as a folksinger. Like Spanky, he too is a former member of the New Wine Singers.

Combining a good amount of comedy and songs in their stage act, Spanky and Our Gang has already appeared at the Bitter End in New York and the Chess Mate in Detroit. Their television credits include the *Mike Douglas Show* and the *Tonight Show* with Johnny Carson. On June 16, they move into San Francisco's hungry i for three weeks.

# The Bee Gees

## *June 17, 1967*

IN 1956, WHEN BARRY GIBB AND HIS YOUNGER TWIN BROTHERS, ROBIN and Maurice, formed an amateur vocal trio in their hometown, Manchester, England, they had no idea that ten years later they would be one of the top groups in the world.

Now the three brothers form part of a quintet known as the Bee Gees. The two other members of the group are Colin Peterson and Vince Melouney, both from Australia. Their current release, "New York Mining Disaster—1941," on the Atco label, is riding high on charts all around the world.

The Bee Gees are now touring Europe as a result of the success of "New York Mining Disaster—1941." Atlantic Records, of which Atco is a subsidiary, does not know whether the disaster mentioned in the song ever occurred or was just made up by one of the imaginative members of the group.

Actually, it wasn't until recently that Colin and Vince joined the Gibb brothers. Back in 1960, when the average age of the three Bee Gees was ten, they had their own weekly thirty-minute TV series in Brisbane.

In 1958, Barry, Robin, and Maurice were building a strong act after leaving England and going to Australia. The Bee Gees spent the next eight years in Brisbane and Sydney, during which time they landed the TV series and had many hit records in the "land down under."

Festival Records released the Bee Gees' first single in Australia when Barry was only fourteen and the twins were just twelve. The record, "Three Kisses of Love," which was released in 1963, made the top twenty and was followed up by "Timber," "Peace of Mind," and "Claustrophobia."

Then, in 1965 and 1966, they had three number one records in Australia: "Wine and Women," "I Was a Lover and a Leader of Men," and "Spicks

43

and Specks." This long line of hits, which they not only recorded, but also wrote, led to the Bee Gees being named "Australia's Best Group of the Year" for 1966.

In February of this year, the Bee Gees returned to Britain and were immediately signed to a five-year management contract. It was then that Colin joined them to form a quartet.

Describing the group's phenomenal writing ability, Robin says: "We write about everything and anything. Day-to-day events, personal experiences, something we've heard on the news or read about in the papers.

"Sometimes we write a song based on our own thoughts. We used to write individually, but today each new number is a collaboration job, a Bee Gees composition with all of us adding something to the finished effort."

Maurice carried on the discussion of song writing: "Obviously, new songs don't come out of the air," he said. "They take time. So composing has to be an occupation and a hobby. What free time we get is used up working on new material. That's the way we like it.

"We don't think of songwriting as a task a job or work," Maurice said. "It's all good fun. It's all worthwhile when a song gets to its final stage . . . when it's there on a demonstration disk so that we can all listen to it and decide about a recording arrangement."

# The Seeds

## *June 24, 1967*

"THE 'HATE MARCH' DAYS ARE OVER, NOW IT'S LOVE AND BE LOVED AND flower music expresses this emotion powerfully and beautifully," says Lord Tim Hudson, manager of a blossoming new West Coast musical combo called the Seeds.

Besides having had three hit singles, "Pushing Too Hard," "Mr. Farmer," and "Can't Seem to Make You Mine," the Seeds have become the spokesmen for a new teenage movement, "the Flower Generation."

The members of the "Flower Generation" are appropriately called "flower children." They believe that since a flower can't harm anyone and is always beautiful, it is a symbol of love and peace.

Sky Saxon, twenty-two-year-old leader of the Seeds, writes most of the group's material. In a recent publication, the lyrics of the Seeds' songs were said to "pierce sensations like tender but determined green seedlings breaking through hard, crusty soil and send flower music crashing through the limits of contemporary rock sounds."

Besides Sky, who was born in Salt Lake City, the other members of the Seeds are Jan Savage, a full-blooded Cherokee from Ardmore, Oklahoma; Daryl Hooper from Detroit; and Rick Andridge from Lansing, Michigan.

When asked why he sang about the flower children, and what he thought about them, Daryl said, "I sing about them because they have a sense of the splendor and power of love which no other generation before has felt as fully.

"They don't riot," he said. "They withdraw from ugliness and cruelty and blossom when peace and friendship warm the air. They know they will grow into beautiful people because they are filled with the joy of loving while they are young."

While discussing teenagers in general, Sky said, "Teenage fans spend so much money buying expensive gifts for singers they admire. I don't want flower children to buy me expensive gifts. I enjoy receiving one, simple, beautiful flower. It's such a perfect symbol of non-violence, love and honest appreciation."

Their manager, Lord Tim, is responsible for much of the Seeds' success. Lord Tim is from London, and before he came to this country, he was a popular British disc jockey. He has traveled with the Beatles, Herman's Hermits, and he discovered the Moody Blues.

When he arrived in America, Lord Tim worked on several radio stations, and while on KFWB in Los Angeles, he was voted the city's Number One DJ. He believes that the success of a group comes from "their treating rock 'n' roll as a regimented form, like any other big business."

In the future, the Seeds intend to go on preaching "flower power," and their latest record, on the Crescendo label, "A Thousand Shadows," does just that.

# The Beatles

## *July 1, 1967*

THE BEATLES' NEW ALBUM, SERGEANT PEPPER'S LONELY HEARTS CLUB BAND, has only been out a couple of weeks, and already it is one of the biggest-selling and most controversial albums to make the music scene.

The controversy has arisen from some of the lyrics of some of the songs, particularly "A Day in the Life," which was banned by the British Broadcasting Company. The particular lyrics that were found objectionable supposedly connote the taking of drugs. For instance, one line goes "found my way upstairs and had a smoke, somebody spoke and I went into a dream." Some people believe this line deals with someone smoking marijuana, but that's not the meaning the Beatles intended it to have.

In a recent interview in a British music trade paper, *Disc and Music Echo*, Paul McCartney said, "If they want to ban 'A Day in the Life' that's their business. Drugs must have been in their minds, not ours. And the point is banning doesn't help. It just draws attention to a subject when all the time their aim is to force attention away from it."

Whether or not the lyrics on the album are objectionable is a minor question, for the Beatles have progressed so far that the album is a musical masterpiece. The lyrics have a poetic quality all their own, and the transition from one song to the next is done smoothly, without a break between cuts, so that the album tells one long story.

In a recent United Press International story, the Beatles discussed the present state of their lives. "We have always said that if we could, we'd leave every job where it was and leave it there, a pleasant memory, then go on and do something else," said Paul. "In other words, every year that goes by try different venues."

Ringo Starr quickly added, "The past is past. That tour thing, for instance. We probably won't do any more tours, at least not like the old ones. We're trying to break new ground. We could spend all our lives making one record. But we must get on to the next one."

George Harrison, who, a few months back, went to India to study the sitar, a stringed Indian instrument, with Ravi Shankar, the world's greatest sitar player, said, "People are always asking where do the Beatles go from here? It's been that way ever since things started happening for us.

"But everything's relative and things don't stay the same," George said. "We're different people now. We've had more experience, been around seeing more of life, expanded our environment. The more we live, the better we ought to get. The better our music ought to get."

The Beatles music has gotten better. They proved this in front of some 300 million people last Sunday on "Our World," a live worldwide television broadcast produced by the BBC. On this program, which was beamed, via satellite, to twenty-four different countries, the Beatles were seen recording a way out new single, which will probably be released in the near future.

To add to the furor over their new album, Paul admitted taking LSD. Incidentally, you might check the lyrics on one of the album cuts, "Lucy in the Sky with Diamonds," then glance at the title of the song to pick out the main words, Lucy, sky, and diamonds. The initials spell out LSD.

The other cuts on the album are "A Little Help from My Friends," "Getting Better," "Fixing a Hole," "She's Leaving Home," "Being for the Benefit of Mr. Kite," "Within You Without You," "When I'm 64," "Lovely Rita," "Good Morning, Good Morning," and the title tune.

Three songs on the album have psychedelic sounds: "Lucy in the Sky with Diamonds," "A Day in the Life," and "Within You, Without You," which was the only song on the album written by George Harrison and in which George plays the sitar.

# Wonder Who

## *July 8, 1967*

Five years ago, when the 4 Seasons first hit the charts with "Sherry," TV personality Dick Clark predicted that, "A lot of new names will come and go, but the 4 Seasons will probably last forever."

So far, Dick's prediction has held true. Not only have the 4 Seasons continued to put out hit after hit, but, changing the name of the group to the Wonder Who, they have done the same. Right now, the Seasons' "C'mon Marianne" is the number 16 tune in the country, according to *Billboard* magazine.

For the past year and a half, Frankie Valli, lead singer for the Seasons and the one who sings with the high-pitched voice, has also put out a number of records as a solo artist. His "Can't Take My Eyes Off of You" is now the number three tune in the country.

As if the accomplishments of Frankie Valli and the 4 Seasons aren't enough, the Wonder Who, who in reality are Frankie Valli, Tommy DeVito, Joe Long, and Bob Gaudio (the 4 Seasons), have just released a new record, "Lonesome Road," which *Billboard* magazine has picked to reach the top sixty in the charts.

As a group, the boys served an apprenticeship singing background on various recording sessions produced by Bob Crewe. Prior to that, Bob Gaudio sang with a group called the Royal Teens, whose record "Short Shorts," written by Gaudio, became a tremendous hit.

While Gaudio was with the Royal Teens, Frankie Valli, Tommy DeVito, and Nick Massi (since replaced in the group by Joe Long) sang with a group known as the Four Lovers.

Explaining how the Seasons develop their new material, Bob Gaudio said, "We never cut a song without a full-scale conference first." In these discussions, ideas for harmony, arrangements, and songs are argued out.

In one such session, the idea that developed into the "Wonder Who" was hatched. Frankie Valli suggested recording under another name just to see if the group could get a hit without the identifying impetus of the established name. Under the new alias, the Seasons released "Don't Think Twice," which eventually became a hit.

Some other reasons for the success of the 4 Seasons are Valli's high voice, the writing of Gaudio, and the production of Crewe.

Dick Clark offers his own formula for the 4 Seasons' staying power with a variety of audiences. "They're not a teenage group fresh up from the ranks," says Dick. "They have a good solid, well-rehearsed act and sound which takes them through nightclubs and concert dates in both the teen and the adult field."

# The Rolling Stones

## *July 22, 1967*

Mɪᴄᴋ Jᴀɢɢᴇʀ, ᴛʜᴇ ᴄᴏɴᴛʀᴏᴠᴇʀsɪᴀʟ ʟᴇᴀᴅ sɪɴɢᴇʀ ᴏꜰ Eɴɢʟᴀɴᴅ's Rᴏʟʟɪɴɢ Stones, is now free on bail after receiving a three-month jail sentence for possession of four Benzedrine-type tablets, but the furor over his sentence has just begun.

Besides Jagger, another member of the group, Keith Richards, also is out on bail after receiving a one-year sentence for allowing his country home to be used for the smoking of a soft narcotic similar to marijuana.

Most of England's younger generation spoke out against Jagger's harsh sentence, and even the London *Times* ran an objective editorial on England's drug laws. One of the best passages in the *Times* editorial was: "If, after his visit to the Pope, the Archbishop of Canterbury had brought proprietary air-sickness pills at the Rome airport, and imported the unused tablets into Britain on his return, he would have risked committing precisely the same offence."

London's Carnaby Street took on a circus-like air by cashing in on the misfortune of Jagger and Richards. Lord Kitchener's Valet displayed handcuffs in their window along with a sign saying, "Be faithful with a pair of Jagger links."

The drug controversy hasn't seemed to hurt the sales of the Stones new album, *Flowers*. The songs on the album are a mixture of old and new. The titles are "Ruby Tuesday," "Have You Seen Your Mother, Baby, Standing in the Shadows," "Let's Spend the Night Together," "Lady Jane," "Out of Time," "My Girl," "Backstreet Girl," "Please Go Home," "Mother's Little Helper," "Take It or Leave It," "Ride On Baby," and "Sittin' on a Fence." Besides Jagger and Richards, the Stones featured on the LP are Brian Jones, Charlie Watts, and Bill Wyman.

Members of the recording industry are paying tribute to the Stones in their own unique ways. According to *Disc and Music Echo*, a British music weekly, the Who have rush-released two Stones songs, "The Last Time" and "Under My Thumb."

The reasoning behind the release of these records, as explained by members of the Who, is that "The Who consider Mick Jagger and Keith Richards have been treated as scapegoats for the drug problem, and as a protest against the savage sentences imposed on them, The Who are issuing a series of Jagger-Richards songs to keep their work before the public until they are again free to record themselves."

The above statement was made before Jagger and Richards were freed on bail. After being notified of the Stones being freed, Who co-writer Kit Lambert stated: "We made this record ("The Last Time" and "Under My Thumb") and released it in twenty-four-hours flat before we knew they'd got bail. It's just a simple gesture and we are not trying to cash in at all. All royalties will go to charity."

Ian Ross, owner of a mod clothing firm in England; Ronan O'Rahilly, a director of Radio Caroline (a pop music radio station located on a ship anchored off the shore of Britain); and Denny Cordell, manager of England's Procol Harum ("A Whiter Shade of Pale"), are planning a "massive" concert to raise money to send flowers of forgiveness to the Chichester (England) judge who sentenced Jagger and Richards.

Rolling Stones in D.C.
PHOTO BY MIKE KLAVANS

# The Monkees

## *July 29, 1967*

THE MONKEES SHOW: BALLADS AND BULLETS

There they were, David Thomas Jones, Michael Dolenz, Robert Michael Nesmith, and Peter Halsten Torkelson, mesmerizing 10,000 adolescents at Baltimore's Civic Center last week. Why? Because they're a relatively new musical phenomenon known as the Monkees.

They played to an almost packed house, and their popularity was reflected in the faces of the thousands of predominantly female ten- to six-teen-year-olds in the audience. As a result of a massive promotion campaign in the District, a big chunk of the audience was from the Washington area.

The Monkees were preceded on the show by a new Decca recording group called the Sundowners and a girl singer from Australia, Lynn Randell. When the Monkees finally came on stage, a deafening roar enveloped the auditorium to the delight of the foursome, but to the chagrin of the many policemen who were on duty to keep some semblance of order.

It was that first roar that proved too great for one officer, who plugged each of his ears with a .38-caliber cartridge. When asked what he thought of the Monkees, the officer removed his ear-plugs and replied: "I don't mind duty at the Civic Center, except for these (censored) rock-and-roll shows."

The Monkees went through all of their popular tunes, including their current release, "Pleasant Valley Sunday." Toward the end of their act, the Monkees went off stage and got out of their red velvet suits. Peter soon strutted back dressed in a white sweater and white pants and sang folk songs, accompanying himself on a banjo.

Then each of the other Monkees made a solo performance. Mike did a rousing job on "Can't Judge a Book by Looking at the Cover," Davy sang a tune from the play *Stop the World, I Want to Get Off*, and Mickey did a weak imitation of James Brown singing "I've Got a Woman."

As a show-stopping finale, the Monkees grouped together and sang "Stepping Stone" as pictures of themselves flashed on a giant screen above their heads and the dark auditorium was filled with searching spotlights and green "stars" reflected from a cut-glass ball suspended from the ceiling.

By the end of the show, the Monkees had finally disproved the rumor that had been circulating before they came on stage . . . that they couldn't play their own instruments. As a matter of fact, the sound the Monkees put out at the Civic Center that night was almost identical to the Monkees records put out by RCA.

The Monkees' rise to stardom began in the final months of 1965 with an advertisement in the show business trade weeklies. The ad read: "Madness. Wanted . . . a quartet of hip, insane, folk-oriented rock 'n' rollers, 17 to 21, with courage to work."

At the time, Peter Tork and Mike Nesmith didn't meet the age requirements, since Mike was twenty-two and Peter was twenty-three. But that was overlooked, and the quartet of Jones, Dolenz, Nesmith, and Tork inherited a new television series that was to begin the following Fall.

The rest of their rise to fame resulted from their popular television series and a number of hit records that followed their initial smash, "Last Train to Clarksville."

Several Monkees fans in the audience said they didn't mind the charge that the group had been put together by adults in a premeditated effort to challenge the Beatles.

"The Beatles are too old," frowned one thirteen-year-old. "Besides, they take drugs and they aren't clean-cut anymore."

Others in the audience said they liked both groups. One teenager pointed out that, "Although there are many different opinions about the musical ability of the Monkees, nobody can doubt the genius of the Beatles."

The Monkees themselves say they are the "greatest fans of the Beatles. After a recent visit to England and a meeting of the two groups, Mickey Dolenz said, "They dig our records too."

# Harpers Bizarre

## *August 5, 1967*

LOSING A CONTRACT WITH A MAJOR RECORD COMPANY "BECAUSE THEY weren't dirty" hasn't stopped a California group, Harpers Bizarre, from making hit records.

Besides the company that turned them down because of their "cleanliness," another company decided they wanted to turn the group into an American "Herman's Hermits." But, the boys put an end to that idea because, as they put it, "We are not going to be versions of anyone else."

The group consists of Ed James, lead guitar; Dick (Scap) Scoppettone, vocals and rhythm guitar; Ted Templeman, vocals and rhythm guitar; Dick Yount, bass guitar; and John Peterson (formerly with the Beau Brummels), drums.

The boys first met in Santa Cruz, a small resort town north of Monterey, Calif. Originally, they called themselves "The Tiki," probably a reference to Thor Heyerdahl's KonTiki, the raft that floated from Peru to Tahiti. At that time, they were under contract to Autumn Records and they achieved quite a following in the San Francisco area—even though they aren't a psychedelic group.

When Warner Brothers bought Autumn Records, the boys came up with their own style and changed the name of the group to Harpers Bizarre. They came up with this name because "Harper" means "a player of stringed instruments," "Bizarre" means weird . . . and "that's us," one of them said.

Their first release, "The 59th Street Bridge Song," better known as "Feelin' Groovy," rocketed the group into the pop charts. They followed up their initial release with another in the "soft rock" style, "Come to the Sunshine." Their current record, "Anything Goes," an old Cole Porter favorite, has been picked by *Billboard* magazine to reach its top twenty list.

Besides having played with the Beau Brummels before joining Harpers Bizarre, John Peterson played for a short while with a group called the Sparklers. Some may wonder why the Brummels broke up since they were such a successful group. The answer to that is the vagaries of the Draft Law. Shortly after the release of Beau Brummels '66, guitarist John Irving left the group when he was inducted into the armed forces.

Ted Templeman is naturally musically inclined, and should be, since his mother is a music teacher and his father once owned a music store. He believes that the current hippie scene will come to a swift end. He also has some pretty sound advice for beginners in the music business. He says: "Learn to listen—one hit doesn't make a record."

His advice has been followed by his own group. All of their singles have been well done, and their album, *Feelin' Groovy,*" is exceptional.

# The New Vaudeville Band

## *August 12, 1967*

WERE THE MEMBERS OF THE NEW VAUDEVILLE BAND REALLY SPIES AND not musicians? Were they planning to burn the White House? These questions were brought to mind when the seven English boys went on a specially arranged tour of the President's home.

At one point in the tour, the guard who guided the boys around asked them if they had been searched for matches. Though he was just joking, it brought back memories of when the British actually did burn down the White House. Later in the tour, one of the musicians wandered off down the hall and was promptly warned that it was too early in the day to get shot.

After their enjoyable tour was over, they went back to the Shoreham Hotel, where they were the feature attraction on the Terrace. Most of the songs they did in their show were reminiscent of the 1930s, as was their first hit single, "Winchester Cathedral." The boys, all able musicians, also did a takeoff on Donovan's "Mellow Yellow."

During an interview at an opening night party, "Pops" Kerr, who plays trumpet and baritone sax, expressed his feelings on America's racial strife. "America has a real problem," he said. "In England, we do have some prejudice against the Indians, but they never existed as slaves in England."

When the conversation switched to flower power and "psychedelic" music, Henry Harrison, the Vaudeville's drummer, said, "This psychedelic thing is on the way out. Flower power is just a craze, but the love that comes with the flowers is basically good.

"We do have light shows in England," he went on. "But we don't have as many, or as good, as in America. The only real psychedelic club in London is the UFO Club."

When questioned about the origins of the New Vaudeville Band, Pops said that most of the members started in Dixieland bands. "When the Vaudeville band formed, we replaced the banjos with electric guitars, and the clarinets with saxophones," he said.

The man who supplies most of the laughs for the band is Tris-Tram, the Seventh Earl of Cricklewood, better known among London professional musicians as Alan Klein, twenty-four-year-old singer. Tris-Tram claims that he "always wanted to be a nobleman," so he gave himself the title.

The band's act is a montage of sight and sound gimmicks. They use smoke bombs, firecrackers, placards, and their own personal antics to keep their audiences laughing. The tremendous appeal of their act is going to keep them in this country until the beginning of November. Most of their appearances will be limited to nightclubs, and they hope their latest album, *The New Vaudeville Band—On Tour*, will please the public as much as their nightclub act.

# Jimi Hendrix

## *August 19, 1967*

IF IT WASN'T FOR A FORMER ANIMAL, THERE WOULD BE NO JIMI HENDRIX Experience.

It was in September 1966, that a former member of the Animals, Chas Chandler, discovered twenty-three-year-old Jimi Hendrix in Greenwich Village's Club Wha? Chandler persuaded Hendrix to try his luck abroad and mated him with two top English musicians in London.

The new partners who were chosen to join Jimi and form the Jimi Hendrix Experience were drummer Mitch Mitchell and bassist/guitarist Noel Redding. Jimi's first engagement with his new group was at the Olympia in Paris . . . just six weeks after he left New York. Their appearances in Paris were all sell-outs, and their next concert tour landed them in Stockholm, where they broke the house attendance record.

Not only were all the group's concerts successful, but their records sold well. All three of the Experience's singles, "Hey Joe," "Purple Haze," and "The Wind Cries Mary," made the top five in the English charts.

Jimi was born in Seattle and, at sixteen, he enlisted in the 101st Airborne Division. A parachute jump that injured his back ended his military career. For the next few years he toured the country as lead guitarist for various rock and rhythm-and-blues singers. Also, under the pseudonym Jimmy James, he played with the Blue Flames in New York for six months. Then the aforementioned break came when Chandler saw him perform.

Hendrix is far from conventional when it comes to performing. Besides playing the guitar with his hands, he plays it with his teeth while lying on his back. During one such display of his "toothy talent," Jimmy

Jimi Hendrix in Car Outside of the Baltimore Civic Center
PHOTO BY MIKE KLAVANS

received an electric shock that threw him part way across stage, but he continues to keep his act intact.

The highlight of the group's short career came when they played at the Monterey Pop Festival in California. Since then, the word has spread that "the" group to see is the Jimi Hendrix Experience.

It's somewhat ironic that Noel Redding auditioned for a place in Eric Burdon's new Animals, when he was heard by former Animal Chandler, and signed to join the other Chandler discovery, Hendrix.

The group's other member, Mitch Mitchell, played drums for a year with Georgie "Yeh, Yeh" Fame and the Blue Flames (not the same Blue Flames that Hendrix played with). After that group broke up, Mitchell decided to produce his own records, but that venture was sidetracked when the Jimi Hendrix Experience was formed.

The Experience's current single release in this country is "Purple Haze" b/w "The Wind Cries Mary." Besides the single, the group's first album, *Are You Experienced?*," is starting to pick up sales momentum.

# Bobbie Gentry

## *August 26, 1967*

WHEN BOBBIE GENTRY FIRST WROTE AND RECORDED "ODE TO BILLY JOE," all she thought about were the handicaps working against her.

She felt that being a new female vocalist with no particular "bag" was one of the main handicaps. Also, the fact that her record is four minutes and thirteen seconds long instead of the usual 2½-minute song added to her fears. But now that "Ode to Billy Joe" is the number one song in the country, according to *Billboard* magazine, Bobbie realizes that she worried for nothing.

Bobbie's song tells of tragic happenings in her native Mississippi. At a recent promotion party for her record at the Shoreham Hotel, Bobbie said, "The events in the record aren't meant to be limited to a particular setting. Although what happens is fictitious, it could happen to anyone anyplace. It just so happens that the part of the country I tell them about in the record is where I come from."

Toward the end of the song, the lyrics mention a bundle being thrown from the Tallahatchie Bridge. Rumors have been spreading that in the bundle was a dead baby. When asked about the mysterious bundle, Bobbie said, "People can think what they want to about it, but I'm not going to say what I meant to be in the bundle."

Originally Bobbie did club work for a living. "I decided I was going to settle down and write," she said. "I rented a studio in El Monte, California, and cut demos to present to various artists.

"I gave the demos to Larry Shayne, a publisher and he sent me to Kelly Gordon, my current A&R (artist and repertoire) man," she continued. "Kelly listened to them and signed me as an artist."

Bobbie's contract with Capitol Records actually came from the flip side of "Ode" called "Mississippi Delta." But, "Ode" had such universal appeal, it was released as the "plug" side.

Because of the record's solid story line and its appeal on all sorts of radio stations, Bobbie has already been approached about the movie rights to the song.

Since her record was released, Bobbie has been traveling all over the country. She recently appeared on *Upbeat*, a syndicated television program from Cleveland. Bobbie is thrilled about her quick climb to the top of the charts. As she puts it, "It's constant elation. It's the greatest thing that ever happened to me, I love every minute of it." And, so far, the public loves every minute, and there are many of them, of Bobbie's record.

# The Who

## *September 2, 1967*

WHO ARE THE WHO? OR SHOULD IT BE WHO IS THE WHO? ANYWAY, THAT question was answered recently when the British foursome toured this country with Herman's Hermits and the Blues Magoos. The Who is one of England's most popular groups, but only recently did they gain fame in this country with two successive hit records, "Happy Jack" and "Pictures of Lily."

The reason for the group not being well known in this country is, as Pete Townshend, lead guitarist, put it, "A lot of our records were banned in America. When we made a record, we weren't concentrating on the States. When 'Happy Jack' went over big, everyone was pleased."

During a show at Constitution Hall, the Who's instrument-smashing act stole the show from Herman's Hermits. Pete explained why he and the drummer, Keith Moon, break their instruments: "It's mainly for audience reaction."

"If our instruments get broken, we try to repair them," Pete said. "I have two Fender guitars—one to play and one to play and break. I try to break the body one job and the neck the next job.

"If I have a lot of quality parts left, I buy cheap guitars and put the parts on them," he continued. "For a while I was buying Fender Stratocasters at one hundred dollars a shot in New York."

Besides Keith and Pete, the other members of the group are Roger Daltrey, singer, and John Entwhistle, bass guitarist. John is also accomplished on the French horn, cornet, and tuba.

When Pete was asked about the flower power and psychedelic scene, his first reply was: "No comment at all." But, after a little coaxing, he went into a lengthy discussion.

The Who (Roger Daltrey and Pete Townshend) in D.C.
PHOTO BY MIKE KLAVANS

"In England it's just another fashion," he said. "People are still basically the same. They're not interested in the philosophy—just the clothes. Everything to do with that scene is just temporary. But what they're saying is valid.

"You know, it's a new Christianity," he said. "It's a new faith. Teenagers have to have faith. No human mind is capable of believing there is no outside influence. There must be something bigger than us. Even if a mind is transferred (reincarnation), it wouldn't remember. Humans go completely from experience."

In a recent letter to *Melody Maker*, a British music trade paper, Pete discussed some of the hot acts in this country. "Jimi Hendrix (a British act) is fairly hot property here now—his new record is an amazing production feat—all kinds of speeded-up passages, and some new, very un-guitar sounding sounds," he said.

"There's a lot of talent here at the moment, and they're coming into line, too," he said. "Some beautiful groups are cutting tracks—Moby Grape, the Paupers, Doors, etc.

"Mother country, watch out."

Pete Townshend (The Who) in D.C.

PHOTO BY MIKE KLAVANS

# Musings . . . Pete Townshend Goes to See
# Jimi Hendrix at the Ambassador Theater

ALTHOUGH MY COLUMN ON THE WHO DIDN'T RUN IN THE NEWSPAPER UNTIL September, I had interviewed them at Constitution Hall in August. The Who was the opening act for Herman's Hermits (although musically, it should have been the other way around). My interview was brief, as Pete Townshend wanted to go across town to the Ambassador Theater to hear Jimi Hendrix.

Hendrix was doing a five-night stand at the Ambassador (D.C.'s answer to the Fillmore) for the whopping paycheck of $1,500 total for his trio for all five nights. I had seen Hendrix at the Ambassador four nights earlier. I didn't go on the night of the Who concert—silly me! I stayed to catch Herman's Hermits.

A young (seventeen years old) Johnny Castle had gone to the Ambassador that night to see a local group called Natty Bumpo. Johnny was a bass player at that time (and an extremely good bass player to this day). While Johnny liked Natty Bumpo, he was completely blown away by Hendrix's playing—not just his command of the guitar but also playing it behind his head, between his legs, and with his teeth. To this day, Johnny has never seen anything like it, and Johnny has seen a lot. Johnny spent years on the road with premier blues band the Nighthawks and has done session work with many great guitarists.

Nils Lofgren (currently guitarist in Bruce Springsteen's E Street Band in addition to touring on his own and in the late 1960s and early 1970s leading the trio Grin) was also at the Ambassador that night. He had been at the Who show earlier in the evening and rushed across town to catch Hendrix. In an interview in the *Washington Post*, Lofgren remembered, "Everyone was standing and mesmerized by obviously the greatest guitar player that ever lived, certainly in rock."

Looking back on that time in 1967, my regret at not going to see Hendrix on that Sunday night is a very minor regret; after all, I saw Hendrix earlier in the week and saw the Who that night (the first of many Who concerts I would attend).

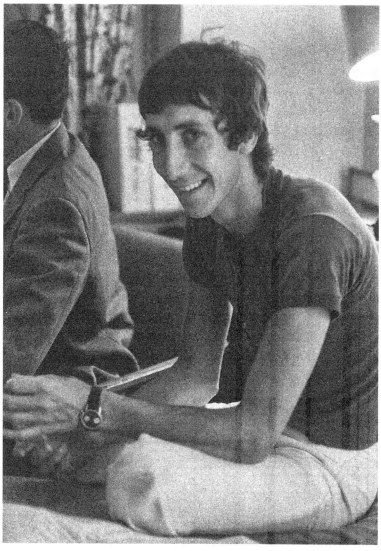

Pete Townshend in a Hotel Room in D.C.
PHOTO BY MIKE KLAVANS

# The Paupers

## *September 16, 1967*

WEBSTER'S SEVENTH NEW COLLEGIATE DICTIONARY DEFINES A PAUPER AS "A person destitute of means except such as are derived from charity." And, paupers, the Paupers aren't. A Canadian recording group, the Paupers, recently played the Ambassador Theater in D.C. and won many new American fans. Skip Prokop, the group's versatile drummer, explained how the Paupers formed.

"We all got together back in Toronto a little over two years ago," he said. "When our lead singer left the group, Adam (Mitchell) took his place. Adam was one of the top folksingers in Toronto, and when he joined us things really started moving."

Now, the Paupers have already conquered San Francisco's Avalon and Fillmore Ballrooms and played with the top groups in the world at the Monterey Pop Festival. During a recent engagement at New York's Café Au Go Go, the relatively unknown Paupers were on the same bill with and stole the show from the Jefferson Airplane.

When asked to compare Canadian groups to American groups, Adam, who plays rhythm guitar besides doing lead vocals, decided, "First of all, Canadian groups are different. They're more into the hit parade bag up there.

"Musically, Canadian groups are better than American groups," Adam said. "Canadian groups are more success oriented and musically disciplined, but American groups are more interesting."

The other members of the Paupers are Chuck Beal, lead guitar, and Dennis Gerrard, bass guitar. Their first single, "Magic People," and their first album, also called *Magic People*, were released simultaneously on the Verve/Forecast label.

The Paupers all thought the Ambassador Theater was one of the best of the so-called "psychedelic ballrooms." But Adam was emphatic about his dislike for being an integral part of the theater's light show.

"The lights bother me," Adam said. "The audience must see the emotions on the faces of the members of the band—with the light show being projected over the band that's impossible."

The rest of the band agreed with Adam about being a part of the light show, but they liked watching light shows. "Especially when they're well planned," Skip said.

All of the Paupers are excellent musicians. In 1963 and 1964, Skip won the Canadian Individual Rudimental Drumming Championship. Dennis and Adam sometimes join Skip in playing the drums—each on their own set—which explains why three sets of drums are on stage at the beginning of each performance by the Paupers.

The city of Toronto can boast of producing such stars as Robbie Robertson, lead guitarist for Bob Dylan; Zal Yanovsky, former lead guitar player for the Lovin' Spoonful; Gordon Lightfoot; Ian and Sylvia—and now, the Paupers.

# Lesley Gore

## *September 23, 1967*

THE INSCRIPTION ON THE NATIONAL ARCHIVES BUILDING READS: "WHAT is Past is Prologue." This just about describes Lesley Gore's careers.

Although Lesley has been making records for more than four years, has appeared in two movies, and has played numerous nightclub engagements, her career is still in its embryonic stage.

Before she begins a full-time show business career, she plans to finish her college education. This means that Lesley must limit her personal appearances to weekends and school vacations. She has arranged her schedule at Sarah Lawrence College so that most of her classwork falls in midweek, leaving her free to fulfill her commitments over longer than normal weekends.

During previous school years, Lesley has flown to California for appearances on variety shows such as the *Andy Williams Show*. She made her TV dramatic debut on a *Donna Reed Show* and was subsequently signed to appear on a two-part *Batman* show as Miss Pink Pussycat, the deadly Catwoman's assistant.

Lesley has also appeared in two films, *Ski Party* and *The Girls on the Beach*. Although those two films weren't exactly Academy Award caliber, Lesley did manage to win star billing opposite England's Tony Tanner in the summer stock tour of *Half a Sixpence*.

Her role in *Sixpence* was a challenging one. She had to emote with both serious and comic overtones, all while using a cockney accent.

Back in 1963, Lesley had no idea of the success she would be now. It was early in that year that she sang at a friend's birthday party and was so well received that some of her friends suggested she make a demonstration record of her voice and submit it to a record company.

Leslie sent the disc, "It's My Party (And I'll Cry If I Want To)," to Mercury Records, and after hearing it once, the company signed her to an exclusive contract. Currently, Lesley's records are produced by Bob Crewe (also the producer of records by the Four Seasons). Crewe, one of the industry's top independent producers, was responsible for Lesley's most recent top ten waxing, "California Nights."

When Lesley isn't singing, she enjoys going out for a spin in her Jaguar XKE. She's also an active athlete and has played golf in celebrity tournaments with Perry Como and other top-notchers.

When not at school, Lesley lives at home with her family in Tenafly, N.J. Her father handles her business affairs and acts as her personal manager.

School and her career have left little time for dating, but she does manage to sandwich them into her schedule. She does think of marriage but not in specifics at this busy time in her life.

# Buffalo Springfield

## *September 30, 1967*

IN THE SPRING OF 1966, FIVE YOUNG MUSICIANS TOO POOR TO AFFORD rehearsal space were practicing at the edge a road in Los Angeles. Suddenly a steamroller roared by, bearing on its sides colorful signs which read "Buffalo Springfield." The group had found itself a name.

The five Buffalo are Steve Stills, Richie Furay, Neil Young, Bruce Palmer, and Dewey Martin.

Each of them had played in other groups before coming to California. Steve and Richie were members of the Au Go Go Singers in New York, while Neil was leader of a Canadian group called the Squires.

Dewey had previous experience with three groups, Sir Walter Raleigh and the Coupons, the MFQ, and the Dillards. Bruce worked as a bassist before joining the Springfield.

Their first engagement as a group came on a seven-day, one-nighter tour with the Byrds. That tour netted them a two-week job at the Whiskey A Go Go in Hollywood.

Charles Green and Brian Stone, who previously managed Sonny and Cher, heard them one night, liked the sound, and signed them to a contract for their York-Pala production firm. Green and Stone quickly recorded the boys and got them a contract with Atco Records.

On July 25, 1966, the Buffalo Springfield became the first group ever to appear at a rock concert at the Hollywood Bowl without having a hit record. They remedied that situation three days later by releasing their first single, "Nowadays Clancy Can't Even Sing."

Their first single didn't do nearly as well as their second, "For What It's Worth," which was an immediate hit. Their current release, "Rock-n-Roll

Woman," is getting airplay in several cities and should bring the group back into the charts.

Of all the boys, Neil had the most unusual musical beginning. He attributes his musical career to Elvis Presley and Arthur Godfrey. After watching Elvis on television, Neil rushed out to buy an Arthur Godfrey ukulele. He quit school to wander around the Canadian countryside, playing his music and writing as well. On impulse, he bought a hearse, packed his guitar and bass guitarist Bruce Palmer, whom he had met along the way, and went to California.

Dewey Martin, the drummer, was once a baseball player. He turned to music in the early 60s, moving from Canada to Nashville and working with the Grand Old Opry, Roy Orbison, the late Patsy Cline, and Carl Perkins.

Not much is known about Bruce. He wears Indian clothes and beaded moccasins and plays with his back to the audience. Rumor has it that he comes from Liverpool, Canada, and that he's twenty years old.

"But one thing is certain," says Richie, "Bruce plays the bossest bass guitar around."

# The Cowsills

## *October 21, 1967*

THEY HAD NO MONEY, THE PHONES HAD BEEN DISCONNECTED, THERE wasn't any oil for the furnace, and it was bitter cold all winter. In desperate need of financial help, the Cowsills came to New York.

There, they met Artie Kornfeld, a record producer and writer. Kornfeld introduced them to a talent manager, Lenny Stogel, who got them a contract with MGM Records. Now, the Cowsills are one of the hottest groups around with their record, "The Rain, The Park, and Other Things," riding high on record surveys all around the country.

The Cowsills are more than just another group with a hit record, they're also a family. Brothers Bill, nineteen; Bob, eighteen; Barry, thirteen; and John, eleven, comprise the nucleus of the group. Whenever her voice is needed, their mother, Barbara, adds to the harmony of the group.

To keep everything in the family, the road managers are brothers Dick and Paul, and their father, Bud, coordinates the whole conglomeration. Susan, the youngest, is the only sister in the otherwise all-brother family.

The Cowsills live in a weird twenty-two-room "Munster-like mansion" in Newport, Rhode Island. Ivy grows all over the walls of the house, windows are broken, screens are hanging, and the grass has grown to a height of three feet.

The interior of the house matches the exterior. The living room contains one large sofa, two chairs, and a TV set. Meals are cooked on a 1917 gas range stove, which "requires a prayer to light it."

What's supposed to be a library houses a ping-pong table and the would-be dining room contains a pool table. There are seven bathrooms and one shower. "Water pressure isn't so great," explains Bob. "The best time to take a shower is around 3 o'clock in the morning."

In John's room there is a cage which used to house a miniature monkey. "I saved my allowance for six weeks to get Clyde," John said. "I waited for him to come and then, the next day after I get him, I woke up in the morning and there he was, lying in the bottom of the cage, frozen!" A little white headstone marks Clyde's grave on the Cowsills property.

Bud Cowsill believes that love is the key to raising a family. "When the kids do the right thing, they know it," he says. "And when they do the wrong things, they know it.

"Whenever any member of the family has a problem, we do like all families, sweat, all the while helping it work itself out," Bud said.

The way that things are going for the Cowsills now, it looks as if most of their problems have been worked out.

# Sonny and Cher

## *October 28, 1967*

Sonny and Cher, although still bound by marriage, seem to be going their own separate ways when it comes to making records.

In 1965, Sonny and Cher recorded "I Got You Babe," which sold over 3 million copies. Ever since, their best-selling records have been solo. And now, Sonny has cut his first album as a solo artist.

According to *Billboard* magazine, Sonny's album *Sonny* is "a blockbuster as his lyrics rise to the status of beautiful poetry." The review of the album goes on to say that "it should establish Sonny in the same category with Dylan and Lennon and McCartney."

Meanwhile, Cher's "You Better Sit Down, Kids," written by Sonny, is number 79 in *Billboard*'s record survey—after only one week.

Cher met Sonny on a double date the week she turned seventeen. She remembers that his Prince Valiant haircut "made him look kind of weird," while Sonny didn't like her at first because he thought she was stuck-up. Nevertheless, they danced all night, and after seeing each other for about a year, they were married on Oct. 27, 1964. It was Sonny's second marriage.

When asked why they are admired by so many young people, Sonny said, "Kids appreciate us because everyone wants to be a little individualistic.

"At first, we tried to be different and found out fast that wasn't us," he explained. "Then we decided to be ourselves. The kids dig this. They know we are what we are. They also know that we understand them."

When they are not performing, Sonny and Cher lead conventional suburban lives. They have a modern Spanish-style house in the San Fernando Valley, and the fans that ring their doorbell are welcomed graciously. This is not an act. Sonny and Cher are friendly and sociable; they enjoy a close rapport with their public.

They also feel a deep obligation to their school-age fans. They wrote a song urging kids to stay in school and recorded it for the Office of Economic Opportunity. The song was distributed to potential dropouts along with a message from Vice-President Hubert Humphrey.

According to Sonny, his and Cher's prize moment came when Mrs. Jacqueline Kennedy asked them to entertain for a private dinner party in New York. They were equally delighted when Princess Margaret asked them to entertain for a charity ball when she visited Hollywood with her husband, Lord Snowden.

Sonny and Cher are very interested in doing charity work and have performed for the Braille Institute for the Blind, Danny Thomas's City of Hope Foundation for children with leukemia, and many others.

# Dusty Springfield

## *November 4, 1967*

FUMBLING AN ELECTRIC TRAIN DEMONSTRATION AND BLOWING THE FUSES for the entire lighting system of a department store were the final steps leading to Dusty Springfield's choosing singing as a career.

The twenty-seven-year-old British pop singer was always interested in music. When she was a youngster, she made music with a copper frying pan and an old cigar box filled with marbles.

After Dusty graduated from St. Anne's Convent High School in England, she became a salesgirl in a record shop. She soon severed this early connection with music in favor of becoming a laundry assistant.

Giving up her laundry job, Dusty went to work in a department store, where she "sold buttons, dustbins and toy electric trains." It was while demonstrating electric trains that Dusty blew the fuses in the department store and decided on singing as a career.

Dusty soon joined a singing group called the Lana Sisters and went on tour with Nat King Cole. In the meantime, Dusty's brother Tom teamed up with Tim Field and asked Dusty to form a trio with them.

Dusty accepted her brother's offer, and they formed a folk singing group known as the Springfields. Their first record, "Silver Threads and Golden Needles," became a worldwide hit.

After singing with the Springfields for a while, Dusty decided to go solo. Two of her biggest hits as a solo artist were "You Don't Have to Say You Love Me" and "Wishin' and Hopin'."

"The Look of Love," which Dusty sings in the movie *Casino Royale*, is her latest entry into the pop charts. It is currently listed as number 22 by *Billboard* magazine.

Originally, the flip side of the record, "Give Me Time," was being pushed by Philips Records. When this side didn't go anywhere, disc jockeys flipped the record and played "The Look of Love." And now it looks as though "The Look of Love" will probably receive an Academy Award nomination.

Recently, two Chicago radio stations, WVON, a rhythm-and-blues station, and WCFL, a top-forty station, got copies of a new Dusty Springfield single that was released in England. This record, "What's It Gonna Be?," drew such tremendous audience response that it will be released as her new single in this country.

Dusty's mother is very proud of her great success. Recalling Dusty's childhood, her mother said, "Well, she was a tomboy. Right from when they were young, she and Tom always made music. She didn't have any lessons, but she sang in the school choir.

"There were always musical instruments lying around," she said. "I remember I would push open doors of the rooms and instruments of all sorts would fall over. The sitting room was a rehearsal room later on."

Dusty's fans will get a chance to see her perform when she comes to this country on Wednesday to do the *Red Skelton*, *Joey Bishop*, and *Tonight* shows.

# The Doors

## *November 18, 1967*

UP UNTIL TWO WEEKS AGO, ONLY THE BEATLES AND THE MONKEES HAD ever had two albums in the top five simultaneously. Last week the Doors were added to this small but elite group.

The Doors' first album for Elektra Records, titled *The Doors*, is currently number four on *Billboard* magazine's Hot 100 album chart. Their second album, "Strange Days," has jumped from number 102 to number three in just three weeks. Both albums have earned the group Gold Records.

Their first hit single, "Light My Fire," was taken from their first album, but it had to be shortened in order to get air play. The Doors' follow-up single, "People Are Strange," dropped from number eighteen to number forty in this week's *Billboard*.

The four young men who have caused such a ruckus in the music world are Robby Krieger, twenty-one, guitar; Ray Manzarek, twenty-five, organ; John Densmore, twenty-two, drums; and Jim Morrison, vocals.

An unusual break got Robby interested in music. "The first music I heard that I liked was 'Peter and the Wolf,'" said Robby. "I accidentally sat on and broke the record. I was about seven then."

Robby studied trumpet at age ten, but nothing came of it. At seventeen, he started playing the guitar. "Records got me into the blues," he said. "I was greatly influenced by Paul Butterfield. If it hadn't been for Butterfield going electric, I probably wouldn't have gone into rock 'n' roll."

Ray's start in music began when his parents gave him piano lessons when he was nine or ten years old. "I hated it for the first four years, until I learned how to do it, and it became fun," Ray said.

"I first heard Negro music when I was twelve or thirteen," Ray said. "I was playing baseball in a playground and someone had a radio tuned in to a Negro station. From then on, I was hooked.

"I used to listen to Al Benson and Big Bill Hill, disc jockeys in Chicago," he said. "From then on, all the music I listened to was on the radio. My piano playing changed; I became influenced by jazz. I learned how to play stride piano with my left hand and I knew that was it, stuff with a beat . . . jazz, blues, rock."

Jim had some strange things to say about his musical beginnings. "You can say that it's an accident that I'm really suited for the work I'm doing," Jim said. "It's the feeling of a bow string being pulled back for twenty-two years and suddenly being let go.

"I am primarily an American; second a Californian; third, a Los Angeles resident. I've always been attracted to ideas that were about revolt against authority. When you make your peace with authority you become an authority.

"I like ideas about the breaking away or overthrowing of established order," Jim said. "It seems to me to be the road toward freedom. External revolt is a way to bring about internal freedom. Rather than starting inside, I start outside and reach the mental through the physical."

The Doors will be making their last appearance in Washington this year in the International Ballroom of the Washington Hilton Hotel. Appearing with the Doors will be the Nitty Gritty Dirt Band.

Jim Morrison (The Doors) Backstage
in Baltimore
PHOTO BY MIKE KLAVANS

# The Turtles

## *December 2, 1967*

THE TURTLES' FIRST CONCERT IN THE WASHINGTON AREA THRILLED MORE than 3,000 fans who jammed the Alexandria Roller Rink to see the Jack Alix-sponsored show on Nov. 22, but it ended with nothing but problems for the Turtles.

During intermission at the show, Mark Volman, the curly-haired vocalist for the Turtles, said that he really thought the crowd was a good one and that he liked playing in Alexandria.

But it's doubtful that he and the rest of the Turtles felt the same way the next day. Early that morning about $4,000 worth of guitars, amplifiers, and other musical equipment—including an electric sitar—was stolen from the Turtles.

Doug Briggman, a teen-age member of WEAM radio's Junior Achievement Corp., Micro-Media, said that the equipment was stolen from a car on the parking lot of the Holiday Inn on Route 1 south of Alexandria, where the group was staying.

Doug is offering a $200 reward for the equipment—no questions asked—since the group may have to cancel a tour to Japan if they don't get it back. To collect the reward, the finders should get in touch with Briggman at xxx-0391.

Besides Volman, the Turtles are Howard Kaylan, Al Nichol, John Barbata, and Jim Pons. Howard's wife, Melita, who accompanied the group to the show, was born in Arlington, VA, but now lives in California.

When asked about the difference between music on the East Coast and on the West Coast, Howard said, "Every group in the East sounds like the Young Rascals, and out West all the groups sound like the Jefferson Airplane."

Howard calls the Turtles' sound "contemporary pop." "It's a happy sound," he said. "We don't try to depress people."

Before the Turtles chose their present name, they were called the Crossfires. At that time, they were putting out a surfing sound, and when that type of music started to die, the boys decided to call it quits. Luckily, before they disbanded, some agents for White Whale Records heard them and signed them to a contract.

After they signed with White Whale, they changed their name and released their first Turtles record, "It Ain't Me Babe," a Bob Dylan tune. Since that time, their biggest selling record has been "Happy Together" (close to 2 million copies).

Right now, the Turtles' newest number, "She's My Girl," is number twenty-four on *Billboard*'s chart, and their album *Golden Hits* is number seventy-six on *Billboard*'s LP chart.

Mark, who bears a strong resemblance to Marty Allen of the comedy team of Allen and Rossi, is married and has one child, but he doesn't take them along when the group tours.

"Being away from home doesn't get me down," Mark said. "I miss my wife, but we talk on the phone all the time. She digs what I'm doing and likes all the guys in the group, so she doesn't mind my being away."

In the future, the Turtles plan to do more concerts, some songwriting, and if their equipment is returned, they will probably tour Japan.

# Musings . . . The Attack

## *December 8, 1967*

THE NIGHT OF DECEMBER 8, 1967, IS EMBEDDED IN MY HEAD IN MORE ways than one. It was a night that changed my life forever.

My memories of that night begin with leaving a club in the Georgetown area of Washington, D.C. I had gone to hear a group called the Cookies. It was getting late, and I made the decision not to stay to interview the group.

What follows is part of a first-person retelling of that night that was published in the *Evening Star* on December 19, 1967. The first person was me, and I was interviewed by *Evening Star* reporter Don Smith. Some things have been omitted and other things corrected and updated:

It was a deserted street, dimly lit by one lamp. On the other side was a string of row houses. On my side there was a parking lot enclosed by a large chain link fence.

They had stopped me to ask directions. I was glad to help them out. They seemed friendly: clean-cut and nicely dressed.

I assumed they were servicemen. All of them had very short hair and looked to be in good physical shape. A lot of GIs come to Georgetown on weekends. You just don't see four guys walking around with short hair like that anymore unless they are in the service.

I had been a short walk from the "Strip" a section of M Street with a number of nightclubs that cater mostly to the college crowd.

I would like to have stayed longer at the club, but I had to be at work at 6 a.m. the next morning. I looked down at the watch my father had given me two weeks before when mine had run down for the last time. It was 10:30 and I had a forty-minute drive to get home.

When I got to about the middle of the block where my car was parked, I noticed them walking toward me, about fifty feet away. They were walking abreast. When they were about five feet away, I stepped off the sidewalk. I didn't give it a second thought. They were looking straight at me and slowing their pace.

When they got beside me, they stopped and one said, "Wait a minute. Could you tell us where some of the action is? Where are some of the good places around here?'

They were all about the same height—a few inches taller than me. There was nothing unusual in their manner or tone. I had been asked directions in Georgetown many times before.

"Go down the next street," I said, pointing toward 28th Street. "Take a left and the next street will be 'M' Street. Then take a right and keep walking and you'll begin to see nightclubs."

They asked me where I had just been and what band was playing. They asked me what the cover charge was. I told them that there were plenty of clubs in Georgetown and they would have no problem finding one.

While I was talking, I noticed one of them begin to move behind me. The other three had started to form a small circle around me. At that moment, I realized I was in trouble. I noticed something sticking out of the jacket pocket of the one standing in front of me. It was a large, empty soda bottle.

There was no place to run. The four of them tightened their circle around me. I tried to diffuse the situation by talking to them. I asked if they were in the service, but they ignored the question and asked me again about how to get to some good places.

The one with the bottle in his pocket was talking. He was standing with his feet apart and his hands on his hips. For some reason I glanced at my watch. It was 10:40.

Out of the corner of my eye I saw a glint of silver. I turned halfway around and saw that the one standing behind me had taken a monkey wrench out of his jacket pocket. He hit me to the left and rear of the top of my head. I saw white light and my body felt hot all over.

I let out a small scream but continued standing. There was a lot of pain. I felt a warm, wet sensation in my nose and tasted blood in my mouth. I saw the wrench coming again. He was swinging it around toward my nose. The blow sent me reeling onto my back and across the sidewalk. I landed on the grass next to the fence. My arms had gone numb and were lying by my sides. I couldn't use them to try to stop the blows.

The three who had been in front of me were just watching calmly, as if they were used to seeing this kind of thing. The one with the wrench shouted excitedly, "Keep quiet or we'll kill you!"

I kept quiet. The one with the wrench continued to beat me with it and was joined by the one with the bottle. I could do nothing but hope it would all be over soon—either I would pass out from the pain or they would leave. Leave me alive.

While I was being beaten the others squatted down and began rummaging through my pants pockets. One pulled out my wallet, another took off my high school ring. One of them slipped my watch off of my wrist, cocked his head as he examined it briefly and put it in his pocket.

The one with the wrench finally stopped hitting me. I believe they thought I was dead. One of them threw my wallet onto my stomach and then they all ran in the same direction they had originally been walking.

When I thought they were far enough away, I stood up and staggered a few feet. I don't know if they saw me or not, but they didn't come back.

I was covered with blood. My nose didn't have any feeling in it but my head was pounding with pain. Somehow, I managed to walk across the street and knocked on a door where there was a light on. Either nobody was home or they decided not to answer the door.

I knocked on the next door and a woman wearing glasses answered it. She looked terrified when she saw me. The door swung shut but immediately opened again, and there were two men standing there. Both, I found out later, were doctors.

They took me into the foyer and put me down on a rug, one of them cradling my head with a towel.

Two policemen arrived. One went across the street to where the attack had taken place. He returned with my eyeglasses. Somehow, they were intact though they had flown off my head from the impact of the initial blow with the wrench. The policeman also had my wallet, emptied of cash by my attackers. The wallet was covered with my blood. The policeman used a handkerchief to wipe the blood off the wallet. That was the first of several mistakes the police made. Any fingerprints that might have been on my bloody wallet had just been erased.

While I was being questioned by one of the policemen, an ambulance arrived. An EMT told me not to worry, that head wounds always bled profusely. I was lifted onto a gurney and the ambulance took me the short distance to Georgetown University Hospital.

In the ER, a doctor put temporary sutures in my head wound. My parents had been called and arrived at the ER as I was being wheeled into a room for X-rays. A police detective had already asked me, just before I was X-rayed, for a description of my attackers.

I was laying on a gurney in the ER hallway when a doctor came out and talked to my parents and the detective. I couldn't hear what was being said. I did see and hear what transpired next. The detective walked over to a payphone in the hallway, called his precinct and said, "Get two homicide detectives over to the Georgetown ER right away!" For a moment I though he was talking about another case. Then, a neurosurgeon walked over to my gurney and said, "Michael, you have a depressed skull fracture. A piece of your skull about the size of a silver dollar was splintered into your brain. Emergency neurosurgery is necessary!"

My first thought was, "What an asshole thing for the detective to say on the phone . . . loud enough for me to hear." My second thought was, "Homicide, neurosurgery . . . it may all be over for me."

I looked over at my mother as I was being wheeled into surgery. I could see that she had been crying. I don't know how many hours I was in surgery. I remember waking up the next day and seeing an Asian man sitting next to my bed. He said, "Michael, my name is Dr. Kashima. I'm a plastic surgeon. Your nose was broken in a number of places. It has already begun to set. I'm going to have to break it again and then I'll put it back in very nice shape."

"Shit," I thought, "I must be having a nightmare." But, no, this was really happening. Dr. Kashima explained that he couldn't work on my nose during the neurosurgery. Now, he couldn't even give me an anesthetic because it might mask signs of a concussion. He put the side rail of the bed up and told me to hold on. He stuck what looked like a small nutcracker up my nostrils and swiftly wrenched it across my face. I saw white light and felt incredibly intense pain as I heard the sound of my nose breaking. Dr. Kashima then took what looked like a tool that you would pick the nut meat out of a walnut and put it up one nostril and began the painful process of setting my nose.

I didn't know that earlier he had asked my mother for a photo of me so he could give me my old nose back. Had I known that, I would have asked if he could give me Robert Redford's nose instead.

After around a week in intensive care, the stitches in my nose and head were removed. I now had a silver dollar–size hole in my skull with skin stretched tight over it. I was told that if after around three months the bone in my skull hadn't grown back together, I would need either a metal plate or a bone graft. Luckily, there wasn't major brain damage. My right hand was kind of numb and has stayed that way.

Well, months went by and the hole in my skull hadn't closed a bit. I went back into Georgetown University Hospital for a second neurosurgery and had a metal plate put in to replace the missing skull. My recovery from that second neurosurgery was even more difficult than from the initial surgery. My body didn't react well to the foreign material that was inserted and screwed into my skull. But here I am over fifty years after that ordeal and I feel good and am able to write about it.

# Cream

## *January 20, 1968*

"It will never work," was the cry of cynics in England when they heard that three of the most successful musicians in the country were planning to band together for "musical freedom."

Now those three musicians, Eric Clapton, Jack Bruce, and Ginger Baker, are members of one of the most successful recording trios in the world, Cream.

Before forming Cream, Clapton played lead guitar for two highly successful British groups, John Mayall and the Blues Breakers and the Yardbirds. Bruce, bass guitar player for Cream, and Baker, the group's drummer, both played with the Graham Bond Organization before joining Clapton.

During an interview shortly after Cream's first album, *Fresh Cream*, was released a little over a year ago, Clapton discussed his feelings about the album. "I couldn't tell you a lie, I am not so happy about it, as it could have been better," he said.

"We were working on it so long and we have greatly improved since then," Eric said. "I am not completely happy with the production. It's good but ..."

Many fans of Cream consider the group a blues group, but when Eric was asked what type of group Cream is, he said, "Pop group is a fair description. I think the reason we have been accepted is because everything else has been done now.

"People have seen everybody and now their minds are wide open," Eric said. "It's a completely open market."

Cream recently released their second album, *Disraeli Gears*, which is among the top fifteen selling albums in this country.

It's been over a year between the release of Cream's first and second albums and in that time Clapton's guitar playing has improved from being excellent on the first album to perfection on the second.

Even after *Fresh Cream*, which has been on the bestselling charts for thirty-six weeks, was released, Clapton was satisfied with his guitar playing. "I have got to the point now where my playing satisfies me technically and I am now realizing the importance of visual impact the same way Pete Townshend (lead guitar player for the Who, who at the end of every act smashes his guitar into the stage) has."

On both albums, and when playing in person with the group, Clapton gets many strange sounds out of his guitar, including a violin-like tone. When asked how he does this, Clapton explained: "I get the violin sound by putting everything full on and using finger vibrato. I work for a long time to get it because I always knew it was the sound I wanted.

"I can't exactly describe how it's done, because it's a freak effect, a lucky combination of guitar and amplifier which I stumbled upon by accident," he said.

Unlike most other recording groups, Cream rely mainly on album sales instead of singles. They have stopped releasing singles altogether in England, but they release an occasional single in this country. Their latest American release is "Sunshine of Your Love," taken from their second album.

# Mitch Ryder

## *February 3, 1968*

If it hadn't been for Little Richard, Mitch Ryder might not have become the blue-eyed soul singer that he is.

It was Little Richard's recording of "Keep A' Knockin'" a few years back that launched Mitch into his musical career. After he heard that record, Mitch began sitting in with local groups around Detroit who were later to become the major acts of the Tamla-Motown record label.

Deciding he wanted to make it on his own, Ryder started touring the country with his back-up band, the Detroit Wheels.

Now Ryder no longer works with the Detroit Wheels, as he would rather have a big band sound backing him. When he goes on tour, he usually has full orchestration and more elaborate arrangements than he had with the Wheels.

Mitch takes pride in his stage show and likes nothing better than an appreciative audience. "I think that the exciting thing about the present-day scene is the excitement itself," he says. "It is marvelous to be on stage and feel the audience reacting.

"I can't understand the performer who is satisfied with polite applause," Mitch says. "The greatest thing in the world is to have the audience right there every step of the way. There has to be this give and take so that the performer and the audience experience the same thing at the same time. That's why they are in the same place."

Since Mitch is on the road most of the year, playing everything from county fairs to college homecomings, he really enjoys getting home to Detroit to be with his wife, Sue, and his young daughter, Dawn. "When I walk in the door," he says, "I go into another world. I'm home."

Mitch's latest disc, "Personality," is a combination of two old records, "Chantilly Lace" and "Personality." Mitch seems to like the idea of combining songs, as this is the third time he's combined two previously released songs as one record. The other two combinations were "Devil with a Blue Dress On" on the same disc as "Good Golly, Miss Molly" and "Too Many Fish in the Sea" combined with "Three Little Fishes (sic)."

Shortly after Mitch dropped the Detroit Wheels, *Esquire* magazine wrote: "Mitch Ryder is special. He is the genuine article . . . intelligent, good looks, and his stage presence is extraordinary.

"The myth of the soul performer is one of identification rather than entertainment," the article went on to say. "It is to Ryder's credit that he can make it work in a new context. Ryder does soul as well as it can be done."

# Boyce and Hart

## *February 17, 1968*

IN THE SPRING OF 1967, TWO YOUNG SONGWRITERS, TOMMY BOYCE AND Bobby Hart, decided to become a singing team and now their recording of a song they wrote, "I Wonder What She's Doing Tonight," is number ten on *Billboard*'s top 100 chart.

Before they launched their careers as singers, Boyce and Hart had written more than thirty hit songs for artists such as Dean Martin, Little Anthony, Tommy Sands, Jay and the Americans, and the Monkees. It was the Monkees, however, who had the most success with Boyce-Hart compositions.

Songs like "Last Train to Clarksville," "The Monkees Theme," and "I Want to Be Free," brought both the Monkees and Boyce and Hart national acclaim.

Both Tommy and Bobby had musical childhoods. Tommy's parents were singers; his father once had his own country and western band. Bobby's father was a preacher, so Bobby developed his musical instincts in church.

When he was twelve, Tommy migrated with his family from his birthplace in Charlottesville, Virginia, to Los Angeles and at the same time, his father began teaching him guitar. While he was still in school, Tommy sold his first hit, "Be My Guest," which was recorded by Fats Domino.

Meanwhile, in Phoenix, Arizona, Bobby had his 18th birthday and left to serve in the army for six months. After his active duty, he went to Hollywood, where he found his first job in show business, printing record labels.

It was in Hollywood that Bobby's and Tommy's paths crossed and they formed a songwriting team. Their first number one song was "Come a Little Bit Closer," by Jay and the Americans.

Although they were writers and friends together, Tommy and Bobby were performers singly for a long time before they decided to pool their singing talents. Tommy had appeared as Tommy Boyce on many tours and television shows, and Bobby had been a soloist and leader of a rock group called the Candy Store Prophets before they joined A & M Records as a singing team last year.

Now that Tommy and Bobby have both fame and fortune, they would like to own their own island. As a matter of fact, they've already picked one, off the coast of South America. It's small, five by twenty miles, but if they have a few more hits, they might just buy it.

The boys' plans for the future include both writing and singing. And, with their feet already planted firmly in both fields, they can't miss.

# Georgie Fame

## *February 24, 1968*

ALTHOUGH THE MOVIE *BONNIE AND CLYDE*, IS A HIT IN NORWAY, GEORGIE Fame's recording, "The Ballad of Bonnie and Clyde," has been banned in that country.

"I don't know why it was banned, but it's certainly amusing to see the different reactions to the record in different countries," Georgie said during an interview before he co-hosted WDCA's Wing Ding with Scott Wallace.

Georgie, who hails from England, is making a whirlwind tour of this country to promote "The Ballad of Bonnie and Clyde," which reached the number one position on the British charts.

"America is such a big place," Georgie said. "This traveling from city to city really wears me out. I'll probably have to leave this country on a stretcher."

It's been three years since Georgie's last hit in America, "Yeh, Yeh." Now his new song, which is not the theme from Bonnie and Clyde, but rather a story about the two murderers, looks as if it may soon top this country's charts.

Traveling with Georgie is his manager, Rick Gunnell. Besides managing Georgie, Rick owns an agency in England that handles some of that country's best talent, including P. J. Proby, Alan Price, Chris Farlowe, and John Mayall and the Bluesbreakers.

When asked to compare the American music scene to the British music scene, Rick said, "There's a much larger young audience in America. In England, most of the acts draw an older audience, except for the Bee Gees.

"Also, we go in for a lot more soul in England then we used to. Then, we've still got sing-a-long types like Tom Jones and Engelbert Humperdinck for the Moms and Dads."

Georgie, who is twenty-four, started singing professionally eight years ago. He was influenced early in life by Fats Domino and Jerry Lee Lewis. His basic sound is sort of jazz-oriented rock.

Georgie, who leaves for home on March 2, will probably be back in this country in June for a concert tour. "If I bring my own band with me, I'd like to do some college gigs," he said. "I don't think I'm ready for the American nightclub scene at this stage of the game."

A concert in a bullring in Spain is just one item on Georgie's agenda for the near future. The concert is being sponsored by Coke and the Spanish government, and Georgie will be paid $14,400 for one performance.

Georgie and Rick both hope that after "The Ballad of Bonnie and Clyde," which is number forty-nine on the American charts this week, fades, Georgie won't have another three-year absence from this country.

# Blood, Sweat and Tears

## *March 23, 1968*

WHAT STARTED OUT AS A FAREWELL EAST COAST PERFORMANCE FOR FOUR young musicians turned into the beginning of a new dimension in pop music.

It was last July when organist-composer Al Kooper, drummer Bobby Colomby, bass player Jim Fielder, and lead guitarist and singer Steve Katz got together in New York's Café Au Go Go to give what was to be their "farewell" East Coast performance before heading to California. Although they didn't realize it at the time, they had formed the nucleus of a new rock group, Blood, Sweat and Tears.

Soon after their "farewell" performance, the group added a skilled horn section comprised of Jerry Weiss and Randy Brecker (trumpets), Dick Halligan (trombone), and Fred Lipsius (saxophone). This horn section, together with the original rhythm section, enables Blood, Sweat and Tears to perform their own compositions, as well as those written by other composers (such as Tim Buckley), with the force and style that is usually lacking in other pop groups.

Al Kooper, who is adept at playing the piano, guitar, bass, drums, and harmonica, besides the organ, played with Bob Dylan at the Hollywood Bowl and was a member of the Blues Project before organizing Blood, Sweat and Tears. Al has written a number of compositions, among them "I Love You More Than You'll Ever Know," "My Days Are Numbered," "I Can't Quit Her" and "House in the Country"—that appear on the group's debut Columbia album, "Child Is Father to the Man."

The co-organizer of the group, Steve Katz, is also a former member of the Blues Project. "My ambition," says Steve, "is to influence music and free thought, the latter both politically and sociologically. I would like to see this generation fulfill all of its long-range ambitions, which I think it is so well starting to do."

Steve has been musically influenced most of his life. "I sang at weddings and Bar Mitzvahs until I was about fifteen," he says. "Then I started taking music more seriously and decided to perform professionally.

"I joined the Even Dozen Jug Band, made an album with them and did a number of TV spots," says Steve. "We also played Carnegie Hall twice. Then I was asked to join the Blues Project, which was really my biggest professional break."

Before playing with Al Kooper for the first time at the Big Sur Folk Festival in July, Jim Fielder played with the Mothers of Invention and Buffalo Springfield. Jim's favorite groups are the New York Philharmonic, Cream, and the Beatles.

"The trend today," Jim says, "is away from trends. To be a competent musician, one must be in tune with all types and styles of music, all these types seem to be fusing into a medium which may only be classified as 'music.' Everything today is valid and has a place."

# The Troggs

## *March 30, 1968*

WHAT IS A TROGG?

In short, the name is derived from troglodyte, an ethnological term that means someone who creeps into holes or caverns or dwells in caves.

The Troggs, a British rock group, do neither, although their first record, "Wild Thing," gave them a caveman type image. Their latest single on the Fontana label, "Love Is All Around," a relatively soft sounding record compared to "Wild Thing," is number twenty-eight on *Billboard*'s top 100 chart and is still climbing.

The quartet, consisting of Pete Staples, Chris Britton, Reg Presley, and Ronnie Bond, is now touring the United States and will appear at Constitution Hall tomorrow at 8:30 p.m. along with the Who, Beacon Street Union, and Orpheus.

According to *Disc and Music Echo*, a British weekly, the Troggs hoped to play to GI audiences in Vietnam, but the State Department told the group that US forces could not protect them as they were British subjects.

"Of course we'll be playing to kids in the US who will wind up in Vietnam, but we wanted to give the troops some of what they're getting back home," says Reg.

However, the Troggs don't give up easily, and they have gone to the Australian and New Zealand governments to try to win Allied protection in case they get to Vietnam. But this could limit the tour to areas in which Australian and New Zealand forces are operating.

"We'll go ahead with the tour if we can get protection from them," Reg says. "We'd be so close to the war I don't think we'd realize it was all happening to us."

When asked about the group's new single, Chris said, "'Love Is All Around' is not so blatantly and obviously sexy, not so aggressive as our other hits. It makes a change."

The Troggs prefer to write their own numbers. "If you do somebody else's material you don't get across the same feeling as if you write it yourself," says Chris. "When you write a song, you can express it better.

"The group now chooses which numbers we want to do and record them the way we want to do them," he said.

"People say we have a different sound," Chris says, " but we can't vouch for that. The sound we produce it's just us, the way we've always played since we joined together."

The Troggs future plans include a new album and a follow-up single. Although they haven't had a record on the American charts for a long time, the Troggs have had seven hits in England, including "Night of the Long Grass" and "Hi, Hi Hazel" (done in this country by Gary and the Hornets).

# Beacon Street Union

## *April 6, 1968*

THEY CAME, THEY PLAYED, THEY CONQUERED.

The much talked about "Boston Sound" came to Washington last Sunday night, and the two groups who brought it to Constitution Hall left a lasting impression on the near-capacity audience.

The first of the two Boston groups that played, the Beacon Street Union, is a hard-rock quintet and the second, Orpheus, has a much softer sound. Headlining the show were the Who and for the first time in America, the Troggs.

It's been almost two years since the five young men who make up the Beacon Street Union got together. Bob Rhodes, the organ and piano player for the Union, organized the group whose other members are Wayne Vlaky, bass; Paul Tarachny, lead guitar; Dick Weisberg, drums; and John Wright, vocals.

During an interview before the show, John explained how the group got its name. "We came up with the Beacon Street Union because Beacon Street is a famous street in Boston, and we're from Boston," he said.

John explained that the "Boston Sound" isn't really a sound, it's just a name given to all the groups that are "making it" in Boston.

"'The Boston Sound' is just a thing that was building up for a long time," John said. "It's like a bubble that burst and now everybody knows that there are good rock groups in Boston.

"There are a lot of hip people in Boston and it's a good place to make things happen," John continued. "Good groups were always abundant there, but only one or two groups were really doing things. Activity kept building until record companies started signing groups."

When asked how the group landed a contract with MGM Records, Dick said: "Wes Farrell, an independent producer, saw us, liked us and signed us. He produced our album, 'The Eyes of the Beacon Street Union,' and sold it in a package deal to MGM. This was before anyone heard of the Boston Sound.

Orpheus, the other Boston group, like the Beacon Street Union, has a new album on the national charts. The album, entitled *Orpheus*, also contains the group's hit single, "Can't Find the Time to Tell You."

The sound put across by Orpheus is unique, because, unlike other rock groups, Orpheus uses two amplified folk guitars along with an electric bass and drums. The four young Bostonians who make up that group are Bruce Arnold, vocals and lead guitar; Jack McKenes, vocals and guitar; John Eric Gulliksen, vocals and bass; and Harry Sandler, drums.

# Blue Cheer

## *April 13, 1968*

"These guys are just like Hells Angels. The only difference is that they don't have motorcycles, they have their instruments."

So says Gut, a former Hells Angel now co-manager of San Francisco's most successful hard rock trio, Blue Cheer.

With more than $20,000 worth of equipment, including six Marshall amplifiers, twenty-four speakers, and a "Coliseum" PA system, Blue Cheer bombards its listeners with a truly mind splitting sound.

Leigh Stevens on lead guitar, Dickie Peterson on electric bass, and Paul Whaley on drums make up the trio, which works basically out of a rhythm-and-blues bag.

"Actually, we just use some of the stuff that's been prevalent in R & B and put it into our own music," says Dickie. "But we are really just starting to get into it."

Blue Cheer is a loud, hard and "heavy" group. They play that way because, as Paul puts it, "The music goes through our bodies, and when we can feel music, it's much easier to experience it."

And, adds Leigh, "We are just saying we feel good by putting as much as we physically can into our music. There are no hidden messages as such in our sound. When anyone listens to a message, it generally gets all twisted around, just like when you whisper something from person to person around a crowded room."

Blue Cheer's first LP, *Vincebus Eruptum* (which means we conquer chaos), is currently number fourteen on *Billboard*'s album chart. The group's single, "Summertime Blues," an old Eddie Cochran hit, is one of the six songs featured on the LP. It's number nineteen and still rising on *Billboard*'s singles chart.

Blue Cheer is working on its second album now and it's recording some of the cuts outdoors at Muir Beach, near San Francisco.

Even before the release of *Vincebus Eruptum*, a DJ on KMPX, San Francisco's underground station, said to his listeners: "If I played all the Blue Cheer requests, I wouldn't have time to play any other records."

Due to the tremendous popularity of the group on the West Coast, their records are finally getting much deserved airplay in the East. This has also resulted in a tour of the East, which will take the group to the Fillmore East, New York, April 26 and 27; the Electric Factory, Philadelphia, May 3 to 5; the Action House, Long Island, May 10 to 12; and Kennedy Memorial Stadium, Philadelphia, May 18.

"I've been following audience reaction very closely," says Gut, "and now when Blue Cheer comes on, there's a far-out response. They're the only band I've seen that's gotten everyone up from sitting on the floor of the Avalon (a psychedelic dance hall in San Francisco) and into dancing.

"It's just outrageous," says Gut. "The reaction is no longer one of just applause. The kids just can't control themselves."

Says Gut about the group's success: "This whole thing has just blown our minds completely."

# The Association

## *April 20, 1968*

A POOR TURNOUT, POSSIBLY BECAUSE OF THE CURFEW IN THE DISTRICT, didn't stop the Association from putting on a great show at Shady Grove last week.

The six-member California-based group went through all their hits from their first, "Along Comes Mary," to their latest, "Everything That Touches You," duplicating the sound of their recordings perfectly.

During an interview before the show, Jim Yester, who plays guitar and organ for the group, explained how the Association ended up on the Warner Brothers label. "Originally we were with Valiant Records, a very small company," Jim said. "Valiant was doing well, and Warner Brothers had been observing the company and decided to buy it."

The name Yester is a familiar one in the music world. Jim's brother, Jerry, is a member of the Lovin' Spoonful, and their father, Larry Yester, plays the organ at the Lancer restaurant on Wisconsin Avenue in D.C.

Besides Jim, the other members of the Association are Terry Kirkman, flugelhorn, tambourine, drums, harp and recorder; Brian Cole, bass guitar; Russ Giguere, rhythm guitar; Larry Ramos, lead guitar; and Ted Bluechel, drums and guitar.

Everyone in the group writes songs, but Terry seems to be the most talented in that field. The tunes he has penned include "Cherish," "Everything That Touches You," "Requiem for the Masses," and some lesser known songs that are on the group's new album, *Birthday*.

According to Terry, "Requiem for the Masses," which appears on the group's *Insight Out* album, is not an antiwar song. "The song was written about people who do things without thinking," Terry said. "The kind of people who drive cars too fast and get into fights."

Larry Ramos, the newest member of the group, was with the New Christie Minstrels before he joined the Association a year ago. He left the Christies because "everyone in the group was an employee, not a member. It was frustrating and stifled all individual creativity," he said.

None of the boys have any favorite musical groups. "We dig everything," Jim said. "I have stacks and stacks of albums, from Wagner to Simon and Garfunkel and from the Rolling Stones to Beethoven."

Being on the road at least 250 days of the year doesn't bother Jim. "I've always had wanderlust and, being with the group, I can satisfy it," he said. "The only thing I hate is being in the same city for more than a day or two."

A new single can be expected from the group soon, probably taken from their *Birthday* album.

# Jefferson Airplane

## *April 27, 1968*

GRACE SLICK, THE LEAD VOCALIST FOR THE JEFFERSON AIRPLANE, IS STILL belting out tunes for the San Francisco–based rock group.

Rumors that Grace had left the group have been circulating for some time but were proved false last Saturday when the Airplane landed at Shady Grove. After Grace and her five male companions did "Somebody to Love" "White Rabbit," and some lesser known songs, Grace talked backstage about the rumors.

"There have been so many rumors about members of the group," Grace said, "that when someone really does leave the group, nobody will know it."

The Airplane, the first rock group to appear on the *Bell Telephone Hour* on TV, and the first to receive an invitation to the Tanglewood Music Festival, were recently honored by having their names appear with other famous Americans in the 1968 edition of *Who's Who in America*.

Besides Grace, the members of the group are Paul Kantner, guitar and vocals; Jorma Kaukonen, lead and rhythm guitar and vocals; Jack Casady, bass guitar; Spencer Dryden, drums; and Marty Balin, guitar and vocals.

So far, the Airplane have three RCA albums to their credit, "The Jefferson Airplane Takes Off," "Surrealistic Pillow," and "After Bathing at Baxter's," but none of the albums was planned in advance.

"If something sounds fantastic when we do it live, we might record it," Grace said. "Some songs are good live, but too difficult to get down on tape. We never know until the last minute what we are going to put on an album."

When it comes to live performances, most of the Airplane's songs are improvised. "They all have a definite chord structure," Grace says, "but everything else is flexible."

When asked if traveling ever bothers her, Grace says that it does. "Sometimes you get the bug to travel, but when you've had too much of it, you get the bug to stay home."

Grace sees no difference between music on the East Coast and on the West Coast.

"Some people say that the East is more blues-oriented, but I don't think so. Of course, there are exceptions, and Frank Zappa of the Mothers of Invention is one of them. The East has Frank, and it's hard to compare him to anyone in this country or for that matter, the world."

The Airplane's latest single, "Greasy Heart," is not doing as well as some of the group's earlier records, but, with their busy personal appearance schedule, it is doubtful that they are ready to feather their props and glide into their hangar.

Grace Slick and Jack Casady (Jefferson Airplane)
PHOTO BY MIKE KLAVANS

# The Youngbloods

## *May 25, 1968*

EARLY IN 1967, WITH A NUMBER CALLED "GRIZZLY BEAR," THE YOUNG-bloods appeared on the record scene with a new American musical sound called "rag 'n' roll."

Based on a happy ragtime beat, underscored with a driving tempo, the sound offered by the group was a fusion of the nostalgic music of the 1920s and '30s with the switched-on pace of the '60s. But after their one hit, the group faded off the rock scene.

Now RCA Victor has launched a promotional campaign (which they call the "groupquake") for the Youngbloods and seven other rock groups.

The Youngbloods have two albums to their credit, the first titled simply *"The Youngbloods,"* and the second, *"Earth Music."* Both albums combine R & B, lyrical soft rock, and touches of country music.

The nucleus of the Youngbloods is Jesse Colin Young, a former Fuller Brush salesman from Memphis. Jesse, who plays the electric bass and sings country blues for the group, went to New York in 1964, made a couple of albums on his own, and worked around Manhattan as a folk-singer.

In the spring of 1965, Jesse met a guitarist and singer named Jerry Corbitt in a Boston coffeehouse, and the two started appearing as a duo.

The idea of the Youngbloods neared reality when Joe Bauer came on the scene. Jerry Corbitt tells it this way: "This little short-haired character from Memphis had just come to Boston looking for work. We told him we were thinking about starting a band. He was hungry and we were hungry, and that's how we got Joe."

At the time, Joe was strictly a jazz drummer, and, since the group was developing its own variety of rock, Joe had to practically re-learn the drums.

The group was completed with the arrival of Banana, whose own musical career had begun with bluegrass banjo. As a guitarist and vocalist, he took on the electric piano. Banana came to the group from his hometown of Santa Rosa, Calif., by the way of Boston University.

After working together and experimenting with various musical styles for six months, the Youngbloods presented themselves to different record companies and were finally signed by RCA.

An underlying theme in most of the Youngbloods' songs is that of peace and brotherhood. As they put it in one of their songs, "Let's Get Together":

*Everybody get together,*
*Try to love one another*

Jesse Colin Young (Youngbloods)
PHOTO BY MIKE KLAVANS

# The First Edition

## *June 1, 1968*

QUESTION: WHAT DO YOU GET WHEN YOU TAKE THREE GUYS AND ONE GIRL from the New Christy Minstrels and team them up with a drummer who has backed up Trini Lopez, Johnny Rivers, and Bob Dylan? Answer: the First Edition.

The First Edition made its first appearance in the area last week on the *Ed Ames Show* at Shady Grove Music Fair. While on stage, they mixed comedy with hard rock, blues, and folk music.

During an interview backstage, the group's drummer, Mickey Jones, explained how the group formed. "Four of the New Christy Minstrels, Mike Settle, Terry Williams, Kenny Rogers, and Thelma Camacho decided to form a rock group and they signed with the Smothers Brothers' managers, Kragen and Fritz," he said.

"One morning, Kenny Fritz called me up and said that he needed a drummer for a new group," Mickey continued. "I joined the group and now we've been together for nine months."

Before he joined the First Edition, Mickey played drums for Trini Lopez for eight years, Johnny Rivers for three years, and Bob Dylan for two years.

"I talked to Dylan three or four days ago," Mickey said. "He'll continue to cut records, but he doesn't want to do live performances anymore. He thinks the secret to life is the fact he digs staying at home in New York State with his wife and kids."

Staying at home is something the First Edition doesn't do much of. Since the success of their first record, "Just Dropped In (to See What Condition My Condition Was In)," the group has been touring the country, making personal appearances and doing numerous TV shows.

Mickey, offstage the most outspoken member of the group, would like to become an actor. Already he has appeared in quite a few movies and television shows. His movie credits include *Planet of the Apes*, *Wild in the Streets*, and *Hell's Angels on Wheels*, while his television credits include *The Daniel Boone Show* and *Custer*.

"In '*Planet of the Apes*,' I played an ape in the scene where the apes were riding horses and shooting at humans and I also played an ape in the scene where Charlton Heston was standing trial," Mickey said.

Onstage, each member of the group only wears black and white. Mickey explained that in the beginning the group was going to have two outfits made up—a white suit with black pinstripes and a black suit with white pinstripes. "Everyone agreed that black and white would be our colors," Mickey said. "Now when we do a color television show, we don't look like the typical rock group with multi-colored uniforms."

Out of all the crowds the First Edition has performed for, they dig college audiences the most. "We like to play for college audiences because they dig music and they don't come to see us because 'it's the thing to do'—they want to hear the group," Terry said. "They make you want to work that much harder for them."

Reprise Records recently released the First Edition's latest single, "Charlie the Fer' De Lance," and plans for a second album are in the works.

# Leonard Cohen

## *June 15, 1968*

CANADIAN-BORN LEONARD COHEN, AN ACCLAIMED AUTHOR AND POET, has now emerged as one of the better songwriter-performers of today.

Cohen's poems and songs explore and teach the ideology of love. *Songs of Leonard Cohen*, his latest album, is a good example of the way his poems can easily be set to music. Although his voice is not the greatest (neither is Bob Dylan's), Cohen always manages to get his message across in his universally poignant songs.

Recognizing Cohen's genius, many singers have recorded his compositions. Among those who have are Judy Collins, Leon Bibb, Chad Mitchell, Noel Harrison, and Spanky and Our Gang.

*Ladies and Gentlemen . . . Mr. Leonard Cohen* is the title of a film shot by the National Film Board of Canada, which followed Leonard as he toured various colleges, singing and giving readings. The Canadian Broadcasting Co. ran the film as an Easter special and the film won resounding accolades.

News of his musical success resulted in Cohen's receiving a commission to write the theme for a NFB project, *The Angel*. After completing that assignment, he was commissioned by Don Owen, of *Nobody Waved Goodbye* fame, to write the title song and entire score for his new film, *The Ernie Game* (in which Leonard will also perform), a most noteworthy assignment since *The Ernie Game* will be the first feature-length NFB production to be commercially distributed throughout the United States and Europe.

Last summer, Cohen was enthusiastically hailed by his fellow Canadians when he appeared with Buffy St. Marie at the Mariposa Folk Festival. His American performance at the Newport Folk Festival prompted the *New*

*York Times* to rate him as "an extremely effective singer who is capable of building a hypnotic, spellbinding effect . . ."

Last July, Cohen made his New York City debut in two standing-room-only concerts in Central Park. American audiences have been further exposed to Leonard's talents through articles in such magazines as *Madamoiselle*, *Vogue*, and *Harper's Bazaar*. In addition, he was the subject of a CBS TV special, *Camera Three*.

Leonard has written two novels, *The Favorite Game* and *Beautiful Losers*, and has had four volumes of poetry published: *Spice Box of Earth*, *Let Us Compare Mythologies*, *Flowers for Hitler*, and *Parasites of Heaven*. The U.S. editions of both Cohen novels are in their second printing, and sales of *Beautiful Losers* have passed the 300,000 mark.

Cohen has a home on the Greek isle of Hydra, but frequently returns to Montreal to renew his "neurotic affiliations." A true poet and intellectual, Cohen is warmed to see his fans, and the public in general, carrying books.

# Tiny Tim

## *June 29, 1968*

TINY TIM IS FOR REAL.

Those who have talked to Tiny Tim and know him best agree that he is sincere and his act is not a put-on. His album, *God Bless Tiny Tim*, is number sixteen in the country and his single "Tip-Toe through the Tulips with Me" is number seventeen.

During a recent written interview, Tiny Tim discussed his beginnings in the music world by supplying answers to written questions. "I come from New York and my dear sweet parents have been so wonderful to me as well as my dear sweet friends," he said. "I have been singing ever since I can remember, years ago appearing in amateur shows in Brooklyn, and just all over the place.

"I sang in hospitals and for the poor in the streets," Tim said. "I even sang in back alleys and on subway trains, just to sing whatever the people wanted to hear. All I wanted to do was to spread joy all over."

Tiny, whose real name is Herbert Khaury, was born in New York City around forty years ago (he never talks about his exact age). After high school, he sang under such names as Larry Love and Derry Dover in Greenwich Village Bars.

He was given the name Tiny Tim from Dickens' *Christmas Carol* and it stuck, even though he is tall and lanky.

Besides his unusual taste in music, Tiny has many personal eccentricities, including brushing his teeth six times a day (three times with toothpaste and three times with papaya powder) and taking a "big shower" once a day for ninety minutes and several "little showers" during the day.

Tiny Tim first started singing and playing his ukulele for money in 1954, at the Alliance Club in Greenwich Village. "I won my first prize for singing 'You Are My Sunshine,'" he said. "It's such a good song. That was my first winning performance. But as far as working for a salary, that wasn't until 1963, when I first sang at the Big Fat Black Pussycat in New York."

When asked what he is trying to do today in his music, Tiny Tim said, "Well, I'm trying to bring back the happiness that was part of the beautiful tunes that were sung in the days of the past . . . the lovely days of vaudeville. Those songs even chill me today when I hear them. And the reason the songs were so unknown then, was that very few people had phonographs. Sheet music was the big thing."

Talking about the singers of the past, Tim said, "What singers we had! Irving Kaufman, one of the first vaudeville singers; Arthur Fields, the first crooner, way before the electric phonograph; and of course Rudy Vallee, Gene Austin, Mr. Jolson, Mr. Crosby, and Mr. Russ Columbo . . . God bless them all! Now as I hear these songs, I believe that they can thrill the people of today just as they thrilled the people of yesterday."

Tiny Tim doesn't believe he is turning back the clock by doing old tunes. "I love rock 'n' roll and popular music," he said. "It's just that the spirits of the singers whose songs I do are living within me. That's why the songs come out in the voices of the original singers. I'm not doing imitations. That's the way they sound inside of me."

Why does he sing a lot of songs but not all, in falsetto? Because, as he puts it, "For me, that voice is all happiness and sunshine . . . a field of flowers and the beauty in the face of a young girl. It is the light, youthful, gay, romantic spirit of my heart."

Tiny Tim will make his first area appearance at the Merriweather Post Pavilion in Columbia, MD, on July 18 at 8:30 p.m.

# Traffic

## *July 6, 1968*

Now, when the pop music highways are as crowded with groups as city streets are with cars, Traffic has come to mean something more than assorted vehicles clogging up congested roads. . . . Traffic is the name of a trio of British musicians that has worked its way up into pop circles with a refreshing new sound.

Traffic's twenty-year-old leader, Steve Winwood, was originally with the Spencer Davis Group, where he sang lead on two hit records, "Gimme Some Lovin'" and "I'm a Man."

Steve was not satisfied with the Spencer Davis Group, so he organized Traffic to suit his more progressive taste in rock. Besides Steve, the members of the group are Chris Wood, twenty-four, and Jim Capaldi, twenty-eight.

Traffic's first album, *Mr. Fantasy* (on the United Artists label), is no. eighty-eight on *Billboard*'s top LP chart . . . quite an accomplishment for a group that has never had a hit single in this country.

The album is almost "Sgt. Pepperish" in that the lyrics and music blend into a sound that takes the listener on a trip through a dream-like world. One song in particular, "Hole in My Shoe," makes use of electronic effects and the voice of a very young girl reading a beautiful, almost poetic, prose selection. The album can't be categorized, for it makes use of the best qualities of jazz, rock, rhythm-and-blues, and folk music.

About the album, Jim says: "The whole thing is crazy, I know. When I listen to it now, I sometimes can't get a grip on it, probably because I'm so close to it.

"The album is a spontaneous part of me and when it's like a part of you, then it sounds incomplete," says Jim. "Unless the song is a little story, the words are chosen for their sound rather than their meaning."

Steve, Chris, and Jim live together in a remote cottage in a secluded section of England known as Berkshire Downs. It was there the boys wrote their two biggest hits, "Paper Sun" and "Hole in My Shoe," which are included on their *Mr. Fantasy* album.

Jim doesn't believe the group is leading a "hermit-like existence," living in the semi-wilderness as they do. "We just use the place to rehearse and work," he says. "We don't like the rush of London or the noise. We can wake up when we want to.

"Most important," Jim says, "is the fact that we can make as much musical noise as we like without having some raving idiot coming in the door to complain. If we want total isolation, we can just pull out the telephone plug."

Traffic has already made one successful tour of this country, playing such clubs as Steve Paul's Scene and the Fillmore East in New York and the Whisky A'Go Go in L.A.

Musically, Traffic is in its own bag. "We might do some rock, but I think we are on our own road," Steve says. "When we started and were living in the cottage, we began by talking together and getting to know each other's ideas on music before we actually did anything.

"What we really wanted to do was to take things that were going on around us and just express them in musical terms," says Steve. "We have reached some of these achievements but there is still a lot we have to do."

Traffic returns to this country for another tour on Sept. 23, and it is hopeful that they will have a single on the charts by then.

# Nilsson

## *August 3, 1968*

"Nilsson is the something else the Beatles are."

That quote, from the liner notes on Nilsson's second album, *Aerial Ballet*, could be taken lightly if it had come from anyone else but Derek Taylor, former Beatles' press agent and close friend. But Taylor did write the liner notes and after listening to the album, one can tell that Taylor knows what he is talking about.

Nilsson, who looks like Mike Nichols in a David McCallum hairdo, was born and raised in Brooklyn, but now resides in Los Angeles. His grandparents toured the circus circuit in Europe about sixty years ago as "Nilsson's Aerial Ballet."

His first album, *Pandemonium Shadow Show*, included six Nilsson originals: "Cuddly Toy," "Sleep Late My Lady Friend," "1941" (recently a hit single by Billy J. Kramer), "Without Her," "Ten Little Indians," and "It's Been So Long."

Besides being a successful songwriter and singer, Nilsson plays piano and guitar. He also has "ghosted" for demonstration records, done TV jingles on the West Coast and an *I Spy* segment (he sang off-camera).

Wanderlust has always been second nature to Nilsson, and between school years, he hitch-hiked across the country. In Los Angeles, he attended St. John Vianney's Parochial School, where he won letters in basketball and baseball, and "moonlighted" as a theater usher.

It was in L.A. that his desire to become a performer took form. As a "gofer" (go for coffee, etc.), he came to meet many young songwriters and record producers who encouraged him to continue singing and to break in by making demonstration discs.

Until recent events convinced him of a solid career as a recording artist, Nilsson was a computer supervisor at the Security First National Bank Computer Center in Van Nuys, Calif. After beginning at the bottom and moving through several promotions in four years, when he left he had thirty-two people working under him.

When Nilsson was signed as an exclusive RCA Victor recording artist, Ernest Altschuler, division vice president and executive artist and repertoire producer, said: "He is one of the truly remarkable writing and performing talents of today, and I expect rapid public acceptance of this young man's remarkable versatility."

Although it has taken awhile for the word to spread about Nilsson, he is now known and admired by most people in the music industry. The biggest compliment Nilsson could ever receive was a recent invitation by John Lennon to come to England and spend some time with four of his greatest admirers, the Beatles.

# The Amboy Dukes

## *August 10, 1968*

QUESTION: WHAT DO A STREET GANG AND A ROCK GROUP HAVE IN COMmon? Answer: their names.

The Amboy Dukes, a six-man Detroit-based hard rock group, borrowed their name from a street gang that operated in the 1930s.

During an interview backstage at Merriweather Post Pavilion in Columbia Maryland, John Drake, the group's vocalist told about the formation of the group.

"Ted Nugent, our lead guitarist, had a group in Chicago," he said. "I was in Detroit, and Ted got in touch with me and told me he was coming to Detroit to form a new band."

John became the vocalist in the new group, and since that time they've recorded two albums and two singles, "Baby, Please Don't Go" and their current hit "Journey to the Center of the Mind."

All the Amboy Dukes records have been on the Mainstream label. The Dukes got their contract with Mainstream through their manager, Bob Hankins. "Bob had produced records for Mainstream, A & M and Motown," John said. "He was the impetus for our signing with the label."

When asked how he would classify their music, John said "You can't really classify our sound. We do everything from symphonies to some of the heaviest sounds you'll ever hear. We did all music, from Beethoven to Stevie Wonder."

Besides John and Ted, the members of the group are Andy Solomon, organ; Greg Arama, bass; Steve Farmer, rhythm guitar; and Dave Palmer, drums.

Steve, commenting on the type of audience the Amboy Dukes prefer to perform for, said, "When it comes to audiences, the bigger they are, the more we like them. We'd much rather play concerts than club dates—but we try to get as intimate with the concert audience as we would in a club.

"You can't fool audiences today," Steve continued. They're more educated. When you go on stage you have to be saying something.

"You also have to be able to duplicate the sound you put down on the record. Groups that can't duplicate that sound are fly-by-night groups."

According to their manager, the group's future plans include more records and continued success. "We'll be doing the whole US concert scene, including tours with Hendrix, Cream, the Doors, Vanilla Fudge, and Tiny Tim," Bob Hankins said.

"We're very lucky to be on these major concert tours," Bob said. "But we've earned the right to appear with people like these."

Bob, worried that the boys might be getting the label of a drug group (their album *Journey to the Center of the Mind*, has a cover photo of various pipes used to smoke marijuana), said: "The boys feel that if you're going to turn someone on, do it with music, not drugs."

# Country Joe and the Fish

## *August 17, 1968*

DON'T LET COUNTRY JOE AND THE FISH FOOL YOU. THEY'RE OUT TO entertain people just as much as they are to put across a message.

During a recent telephone interview with the Berkeley-based rock group, Barry Melton, guitarist and vocalist, said that too many people think of the group as strictly a protest group.

"Look at our three albums," Barry said. "Only around one-fourth of the songs are protest songs. We fall in love and do other things besides protest."

Country Joe and the Fish was formed as a jug band in October, 1965, during peace demonstrations in Berkeley. Their first song, "I Feel Like I'm Fixin' to Die Rag," was released on their own label and sold 5,000 copies at the peace demonstrations.

Barry, Country Joe McDonald, and the other Fish (Bruce Barthol, Chicken Hirsh, and David Cohen) signed with Vanguard Records because of the freedom that company would give them. "They offered us total artistic control," Barry said. "The only other company that offered us that kind of control was ESP Records—but we chose Vanguard."

The cover photo of *Together*, the group's third and most recent album release (currently number twenty-four on *Billboard*'s album chart), shows Country Joe's wedding.

"Country Joe's wedding just sort of happened." Barry said. "We voted to use the picture as our album cover. It's representative of the three of us in the group who have been married.

"It's important for the audience to know we're not weirdos—we get married and old just like everyone else," he said. "Honesty is where it's at. Don't lie to your audience."

Country Joe and the Fish definitely are not in the music business for the money. They've donated their talents to numerous student causes, political rallies, radio stations, and publications. As Joe puts it: "Money is just another way of keeping score of how you're doing.

"I'm not sure I even know what affluence means anymore," he said. "We travel around and stay in fancy hotel rooms. There's no affluence there. They're clean, but the furniture is horrible and the beds are uncomfortable. You got color TV, but there's nothing on TV. So why do we need bread for these things?"

Some of Country Joe's favorite groups are the Beatles, the Grateful Dead, Quicksilver Messenger Service, and the Bob Seeger System.

"Blue Cheer are doing something, but we don't know what it is," Barry said. "They're hippies. A bubblegum group. I don't consider them serious musicians—yet. They may develop. Most of the serious rock musicians are older than they are.

"If we play for SDS (Students for a Democratic Society) or another left-wing group, we may do four protest songs in a row. No matter where we play, we never delete all of our protest material. But I can't stress enough that we don't go on stage just to protest."

Area fans can see Country Joe and the Fish next Saturday night at the Merriweather Post Pavilion in Columbia, Maryland. Included on the bill will be Iron Butterfly.

# Janis Joplin

## *August 24, 1968*

Soul is where it's at, and Janis Joplin has more than her share.

Janis, the lead singer with Big Brother and the Holding Company, puts herself in a class with Aretha Franklin with the release of Big Brother's second album, *Cheap Thrills*, on the Columbia label.

Janis is at her best in "I Need a Man to Love," "Ball and Chain," and "Piece of My Heart," the latter recorded live at Bill Graham's Fillmore Auditorium in San Francisco.

Big Brother and the Holding Company came onto the scene in the summer of 1967 at the Monterey Pop Festival when Janis grabbed the microphone and split the air into shockwaves with the first notes that bolted from her astounding throat.

Janis was born in Port Arthur, Texas, an oil refinery town described as being populated by some 60,000 middle-income-bracket people who like their drive-in movies, corner drug stores, and get-married-to-the-guy-next-door way of life left undisturbed. Janis decided that kind of life wasn't for her.

"I was a sensitive child," she says. "I had a lot of hurts and confusions. You know, it's hard when you're a kid to be different. You're all full of things and you don't know what it's all about."

Janis tried to break away from the conformity of Port Arthur by painting, reading poetry, and being as beat as the town would tolerate. When she was seventeen, Janis ran away. She dropped in and out of four colleges, worked a little, and drew unemployment a lot. Somewhere along the line she began to sing.

"Back in Port Arthur, I'd heard some Leadbelly records, and, well, if the blues syndrome is true, I guess it's true about me," she says. "So I began listening to blues and folk music. I bought Bessie Smith and Odetta records, and one night, I was at this party and I did an imitation of Odetta. I'd never sung before, and I came out with this huge voice."

Janis sang for a while in the folk clubs and bars of San Francisco, but she eventually wandered back to Texas where she worked in the hillbilly bars of Austin. It was there that a friend saw her and brought her back to San Francisco.

"He told me Big Brother was looking for a chick singer, so I thought I'd give it a try," she recalls. "I don't know what happened. I just exploded. I'd never sung like that before. I'd been into a Bessie Smith type thing, you know. Big open notes. I stood still and I sang simple. But you can't sing like that in front of a rock band, all that rhythm and volume going.

"You have to sing loud and move wild with all that in back of you," she says. "It happened the first time, but then I got turned on to Otis Redding, and I just got into it more than ever. Now, I don't know how to perform any other way. I've tried cooling myself and not screaming, and I've walked off feeling like nothing."

Besides Janis, the other members of the Holding Company are Peter Albin, bass and vocals; Sam Andrew, guitar and vocals; James Gurley, guitar and vocals; and David Getz, drums and vocals.

In order to fully appreciate Big Brother and the Holding Company, one must see them in person. Janis has a complete rapport with the audience. As she puts it: "If you're on stage and if things are really working and you've got the audience with you, it's a oneness you feel. I'm into me, plus they're into me, and everything comes together. I just want to feel as much as I can. It's not wise always, but it's super valid, and maybe it's much wiser. It's what soul is all about."

# Jerry Lee Lewis

## *September 28, 1968*

FROM COUNTRY-AND-WESTERN TO POP AND BACK TO COUNTRY-AND-western—that's the story of Jerry Lee Lewis' musical career.

Jerry was born in Ferriday, La., on Sept. 29, 1935. His father, Elmo, played both guitar and piano. Jerry first started playing his father's guitar and then took up the piano. It was nothing for Jerry to sit at the piano for two or three hours a day, wailing everything from Tampa Red or Sunnyland Slim blues he heard on a record to the latest country hit.

During his late high school years, Jerry built up a local following with material ranging from "Stardust" to "Boogie Woogie" and "Cheatin' Heart."

In February 1956, Jerry drove 300 miles to Memphis to see Sam Phillips, a local recording producer-executive who had discovered Elvis for his Sun label. Phillips wasn't there, but Jack Clement, who was a member of the Sun staff, cut some tapes with Jerry.

After failing to hear anything from Sun records for a month, Jerry returned to Memphis. He was told that his record, "Crazy Arms," had something and would be his first release.

"Crazy Arms" was big where country-and-western was big. Jerry Lee's one-night price went up to $50 and rose again to $100 when the record made it on the pop charts. Final sales for the record were 300,000.

Jerry's second record exploded. "Whole Lotta Shakin' Going On" eventually sold 6 million copies to become one of the record industry's greatest sellers. That record was No. 1 in the Pop, R & B, and C & W charts simultaneously, a unique experience in the history of logging the popularity of recorded music.

Jerry's price jumped to five figures. Offers started pouring in from every state after he appeared on the *Steve Allen Show* on TV. Jerry's second biggest seller was "Great Balls of Fire," which has sold over 5 million copies. A rundown of sales for Jerry's first eighteen months on the charts showed that he had sold over 25 million singles and LPs.

It wasn't until recently that Jerry realized how important his country-and-western background was to him. After years on the rock charts, Jerry's present label, Smash records, decided to cut a C & W session with Jerry. The record that came from that session, *Another Time, Another Place*, was the biggest record that Jerry had in six years.

Jerry's next release, "What Made Milwaukee Famous Made a Loser Out of Me," kept him on the country charts until his current release, "She Still Comes Around (to Love What's Left of Me)" replaced it.

Jerry also started an acting career this year with his part in *Catch My Soul*, a rock version of Shakespeare's *Othello*, which ran for six weeks at the Ahmanson Theater in Los Angeles.

The show was so successful that it has a good chance of opening on Broadway later this year.

# Jeff Beck Group

## *October 26, 1968*

On June 15, 1968, the Jeff Beck Group made its first American appearance at the Fillmore East in New York and was a smash hit.

Last Sunday the British blues group finally made it to the Washington area and proved their versatility to 7,500 fans at the Alexandria Roller Rink.

Beck made his guitar talk on such numbers as "I Ain't Superstitious," "Let Me Love You," and "Shapes of Things," all included on his first album on the Epic label, *Truth*.

During an interview after the show, Beck said, "The name of the album is 'Truth' because the group feels that it is an honest album without any electronic tricks."

Besides Beck on guitar, the group consists of Ron Wood on bass, Mick Waller on drums, and Rod Stewart as vocalist. The piano accompanist during the group's current tour of the United States is Nicky Hopkins, who has worked with the Beatles, the Rolling Stones, and the Who.

Jeff was born June 24, 1944, in Surrey, England. He studied music as a child and sang in the church choir. After studying four years at Wimbledon Art College in London, he turned professional musician. Soon after, he joined the Yardbirds and toured throughout the U.S. and Europe.

Jeff, a strict vegetarian, belongs to the British League of Racing Cyclists and has an Afghan hound that is currently sharing his London apartment with thirteen cats.

When asked why he left the Yardbirds, Jeff said: "The types of sounds I wanted to play didn't mesh with the Yardbirds, so we parted peacefully. I want to play the blues, so I formed this combo. Blues is the simplest form of music, but you can elaborate on it and make it complicated."

"The American Negro sold the blues to England," Jeff continued. "Two years ago, a Negro blues artist couldn't make more than $50 a night. But now that there's been a revitalization of the blues, artists like Muddy Waters are really making it."

Although British groups are accepted readily in the U.S., American groups have a hard time in England.

"We just don't accept American groups, and I don't know why," Jeff said. "Groups like Big Brother and the Holding Company, the Grateful Dead, the Jefferson Airplane, and other progressive groups have a hard time selling records in England."

When his group's tour of this country is over, Jeff plans to take a long rest and finish working on his second album.

Jeff Beck (at the Alexandria Roller Rink 1968)
PHOTO BY BILL PERRY

Rod Stewart (Jeff Beck Group at the Alexandria Roller Rink 1968)
PHOTO BY BILL PERRY

Jeff Beck Group (Backstage Alexandria Roller Rink 1968 l. to r. Nicky Hopkins, Keyboards; Ron Wood, Bass Guitar; Jeff Beck, Lead Guitar; and Rod Stewart, Vocals)
PHOTO BY BILL PERRY

# The Legendary Stardust Cowboy

## *November 2, 1968*

EVERY SO OFTEN A RECORD SO HORRIBLE AS TO MAKE PEOPLE LAUGH IS released and becomes a hit.

Such is the case with a record titled "Paralyzed" by the Legendary Stardust Cowboy. The record starts off normally, with several soft guitar chords. Then comes a piercing scream, a hard rock beat, drum rolls, a bugle solo, and lyrics that are nothing more than gibberish.

The composer and singer of this masterpiece, the Legendary Stardust Cowboy, was in town last week to do Jack Alix's Wing Ding TV show. During an interview after the show, Stardust (he refuses to give his real name and one can't blame him) explained how he picked up his alias.

"Well, I picked the word Stardust because it has to do with space and I'm very interested in that subject," he said. "I took Cowboy because I like country and western music and legendary because I'm a legend in my own time."

Stardust was born twenty-one years ago in Lubbock, Texas. He's been writing and singing for the last eight years and says he has enough material to last him another decade.

Besides singing, Stardust has written two books, one science fiction, the other romance, and hopes to have them published. "I also want to make a motion picture that will tell the true story of who and what the legendary Cowboy is and what he does," he said. "Two companies have already offered to make the movie, but I've turned them down."

"Paralyzed" has only been out a few weeks, but Stardust has already taped *Rowan & Martin's Laugh-In*, and will be doing the *Johnny Carson Show*, *American Bandstand*, *Upbeat*, and the *Smothers Brothers Show*.

When asked what "Paralyzed" is about, Stardust replied, "There's really no message in the song. It's just a hard rock song meant to relieve tension and relax people.

"The song is definitely not a put-on," he said. "It's as serious a piece of music as any other song."

On his visit to town, Stardust wore yellow cowboy chaps emblazoned with his pseudonym, a high-domed white cowboy hat, boots, and spectacles. He designs his own clothes.

Included in Stardust's future plans is a soon-to-be-released Mercury LP titled *Here Comes the Legendary Stardust Cowboy*. The album will include all original material and will probably be released within a month.

According to Stardust, the material on the album is better than "Paralyzed." He says it will be understandable and have meaning. One can only hope so.

# Musings . . . The Legendary Stardust Cowboy and David Bowie

THERE WAS NO WAY FOR ME TO KNOW HOW THE WRITER/SINGER OF "PAR-alyzed" would influence David Bowie. I mean, when I interviewed "Ledge," I didn't even know David Bowie existed.

It wasn't until 1971 that my brother Ron handed Bowie a copy of "Par-alyzed," and Ziggy Stardust was born. Details later in this book.

# Spencer Davis

## *November 30, 1968*

EXCEPT FOR THE BEATLES AND THE ROLLING STONES, NOT MANY BRITISH rock groups have survived the very competitive music scene.

One unique British group that has gone through a major change of personnel and survived is the Spencer Davis Group. A few years back, Spencer recorded "Gimme Some Lovin'" and "I'm a Man," both hits in this country.

It was after "I'm a Man" was released that Spencer's lead singer, Stevie Winwood split from the group to form another group called Traffic. Since that split, Spencer has added new musicians to his group, but he hasn't had the success on record in this country that he had when Winwood was with the group.

During an interview after a recent concert Spencer gave at American University, he explained why Stevie left the group. "Steve and I decided we wanted to do our own thing," he said. "We both felt better for it in the beginning."

"We were holding each other back," Spencer said. "Now we have more freedom lyric-wise and power-wise as well."

Besides Spencer, the current group consists of Dee Murray, Dave Hynes, and Ray Fenwick. Their next single release on the United Artists label will probably be "Short Change," a very heavy number with an excellent guitar break.

When asked what he thinks of the artistic freedom recording artists are getting, Spencer said, "The freer the better. It's a gas. The cover of the John Lennon/Yoko Ono album, with them in the nude—what they're showing has been around for years, it's nothing new.

"I think that society has repressed and depressed us to the point where we're afraid of saying what we want," Spencer added.

Spencer attended both Birmingham University in England and the University of Berlin, where he studied German poetry.

Since the group is named after him, the spotlight does fall on Spencer. But Spencer feels that the workload must be divided equally. "For the most part we split up the vocals in the group," he said. "Everyone can sing well and besides, I think it's damaging to a group when any one individual gets sorted out by the fans as the one who makes the group."

Spencer now lives in Potters Bar, a suburb of London with his wife, two children, and his highly prized collection of electronic gear.

"My father is now an engineer and he taught me a lot," Spencer said. "I've built many parts of my hi-fi system myself, and I just keep adding to it. I use it a lot for making demonstration discs because I'm very interested in record producing, both our own and other artists."

Spencer will be in this country doing a college tour until Jan. 1. Not wanting to miss Christmas with his family, Spencer's wife and children will be flying to this country to spend the holiday with him.

# Joni Mitchell

## *December 7, 1968*

HER SONGS HAVE BEEN RECORDED BY MANY ARTISTS, BUT IT'S BEEN ONLY recently that Joni Mitchell has made a mark as a singer herself.

Joni, who hails from a small town in Saskatchewan, Canada, has had her material recorded by artists such as Judy Collins, Tom Rush, Dave Van Ronk, Leonard Cohen, and Frank Sinatra. But Joni proved to sell out houses at the Cellar Door that no one can sing her songs the way she does.

During an interview after one of her performances, Joni discussed her views on many subjects. When asked who, besides herself, does the most justice to her songs, she said: "That's difficult to say. I like the way different people bring out things I can't."

One of Joni's compositions, "Both Sides Now," recorded by Judy Collins, is riding high on the charts. "When Judy sings my songs," Joni says, "they are similar in approach to the way I do them. But I'm more excited when a man does one of my songs.

"Frank Sinatra just recorded 'Both Sides Now,'" Joni said, "but my favorite version of the song is by Dave Van Ronk."

Many of the songs Joni writes deal with life in the city. Explaining this, Joni said: "I just write about what I feel like writing about. Whatever happens to be on my mind at the moment. I'm a little in awe of cities, being raised in a Prairie city and Saskatchewan."

Joni moved from bigger city to bigger city, until she reached "THE City," New York.

"As a child, I thought cities were beautiful," she said. "I judge them by their neon. Then, in New York, I found that cities are really vulgar.

"I saw the dirt of the city," she went on. "I found they were plastic and there's always a rush for the dollar. Now I'm ruralizing myself again. I don't like to live in the cities. I owe it to myself to live where there is greenery."

Joni's first album on the Reprise label, does a good job of showing off her writing and singing talent. Some of the songs on that album are, "Marcie," "I Had A King" and "Michael from Mountains." Some of her other well-known songs, not contained on the album, are "Circle Game" and "Chelsea Morning."

When it came to choosing a company to record for, Joni had a tough job. "My recording contract came down to three labels," she said. "Vanguard didn't take me seriously. Elektra was pretty much the same, and they had Judy Collins already. They wouldn't have done me justice.

"I chose Reprise because their contract gave me a lot of control," Joni said. "I have freedom to make my music my own way. Reprise is good to its artists."

# Musings ... Joni, Jim Morrison, James Brown, and an Answer to a Frequently Asked Question

THE QUESTION I AM ASKED MOST OFTEN WHEN FRIENDS (AND EVEN strangers) realize I interviewed so many famous artists: "Who was your favorite person or group that you interviewed?"

Thinking back decades, I have to break my answer into two parts. Part 1 is that there were so many artists whose music I loved that the list would be long. Part 2 is that there were artists like James Brown, whom I got to know over a number of years and a number of interviews, and there were artists like Joni Mitchell and Jim Morrison, whom I never expected would agree to be interviewed. They were like royalty to me. I wasn't in awe when I was with them, but they were so famous and so talented that I felt honored not just to be in the same room with them but also to be able to ask them questions.

If I had to name one artist out of all my interviews, it would be tough, but I would have to say David Bowie. It's not because David's music is my favorite, but it's because I got to know him and spend time with him two years after interviewing him. Plus, the time I spent with him was his first day in the United States. Read on, and what happened on that day in January 1971 and his subsequent days here leading to his "becoming" Ziggy Stardust will shed some light on why I would call Bowie my favorite of favorites.

# Mother Earth

## *December 14, 1968*

OVER THE LAST FEW YEARS, MORE AND MORE FEMALE VOCALISTS HAVE come to the forefront on the rock scene.

Now, added to the list that includes Aretha Franklin, Janis Joplin, and Grace Slick, is a five-foot-three powerhouse vocalist from Madison, Wis., Tracy Nelson.

Tracy, the lead singer for a San Francisco group, Mother Earth, took up singing in the coffeehouses surrounding the University of Wisconsin. After tiring of the coffeehouse circuit, Tracy joined a Motown-type group, the Fabulous Imitations.

The musical turning point in Tracy's career was when she was turned on to the gospel family act, the Staples Singers.

"Although gospel isn't that strong with the rest of the group," Tracy says, "it is something I'm very interested in that, quite naturally, influences much of our music."

Besides Tracy, the members of the band are Mark Naftalin (a graduate of the Butterfield Blues Band), organ; George Rains, drums; Bob Arthur, bass; John (Toad) Andrews, guitar; and Powell St. John, harmonica and vocals.

Mother Earth's first Mercury LP, *Living with the Animals*, was the result of several months of work. "It's representative of all of us, especially Tracy," says Powell. "There's a lot of gospel influence as well as country, blues, and jazz."

Tracy formed the band after she won a round-trip ticket to L.A. in a folk-singing contest at Milton College in Wisconsin. After settling in San Francisco, she sang with a few different groups before deciding to form her own.

"It wasn't hard to gather a band," Tracy says. "Musicians in San Francisco get acquainted fast. We were lucky because we clicked together from the start."

Summing up her feelings about Mother Earth's sound, Tracy says: "I'm just personally concerned with making a certain kind of music; a kind of music that's just a groove. Although my particular interest is just a type that compares with gospel voicings as opposed to those in straight rock, jazz or rhythm-and-blues," she says. "And, too, we're into more changes than most gospel songs have."

Besides their Mercury LP, Mother Earth is featured on a United Artists soundtrack album from a documentary film on hippies, *Revolution*.

# Led Zeppelin

## *December 21, 1968*

JIMMY PAGE, A FORMER MEMBER OF THE YARDBIRDS, THE GROUP THAT spawned the careers of two other great musicians, Eric Clapton and Jeff Beck, has formed his own super group, Led Zeppelin.

Atlantic Records signed the hot new English group to a long-term exclusive recording contract. This marks the eighth signing of a British group by Atlantic Records in the last two years.

In addition to guitarist Jimmy Page, those in the group are John Paul Jones, bass; John Bonham, drums; and vocalist Robert Plant.

Besides being an outstanding bass player, Jones is considered one of England's finest arrangers. He is the arranger of Donovan's "Mellow Yellow," "Sunshine Superman," and "Hurdy Gurdy Man" and of the Rolling Stones' "She's a Rainbow."

Talking about the new album, which is to be released in January, Page says: "The statement of our first two weeks together is our album. We cut it in fifteen hours and between us wrote eight of the tracks.

"Our main problem was knowing what channel to take it along musically. Everyone in the group had such a high musical content, we thought each of us would be into our own thing. But it all fell in together,

"We'll probably always be faced with the fact that individually each member could cut his own album going in his own direction and it would be great," Jimmy Says. "But all those ideas in one outfit . . . well, that's pretty fantastic too."

Before Jimmy joined the Yardbirds in 1966, his forte was session work. Backing up such artists as Mick Jagger and Keith Richards, the Kinks, and

Donovan, Jimmy gained a sound knowledge of production, put to good use with the Yardbirds, and now in the first Led Zeppelin album.

"When I joined the Yardbirds, my main reason was to give myself the opportunity of playing my own music," Jimmy says. "Before that, my only interest was session work. I began to feel limited, not being able to express myself.

"When I left, it was almost for exactly the same reasons," he says. "The group split because everyone began to feel the need to go in his own direction. The pity is, there would have still been great potential."

When asked how he would classify Led Zeppelin's music, Jimmy said: "I can't put a tag to our music. Every one of us has been influenced by the blues, but it's one's interpretation of it and how you utilize it. I wish someone would invent an expression, but the closest I can get is contemporary blues."

# Musings . . . Jeff Krulik, *Heavy Metal Parking Lot*, and *Led Zeppelin Played Here*

Dᴉᴅ Lᴇᴅ Zᴇᴘᴘᴇʟɪɴ ᴘʟᴀʏ ᴛʜᴇ Wʜᴇᴀᴛᴏɴ Yᴏᴜᴛʜ Cᴇɴᴛᴇʀ ɪɴ Wʜᴇᴀᴛᴏɴ, Maryland, on January 20, 1969 (the night of Richard Nixon's inauguration), before fifty people—and not get paid? Was deejay/promoter Barry Richards threatened by Led Zeppelin's manager, Peter Grant, finally handing Grant gas money for Led Zeppelin to get to their next concert? Jeff Krulik's feature-length documentary *Led Zeppelin Played Here* may answer these questions (or not). The film is more than just a film about that "mythical" Led Zeppelin show; it is also the story about how teen centers and high school gyms were the birthing places for the major concert promotion industry.

I'll get to "Led Zeppelin Played Here" in a bit. In the late 1980s, I walked into my favorite video rental store in D.C. Chatting with Vas, the manager, was always fun. Hanging out in the store was sometimes a surrealistic experience. Besides Vas turning me on to quirky and obscure films, the store often became the neighborhood "coffee klatch." One person who often stopped by to participate in discussions that ranged from Bulgarian underground films to rarities like the Rolling Stones documentary *Cocksucker Blues* was Daniel Ellsberg.

If the name Daniel Ellsberg rings a bell but you're not sure why, here's a quote from Wikipedia: "Daniel Ellsberg (born April 7, 1931) is an American economist, activist and former United States military analyst who, while employed by the RAND Corporation, precipitated a national political controversy in 1971 when he released the Pentagon Papers, a top-secret Pentagon study of the U.S. government decision-making in relation to the Vietnam War, to The New York Times and other newspapers."

"On January 3, 1973, Ellsberg was charged under the Espionage Act of 1917 along with other charges of theft and conspiracy, carrying a total maximum sentence of 115 years. Due to governmental misconduct and illegal evidence-gathering, and the defense by Leonard Boudin and Harvard Law School professor Charles Nesson, Judge William Matthew Byrne Jr. dismissed all charges against Ellsberg on May 11, 1973." Okay, enough of a history lesson.

One day, Vas asked me, "Have you seen *Heavy Metal Parking Lot*?" I said that I had never heard of it. Vas told me it was a short documentary by Jeff Krulik and that I had to see it. He wouldn't tell me anything else. I asked if he could get me a copy, and he said he could—and he did.

Short and funny, *Heavy Metal Parking Lot* was a quirky look into heavy metal fandom. A film crew of two, Jeff Krulik and John Heyn, simply took their video equipment to the Capital Centre in Landover, Maryland, and began interviewing metal fans in the arena's parking lot before a Judas Priest concert. To quote from Wikipedia again, "Most of the fans appear drunken and drugged, with bare feet, muscle shirts, bare-chested, bleach blonde frizzy perms, mullets from hell, big hair, bad teeth, scar tissue, and by far the largest collection of late '70s Camaros ever seen in one location." Cult director John Waters said of the film, "It gave me the creeps."

I thought to myself, I've got to meet Jeff Krulik. I didn't realize that more than twenty years would go by before I not only met Jeff but also had a speaking role in his feature-length documentary *Led Zeppelin Played Here*.

Not really a spoiler alert, but in *Led Zeppelin Played Here*, I am a debunker. Although Barry Richards has been a friend of mine, on-screen I say, "he's kind of an embellisher." Although Barry and a number of other people who frequented the Wheaton Youth Center swear that Led Zeppelin played there on January 20, 1969 (the day of Richard Nixon's inauguration), in front of a crowd of fifty-five people, I still don't believe it happened. Barry Richards did promote many shows at the venue. Supposedly, because no one knew of Led Zeppelin yet, they were billed as the New Yardbirds. While Zeppelin's first album had just been released and it wasn't unheard of for a "new" act to play a low-paying or free gig to promote their album, there is no hard evidence that they ever played at the Wheaton Youth Center—no posters, no flyers, no ticket stubs, and no photographs. In the half-dozen plus years since the film was released and continues to play film festivals, no one has come forth with concrete proof of Zeppelin in Wheaton.

Barry Richards says that they played but that, because of the low turnout (and splitting the door between himself and the group), he was able to pay the group only "gas money" and only after their manager, Peter Grant, threatened Barry.

Like Bigfoot and UFOs, there is no concrete proof that Led Zeppelin played in Wheaton. At one time, the official Led Zeppelin website did not have Wheaton listed as a tour date, and another time that it was listed, it was listed as "maybe."

I am not a big believer in conspiracy theories. I don't think several dozen people got together and conspired and came up with a tall tale about Led Zeppelin playing for gas money. I do believe that confabulation can be like a virus. When one person believes something has happened and that belief isn't necessarily true, that's confabulation, or "honest lying." Part of me wants to believe that Led Zeppelin played the Wheaton Youth Center the night of Richard Nixon's inauguration. But if everyone believed that, there probably wouldn't be the wonderful, wacky, mythical documentary *Led Zeppelin Played Here*.

Unfortunately, *Led Zeppelin Played Here* has never gone into general release. The documentary has played all over the United States at film festivals and special screenings and as far away as Australia. Jeff Krulik never procured the licensing rights for the music in the film; songs by Led Zeppelin, Alice Cooper, Iggy Pop, and others, unlicensed, have kept the film in the world of "can you get me a DVD copy of it?"

Robert Plant (Led Zeppelin) and Fans
PHOTO BY MIKE KLAVANS

Jimmy Page (Led Zeppelin, Backstage with Unidentified Friend)
PHOTO BY MIKE KLAVANS

# Musings . . . 1969 . . . The Year of the Bong . . . Gene Wishnia

I FIRST MET GENE WISHNIA IN 1964. HE WAS TWO YEARS OLDER THAN ME and moved onto the street where I lived with his parents, Ruby and Helen, and his older brother, Jimmy. I was a junior in high school, and Gene had already graduated from high school. Although the age difference was a lot in those days, we had some mutual friends. I remember shooting pool with him in the rec room of his house.

It wasn't until the late 1960s that we became good friends and ran in the same circles. Gene got a job as a bouncer at a Georgetown nightclub called the Bayou. When I graduated from high school, the drinking age in D.C. was eighteen for beer and wine. The Bayou was one of the clubs where you could hear live rock 'n' roll and grab a cold brew. Gene would often be working the front door of the club when I would go there. Little did I know at the time that Gene would eventually be integral in bringing a new marijuana smoking device to the forefront of the D.C. "pot scene."

In August 2019, I sat down with Gene and let him tell his story—a story I knew well, as he and I have remained friends for more than fifty years:

When I first started working for the Bayou, they didn't open on Sundays because of the blue laws in D.C. Alcohol had to stop being served at midnight on Saturday night and couldn't be served again until Monday. Sundays were dry days. So, the Bayou on Sundays would rent the club out to Mike O'Harro for his Junior Officers and Professionals Association (JOPA). You could pay $5 and drink all the beer you wanted and socialize and meet other JOPA members, which was b—— because it was mostly a bunch of drunk soldiers.

So, Monday morning when the Bayou would reopen, the place looked like a hurricane had come through. Everything was a mess, the floors were disgusting, there was beer spilled everywhere. We decided one night we were going to get even with them. One of my friends, Eddie Wolfman, was in the National Guard in Hyattsville. He stole two tear gas bombs from the National Guard. On Sundays, when the Bayou was rented out, one employee of the Bayou was always there to guard the downstairs bar. There was no way to close it off. He stayed behind the bar to keep people from stealing the booze.

So, there's this guy Earl, who was a waiter. I called him up and said Earl do us a favor and leave the back door unlocked because we want to sneak into the JOPA. Earl left the back door open, and my friends, Dave and Louie, go in, and we're sitting outside in a car, and we're waiting for them to set off the tear gas bombs. They'd never set one off before, so they go inside thinking that it's just going to make a small noise. When they pull the canister open, instead it sounded like a gun going off.

I'm sitting outside in the car with my friend Harry, and we're waiting. All of a sudden, the place emptied out like there was a plague—two hundred and fifty people running out coughing, tears in their eyes, throwing up, everything . . . you name it. They had put the tear gas right in front of the air-conditioning duct, which blew all the tear gas into the club. It made the newspapers the next day.

The police found the tear gas canisters and traced the serial numbers back to the Hyattsville National Guard. Then they took the fingerprints off of them and compared them with the fingerprints of all the soldiers in that National Guard unit. The police went to Eddie Wolfman and said, "Your fingerprints are on these tear gas canisters. What do you know about them?" Eddie says, "I don't know anything about them." The police told Eddie he might go to jail. Eddie said, "I might have handled them in the armory, but I don't know what you're talking about." He continued to deny that he had anything to do with the incident at the Bayou. It seemed to be a stalemate. Two months later, Eddie walked into the Hyattsville National Guard and said, "I think I've had enough of the National Guard, I quit." They told him he had three more years in his contract. Eddie said, "Go ahead and arrest me, put me in jail, I'm not coming back!" Eddie turned to the sergeant, saluted him, and walked out.

So, when I left the Bayou, I didn't have a job, and I was with somebody one night, and they had a bamboo bong, and it was the first time I had seen a bong. Getting high off of a bong was not the same way as any other way of getting high. It was a real instantaneous rush. There was only one place that sold bongs, and that was over in D.C., where this guy Michael Willis had a head shop. I went in there and bought a bong, a bamboo bong, and took it home and took it apart and saw how it was made: just a stem and a piece of bamboo with a plug on one end. I went to a plastics place, bought some pieces of plastic, and crudely made a bong. Me and my friend Jack Rosenberg worked on it. It worked great. I took it to a party at Mike Klavans's house.

I was in a bedroom upstairs, and Mike was telling everybody who got high, if you really want to get high, go upstairs. I was having one after another come up and take a couple of hits off the bong. I had to teach them because everybody didn't understand the principle. I was having people say to me, where can I buy one? We only had the one. So, Jack and I, we went to a place in Hyattsville called Commercial Plastics and bought some plastic. We had a very crude way of making bongs. Then Jack, being very creative, started building a process where we could do sixteen bongs at a time and put the stems in the bongs and not have any leakage around them. We found a glue that was waterproof, very thin glue. Eventually, we found a process of being able to put the stems in with such a tight fit that we just used one drop of glue, and it would seal the whole thing up. The glue literally melted the two pieces of plastic together. So, we started making bongs, and I was selling to local head shops. After we sold them to a few head shops in the area, we took an ad out in *Rolling Stone* magazine. I think it was $65 for a three-inch-by-three-inch. Suddenly we had orders from thirty-five states.

Some of our biggest customers were drag race car drivers. Somehow, they found out about the bongs, and boy did they buy them. This one guy named Jungle Jim Liberman, he's now deceased, killed in a car crash, not drag racing, but on the road. He bought like twenty-five bongs for his drag racing crew. We stayed in the bong business for probably about six years until Maryland started cracking down on paraphernalia. Then Virginia started cracking down on paraphernalia. I had a store we did business with in Vienna, Virginia, called Penguin Feather. They used to buy maybe fifty bongs a week. The owner called me up one day and said, "They came and took my inventory, can you supply me with more?" I said we could. We drove down there, delivered more bongs to him, and three days later the police came and confiscated their inventory again.

The same thing happened with a place called Sunflower Seed in College Park, right near the University of Maryland. The police would come in, confiscate their inventory, we'd deliver more, and police would continue confiscating. There was no law that said you couldn't sell paraphernalia, but they enforced something which they said was "because marijuana was illegal, you couldn't sell anything that was used to smoke marijuana, including cigarette papers." Even though you could use cigarette papers to roll regular cigarettes, you could no longer sell papers.

Pretty much that was the end of our bong business. After that, I did various jobs for Cellar Door Productions. One of the fun and sometimes wacky jobs was picking up musicians at the airport when they would arrive to play a concert for Cellar Door. I would also pick up equipment and luggage for the acts.

One of those artist pick-ups stands out in my mind. We went out to Dulles Airport about one o'clock in the morning to pick up the Rolling Stones. Bill Wyman had just left the group, so it was the next tour after he had left (the Voodoo Lounge Tour). We had station wagons to pick them up. For some reason, they didn't want limos, so there were three station wagons and one truck (for their luggage). In my station wagon, I had Keith Richards, the new bass player Darryl Jones, and two roadies.

We were going up the Dulles access road toward D.C. There was nothing out there except the airport. So, as we were going up the road, I heard from the backseat, "Hey mate, can you pull over? I've got to take a pee!" I pulled over to the side of the road. This guy climbed out of the backseat and goes into the woods to pee.

Somebody in the backseat tapped me on the shoulder and says, "Leave." I said, "Leave, what do you mean. He's in the woods." He says, "Leave, he works for me." I turn around, and it was Keith Richards telling me to leave.

So, I left this guy in the woods peeing, and I drove to the hotel. I got to the hotel and dropped everybody off, and I was waiting for the truck to arrive with the luggage. The truck arrived, and who jumped out? The guy I had left in the woods. He started screaming, "You motherfucker! You left me in the god damned woods!"

I looked at the enraged roadie and said, "Excuse me. Keith told me to leave you. I had nothing to do with it." Okay that was it if it wasn't for the fact that the truck with the luggage passed this guy standing out there in the middle of the Dulles access road waving people down because he had no idea where he was. Luckily, the truck driver saw him, but I caught the shit for it because I'm the one who left him in the woods.

Another time, I went out to National Airport for Earth, Wind and Fire. They had about a hundred and ten pieces of luggage because they're such a large group. We had to unload all of this into two trucks and go to the Mayflower Hotel on Connecticut Avenue. We pulled up and unloaded all of the luggage into the lobby. We were in the lobby, and all of a sudden one of the managers for Earth, Wind and Fire turned around and says, "We don't want to stay here. There's no black people here." We looked around, and he was right—all we saw was white faces. We loaded up all the luggage again and drove it out to the Sheraton near the Capital Centre, which is where they should have stayed anyway since they were playing at the Capital Centre.

Postscript: Gene is now an executive with a wholesale bakery. We remain friends. I wish I still had my bong from 1969.

Gene Wishnia with Bong
PHOTO BY MICHAEL OBERMAN

# The Fool

## *January 4, 1969*

A TAROT DECK IS A PACK OF COLORFUL PICTURE CARDS THROUGH WHICH some people claim one can find the key to the "wisdom of the ages."

One particular card in the deck, the Fool at Zero, refers to that "foolishness of God which is wiser than man." The Fool is the point at which all things proceed. It symbolizes the creative energy of universal cultural activities. The Fool is also a new rock group.

There isn't too much that can be said of the Fool's musical achievements, since their first album was just released. The album, produced by Graham Nash (formerly with the Hollies), incorporates rock with unusual instrumentation such as bagpipes and lutes.

Although the Fool began performing just recently, they have been known around the musical world for some time. Their real claim to fame came when they opened the Apple boutique for the Beatles in London.

The Fool's creative lineage can be traced to the summer of 1964 and the Dutch metropolis of Amsterdam, where a young leader in avante garde art, Seemon, and two young fashion designers, Marijke and Josje, joined forces to open a trend-setting boutique.

In September 1966, Seemon and Marijke went to London, where they met Barry Finch and Simon Hayes, who co-headed Mayfair Public Relations. The company was looking for a new approach in design for the program cover of the Saville Theater, music center of London, owned by Brian Epstein. Seemon and Marijke were hired and reaction from theater-goers soon brought a wave of business to the couple.

Some of the more interesting chores that were assigned to the duo included painting Cream's instruments, designing stage outfits for Procol Harum, and designing the cover of the Hollies' best-selling *Evolution* album.

As fame spread for Seemon and Marijke, Josje, still in Amsterdam, read about them in a Dutch newspaper and took off for London to join them. Shortly thereafter, Barry Finch became their personal manager, and the foursome decided to call themselves the Fool.

After the rapid opening and closing of the Apple boutique, the Fool were asked to design the sets, titles, and costumes for an eighty-minute film, *The Wonderwall*. At their suggestion, George Harrison was commissioned to do the music.

Their musical career began when George asked them to record their own music for the four-minute sequence in the film in which they appeared.

Immediately after finishing *The Wonderwall*, the Fool were commissioned by World Film Services to produce a picture in association with John Heyman (producer of most of the Elizabeth Taylor–Richard Burton films) based on a story by Wolf Mankiewicz. This film, *Seventeen Plus*, will find the Fool acting as set designers and costume creators as well as members of the cast.

# Musings . . . Management . . .
# Part One . . . Claude Jones . . . 1969

FOR A BRIEF TIME, I HAD A DESK AND PHONE AND OPERATED AS A BOOKING agent for Barry Rick Associates—free office space for booking bands that played original material. Barry Rick Associates booked mostly cover bands. Barry's office was in Chuck Levin's Washington Music Center. What better place to come in contact with bands than a store that was well known for selling a wide variety of musical instruments, PA systems, and accessories.

One day, a drummer named Reggie Brisbane came into Chuck Levin's and said he was in a band called Claude Jones. We chatted about the band's music, and Reggie invited me to hear the band rehearse in their group house, Little Grey, on Military Road in D.C. I went to a rehearsal and was blown away, especially by vocalist Joe Triplett. Joe had been in a local D.C. band called the Reekers. They garnered some airplay with a single, "Don't Call Me Flyface." Later, Triplett would supply lead vocals on the Hangmen's hit "What a Girl Can't Do." It took that one rehearsal to sell me on Claude Jones and lead me on almost a three-year journey as their manager, my first time managing a band.

I had already been writing my weekly music column in the *Evening Star* newspaper. Claude Jones was the only band I would defer to fellow *Star* writers to stay away from conflict of interest.

Claude Jones, collectively, was a socialist group when it came to money and living arrangements. Money from gigs paid for the group's rent, food, cigarettes, and other smoking items. Each band member was paid $1 per gig. This arrangement worked well when the band moved onto a 100-plus-acre farm in Culpeper, Virginia. The owner of the farm, Mr. Carter, liked the band and may have been the only farmer in a fifty-mile radius who would rent to a hippie band with a black drummer. The year was 1969.

Claude Jones didn't take long to become *the* band in the D.C. hippie scene. From gigs in clubs and colleges to opening for acts like the Allman Brothers, crowds grew to sell-out size. Free gigs at the Sylvan Theater on the grounds of the Washington Monument might draw from 5,000 to 20,000 music lovers.

One fan of the band was a D.C. cardiologist, Dr. Michael Halberstam. He offered everyone in the band plus roadies and management free health care in return for playing two gigs a year for him: one for a liberal political cause and the other for a personal party he would throw. It was great: you could go to his office, he would take care of your health, and no one was ever billed.

I kept Dr. Halberstam as my personal physician after Claude Jones broke up. Unfortunately, in 1980, he was shot in the chest after he and his wife surprised a burglar after coming home one evening. He insisted on driving himself and his wife to nearby Sibley Hospital despite being grievously wounded. On his way to the hospital, he spotted the burglar, hopped his car over a curb, and ran over the burglar. Dr. Halberstam died of his wounds that night. The burglar turned out to be an escaped convict named Bernard Welch, one of the biggest "cat burglars" in D.C. history.

Ironic that Dr. Halberstam captured the man who killed him. Welch lived in a mansion that included a smelting oven where he could melt down the gold and silver he stole. Welch was sentenced to 143 years in prison and died there in 1997.

To friends and associates, Claude Jones was collectively known as the Amoeba. At any given gig, there might be five musicians onstage, or there could be up to a dozen. One of their roadies might hop on stage and sing "Not Fade Away." The road manager might play a guiro. The band had great original songs and much interest from record companies.

There was so much interest that Mercury Records' vice president Irwin Steinberg and president Irving Green flew from Chicago to D.C. to hear the group play at a club called Emergency. Claude Jones always filled the club, and that night was no exception. Before Steinberg and Green came to D.C., the band had already wowed Mercury's A & R department and their marketing and public relations personnel. That night after a great performance, Steinberg and Green came up to me and said, "We want this band."

I agreed to come to New York in a week or two and begin negotiations. The band, having this socialist, anticorporate philosophy, wanted at least one band member to accompany me. That was a big mistake. Mercury was offering $40,000 for the first album and an option for additional albums.

Band members pretty much scotched the deal. I recall hearing one or two of them say that Mercury was part of the "corporate war machine." I said to the band, "Guys, this is a lot of money, but if it doesn't work out, then your lives aren't over." But the band said no to the Mercury deal.

One of the people in the Mercury A & R department told me a about a guy named Don Johnson (not the *Miami Vice* actor). Don had some money, liked the band, and agreed to invest enough for the band to record and press a five-song EP (extended play) record. Don lived in Manhattan but came to D.C. to co-produce the record. While in D.C., Don was pulled over for a minor traffic violation. Police searched the car and discovered "possible" drugs in the trunk.

While the police stop was bad luck for Don, it turned into good fortune for me. Don called me one evening to tell me about the D.C. attorney he hired to keep him out of jail. He mentioned that he had begun dating a woman in his attorney's office. "Michael," he said, "you've got to meet this woman's roommate." I ended up meeting her. Dawn was seven years older than me (she was thirty, I was twenty-three), divorced, and secretary to the ambassador from Libya. At first, my parents were not happy—their son, raised Jewish, in love with a divorced, Gentile woman who works for the Libyans (Gaddafi had just come to power).

A few months later, Dawn and I were living together. Once my parents met her, they warmed to her. Okay, enough about that. The EP was recorded and titled after the first song on it, "Sykesville." Sykesville is a town in Maryland where the Springfield State Mental Institution was located. John Guernsey, piano player in the band, wrote the song. It was autobiographical, about his forced stay at Springfield State. Shortly after the recording was finished, there was a story about the Sykesville train station in the *Washington Post*. The black-and-white photo that ran with the story was of the train station with the sign over the doorway reading "Sykesville." I called the newspaper, and they gave me the name of the photographer. I rang him up and asked if we could use his photo on the cover of the EP. He said, "Absolutely."

The EP began getting a fair amount of radio play, and one day I got a call from the administrator at Springfield State Mental Hospital. I was told that the nurses, staff, and patients loved the song "Sykesville." Then I was asked if the band was available to play for the patient/staff Halloween party. Of all the gigs Claude Jones played, from clubs to concert halls, the most memorable gig for me was the Halloween show at "Sykesville."

When we pulled up to the hospital that Halloween night, it was like we drove into a Diane Arbus photograph. Some patients in costume, others not—almost all of them excitedly asking band members, "Got a cigarette?" A recording of that gig was made at the sound board and can be heard on the Claude Jones website (along with the Sykesville EP and a few other recordings) at ClaudeJonesArchive.org.

Meanwhile, down on the farm. One day, back at my house in Takoma Park, Maryland, I received a phone call from a guy named Milan Melvin. Milan had been married to Mimi Farina, the sister of Joan Baez. He was a prominent figure in the West Coast counterculture scene. (I didn't know that at the time of the phone call.) After introducing himself, Milan said, "We are looking for a farm near Washington, D.C. I understand that you manage a band that lives on a farm near Warrenton, Virginia." I told him that was true, and he said, "There are 165 of us traveling across the U.S. Our last stop before flying to Europe is Washington. There are several bands on the road with us, including Hot Tuna and Alice Cooper. We'd love it if you would let us camp out on your farm for a few days before the D.C. concert. We call our road show the 'Medicine Ball Caravan.'"

Kind of as an afterthought, Milan said, "By the way, French director Francois Reichenbach will be with us filming the entire thing for Warner Brothers. Maybe a movie and an LP."

I took the idea to the band, and, thinking it would be fun, the band agreed to let the Medicine Ball Caravan camp out on the farm. I called Milan back and said that we would happily meet them at a nearby gas station and guide the Caravan to the farm. A date and approximate time were agreed on.

When the day came to meet them, we arrived at the gas station to find the Caravan already there. Milan Melvin was leading the Caravan on a chopped Harley-Davidson. Milan and the motorcycle looked like they drove out of the movie *Easy Rider*. The Caravan consisted of multiple vehicles, including a psychedelically painted bus that was flying Vietcong flags and had a sign painted on the front that read, "We Have Come for Your Daughters."

I thought to myself, "We're in redneck country. This isn't going to go well." We proceeded to the farm, where members of the Caravan pitched ten or eleven twenty- to thirty-foot-tall tie-dyed teepees. The assistant to the director was a man named Martin Scorsese, the same Martin Scorsese who would go on to direct *Mean Streets*, *Taxi Driver*, *Raging Bull*, *Goodfellas*, and so many other great films.

Wavy Gravy (he of Woodstock, the Hog Farm, et al.) was a member of the Caravan. Somewhere between 150 and 170 hippies led by Wavy Gravy and Milan Melvin plus a film crew were now camped out on the Amoeba farm. Lots of LSD was being taken, but the vibes seemed calm, though a lot seemed staged for the film. At one point, while sitting around a bonfire and singing "Happy Birthday" to a member of the caravan, Francois Reichenbach yelled, "Cut! Let's try that again." My epiphany came at that moment. The only thing we (the Claude Jones band and I) had in common with this large group of visitors was long hair, a love of music, and the smoking of reefer.

Warner Bros. ended up releasing a Medicine Ball Caravan LP but was unhappy with the documentary film that was produced. They had Scorsese do some editing to the footage, and eventually the film was released, but I don't think it ever made it to theaters. If you search the Internet, DVD copies are available. But my one-word review of the movie is "dreadful."

Claude Jones broke up after playing one last gig on New Year's Eve in 1971. The band's musical DNA lived on and led me to managing a group called the Rosslyn Mountain Boys (RMB). RMB included three musicians from Claude Jones, and you can read about the RMB years in my "Musings ... Management ... Part Two ... The Rosslyn Mountain Boys."

# The Chambers Brothers

## *January 18, 1969*

TAKE FOUR GOSPEL-SINGING BROTHERS, ADD A DRUMMER, AND WHAT DO you have—the Chambers Brothers.

The Brothers, Willie, George, Lester and Joe Chambers, and their drummer, Brian Keenan, have risen from playing the underground palaces in San Francisco to nationwide fame with hit singles like "The Time Has Come Today" and "I Can't Turn You Loose," and albums like their latest, *A New Time, A New Day*.

In a recent interview, George, eldest of the Chambers, explained how the group formed. "Until I was twenty-one, farming was my only occupation," he said. "It was a groove then, because I knew nothing else.

"I suppose every farmer finds something to make the time go faster, or seem to," George said. "I chose singing to ease the hard strain."

After a stint in the Army, in which George formed a singing group called the Soldiers, he moved to L.A. The rest of his brothers shortly followed.

"My three younger brothers were growing up. And we began to sing together," said George. "Every Sunday we would go to church and sing, using our family name as the name of the group. In 1961, we all quit our jobs and went professional.

We were still gospel singers and played coffee houses and small clubs. We went on like this for two-and-a-half years. Then we decided to do some pop songs and blues.

"We were all too busy playing different instruments to do hand-claps, so we had to get a drummer," he said. "We tried out a few and then we met Brian (an American, who at one time played drums with Manfred Mann in England). As far as we're concerned, he's the best around."

The Chambers Brothers live, write, and jam in a big house in Stamford, Conn., where among "trees and rabbits and woodchucks and chipmunks and birds," they get into their own fraternal thing.

The talent of the Chambers Brothers has won them a large and diversified audience. They've performed at the Fillmore in San Francisco, the Shrine in L.A., the Electric Circus, Apollo Theater and the Scene in New York, and major colleges and universities all over the country.

They appeared on *Showcase '68*, a network television program which features the best of today's pop performers. They were invited back for a return engagement and a chance to win the *Showcase '68* award for the most exciting professional performers of the year.

The Chambers Brothers lost the *Showcase '68* award to Sly and the Family Stone, but for the Brothers it is "a new time and a new day" for their "time has come."

# The Everly Brothers

## *January 25, 1969*

STARTING THEIR PROFESSIONAL CAREERS AS CHILDREN, THE EVERLY Brothers have retained their popularity longer than most singing duos.

Born in Brownie, Ky., they started their professional careers when Don Everly was eight years old and Phil was six. It wasn't until about twelve years later that the brothers had their first big hit, "Bye-Bye Love."

Since that first hit in 1957, the Everlys have sold over 35 million singles, have appeared on most network television shows in the U.S. and Great Britain, and have done concert tours in most European countries and parts of the Orient.

In town recently for a two-week engagement at the Cellar Door, the Everlys proved to capacity crowds that their brand of country-rock hasn't lost its appeal.

During an interview between shows, Don and Phil talked about some of their likes and dislikes. "I like an audience to listen," Don said. "The days of screaming crowds are over.

"It's more satisfying to appeal to adult crowds," he continued. "I never enjoyed the screaming bit. It's not a good showcase for talent."

When asked how their music has changed over the years, Phil said, "We're still basically a country-rock group. That's what they called us in the beginning and that's what we are now. Our music definitely is not rock 'n' roll."

On the Warner Bros.-Seven Arts label, the Everlys have recorded fifteen albums, including their newest release, "Roots."

Some of their hit singles over the years include "Wake Up, Little Suzie," "This Little Girl of Mine," "All I Have to Do Is Dream," "Bird

Dog," "Problems," "Till I Kissed You," "Claudette," "Let It Be Me," "Cathy's Clown," and "Walk Right Back." During their Cellar Door engagement, they sang their old numbers plus songs from their recent albums. But they all have the Everly Sound.

Don is married to former film actress Venetia Stevenson. They were married at the San Diego Naval Training Center on Feb. 13, 1962, on the day Don completed boot camp for the Marines. Phil, also a former Marine, has been married six years.

On tour a good part of each year, Don admits that traveling can be bothersome. "Traveling gets you down every now and then, but for the most part we like it," he said. "But we'd rather stay in a club for an extended period than do one-nighters."

The Everlys have used the same excellent back-up band for the last four years. Consisting of electric guitar, electric bass, and drums, the band adds a great deal to the stage show.

One can only hope the Everly Brothers will come back to the Cellar Door and that when they do, the Georgetown night spot will have been allowed to expand its size.

# Creedence Clearwater Revival

## *February 1, 1969*

IT TOOK A SONG FIRST RECORDED IN THE MID-1950S TO GET THEM IN THE charts, and the musical ability of Creedence Clearwater Revival should keep them there.

The Revival's first hit, "Susie-Q," was originally recorded by Checker Records' Dale Hawkins. Though "Susie-Q" put the group in the national spotlight, they had been together long before the record was released.

Formed in 1959 as a junior high school trio called the Blue Velvets, the group consisted of three young Californians, John Fogerty, Stu Cook, and Doug Clifford.

"We were all on the same wavelength, really," John says today. "Once we got started, we were the only group playing in school. We were playing blues, not rock 'n' roll, but most people didn't understand what we were talking about musically. They didn't know the difference."

Soon after they formed, John's older brother Tom joined the group. With high school jobs plentiful, the Blue Velvets built a substantial reputation for themselves.

After high school, a San Francisco label, Fantasy Records, signed the group. After clearing countless hurdles, the group came up with a new name, Creedence Clearwater Revival.

"Creedence," John says, "was the name of a friend of ours, believe it or not, and it also means 'to believe in.' I got 'Clearwater' from watching a beer commercial, which shows the beautiful clear water they use for the beer. The idea really appealed to us because it seemed to symbolize purity. With 'Revival,' we feel there's excitement and fervor."

In February 1968, the group had a basic repertoire of original material. By spring of 1968, they released their first album, titled simply *Creedence Clearwater Revival.*

Explaining their music, John says: "I was on a blues kick at seven. When I started listening to radio in 1953, there was no pop station in our area. All we had was rhythm-and-blues.

"We just all got into that music early in life. And today, our music bears this trademark. It's not that we're a blues group. I don't think that's true at all. But I think many good things in music come from blues roots."

The group, like many others, has been influenced by musicians like Duane Eddy, Chet Atkins, Howlin' Wolf, and Lefty Frizzell. They all had an honest blues feeling, which, says John, "is the most pleasing basic form, the most natural progression."

The group's latest LP release, *Bayou Country*, which includes another old hit, "Good Golly, Miss Molly," should keep them in the charts.

# Canned Heat

## *February 22, 1969*

TAKING TRADITIONAL BLUES AND ADAPTING THEM TO THEIR OWN STYLE, Canned Heat made their first appearance in two years in the Washington area last Sunday.

Playing before a poor turnout at the Alexandria Roller Rink, the San Francisco–based quintet played two shows, sharing the bill with B.B. King.

During an interview after the first show, Bob "Bear" Hite, vocalist for the group, explained how he got interested in the blues. "I first became interested in blues by hearing old blues records at the tender age of six," he said. "I was a record hunter. I loved records at that age.

"I would buy anything that cost nine cents," Bob said. "They had used records in those days for nine cents and up and I'd buy all those records. It seemed like all the nine cent ones were funky old blues records."

Besides Bob, the others in the group are Henry Vestine (born in Takoma Park, MD), lead guitar; Al Wilson, slide guitar and rhythm guitar; Larry Taylor, bass guitar; and Fito de LaParra, drums.

The group's original drummer, Frank Cook, left Canned Heat after their first album was released. "Frank left us and went to L.A. to form Pacific Gas and Electric Blues Band," Bob said. "They're doing quite well."

When asked who he thought was the first white group to bring blues back into the musical scene, Bob replied, "Butterfield (of the Paul Butterfield Blues Band) started up a few months before we did and had an album out before we did. As far as I know, we were the second white blues group to get together in this country."

Bob believes that blues, as a music form became popular only recently. "When it first happened, it only happened for the black people, not for the masses," Bob said. "Now, everyone's hearing the blues. For the first time, people are getting turned on to it because of the progressive FM stations and because of shows like the one we're playing tonight."

Bob and Al are the only members of the group who had never performed before forming Canned Heat. Larry had played with Jerry Lee Lewis, Henry with the Mothers of Invention, and Fito, who is from Mexico, had played with four top Mexican groups.

Bob and Henry have two of the most extensive collections of old blues records in the country. It was their idea for Liberty Records to start a series of albums with old blues cuts on them. The series, called *Rural Blues*, is one of the best-selling reissue series any record company has released.

Canned Heat's latest single venture, "Time Was," has just been released and should keep the group in the charts.

# Buffy Sainte-Marie

## *March 22, 1969*

BUFFY SAINTE-MARIE IS MORE THAN JUST A SINGER AND COMPOSER. SHE'S also a Cree Indian who cares about the plight of her fellow Indians.

During an interview at radio station WWDC, where she was a guest on Fred Gale's *Comment Show*, Buffy discussed some of the problems facing Indians in America today.

"People think about 'the' Indian and what does 'he' want today," she said. "They don't realize that the Indians were never one people. They are many different tribes.

"Things aren't getting any better for Indians," Buffy said. "Life expectancy is only forty-eight years. A few hundred years ago, Indians had healthy teeth, strong bones, good bodies, and a good way of life."

Buffy was trained to be a teacher and is trying to improve the education of the Indians. "I wasn't ever taught to question the history books," Buffy said. "But they need questioning because they are not true; they're one-sided and grossly slanted."

Buffy's music is always meaningful and from the point of view of one person. When she last counted how many songs she had written, the figure was 400. That was three years ago.

"Every now and then, Vanguard grabs me by the hair and puts me in front of a microphone and tells me to sing," she said. "If I had my way, I'd be writing songs all the time and never get around to recording them."

Buffy has had five LP's on the Vanguard label: *It's My Way*, *Many a Mile*, *Little Wheel, Spin & Spin*, *Fire & Fleet & Candlelight*, and *I'm Gonna Be a Country Girl Again*. Her sixth album, *Illuminations*, will be released shortly.

"My new album has to do with the supernatural as it exists today," Buffy said. "It's very real."

Something else that is very real to Buffy is the Bureau of Indian Affairs (B.I.A.). She feels that it is a useless organization. "American people think that because there's a Bureau of Indian Affairs, then there exists a big white brother for the little Indian," she said. "It just doesn't work that way.

"The problem of the Indians was originally handled by the War Department. Their policy was annihilation. Finally, when the government got a little cooler, they turned over the Indians to the B.I.A. All they've done is change the wording from annihilation to assimilation."

Buffy used to be in plays when she was in college, but it wasn't until she landed a role on *The Virginian* that she had the chance to play an Indian. Now she has in her contract that if she plays an Indian in a show, all the other roles of Indians must be filled by real Indians.

"I want the production to come out as genuine and authentic as it possibly can," she said. "Nobody in Hollywood has given me a hard time because of that clause in my contract, but, then again, I've only been hired to do one show so far."

# Tommy Roe

## *April 5, 1969*

Like it or not, "bubblegum music" has made an unmistakable impression on the American musical scene.

Groups like the Ohio Express and the 1910 Fruitgum Company keep churning out simple bubblegum tunes, generally to the chagrin of those over the age of fifteen. This type of music is not new (remember "Itsy Bitsy, Teenie Weenie, Yellow Polka-Dot Bikini"), but it's very profitable to the artist.

The latest to cash in on this trend is Tommy Roe, whose record, "Dizzy," has occupied the number one spot in this country for the last month, according to *Billboard* magazine.

Tommy, who was born May 9th 1943, in Atlanta, has been singing since he was in the ninth grade." I had learned to play the electric guitar from my father and began writing my own songs," he says. "I got together with some friends and we formed a group called Tommy Roe and the Jordanaires."

Tommy decided to turn professional after Bill Lowery, his present manager, stopped by the club where he was playing and asked him who wrote the song, "Sheila."

"I told him that I wrote it and then he asked me if we were both available, I and the song," Tommy says. "I signed with ABC Paramount and the first record I cut for them was 'Sheila.'"

With "Sheila," Tommy had his first million-seller and began touring the country and the world. "I went to Europe on tour and had a lot of fun," he says. "Chris Montez and I headlined the bill and we had good acts with us. One of the acts was the Beatles.

"We got to be pretty good friends, and when they came to the United States, they invited me to tour with them," says Tommy. "It worked out just fine for all of us."

Tommy was soon drafted and went into the army for six months. "When I came out things had changed," he says. "Groups had taken over. Solo artists had all begun to do other things.

"I had been thinking about acting, and this seemed to be the time to do it. I pulled up stakes and moved to New York City, where I signed up with Wynn Handmann, one of the top drama coaches in the country.

Before Tommy's acting career could take off, he recorded another hit, "Sweet Pea." "After that song, I moved to Hollywood and wrote songs for Billy Joe Royal and Floyd Cramer among others." It was on the West Coast that he also wrote another of his hits, "Hooray for Hazel."

Summing up his philosophy of life, Tommy says, "Too many people who have had an early success think that everything's got to run smoothly. A man has got to take time out occasionally and do some deep studying, and to find out where he's going and how he's going to get there. I think I know now."

# Johnny Winter

## *April 26, 1969*

"I'M REALLY GASSED TO FIND PEOPLE DIGGING BLUES," SAYS ALBINO BLUES guitarist Johnny Winter.

Blues seems to be the thing now. The record-buying public is paying for blues artists. A case in point is the signing of Johnny Winter by Columbia Records for a reported $500,000.

Winter, like Janis Joplin, Steve Miller, Doug Sahm, and many other blues artists, comes from Texas. He was born Feb. 23, 1944 in Beaumont. His father sings in church choirs and plays sax and banjo; his mother played the piano.

"Soon as I could walk and talk, I was singing and playing," says Johnny. "My dad always encouraged my kid brother Edgar and me. When I was eight, Dad taught me the ukulele. I learned the guitar when my hands got bigger."

While still in high school Johnny and Edgar formed a group called It and Them and later changed the name to Johnny Winter and the Black Plague. "At that time, I couldn't imagine playing blues for people," Johnny says. "In Beaumont, nobody knew what blues were, let alone liked them."

After high school, Johnny tried a semester at Lamar Technical College, but gave that up to play blues in Chicago. "I didn't know it at the time," he recalls, "but I played with a lot of good people like Barry Goldberg and Mike Bloomfield.

"Mike had a club called the Fickle Pickle on State Street," Johnny says. "He booked in people that nobody else would touch. As a result, he wasn't making any money. I walked up and started playing my harp (harmonica)."

Bloomfield hired Johnny that night six years ago. Working at the club on and off for a couple weeks at a time, Johnny tired of the Chicago scene and headed back to Texas and temporary obscurity.

It was the December 7, 1968 issue of *Rolling Stone* (a bi-weekly rock newspaper) that helped rocket Johnny to stardom. An article on the musicians of Texas said of Johnny, "He's a 136-pound cross-eyed albino with long, fleecy hair who plays some of the gutsiest fluid blues guitar you have ever heard."

After reading that article, Steve Paul, owner of Steve Paul's Scene (a New York rock club), flew to Texas and hired Winter to play at his club. Now Winter has one of the hottest acts around.

Winter's first album, *The Progressive Blues Experiment*, on the Imperial label, consists of some old tapes of Winter that were sold to Imperial by Sonobeat , a Texas label. His second album, simply titled *Johnny Winter,*" is on Columbia, the company Johnny signed a five-year pact with.

# The Byrds

## *May 31, 1969*

ONLY THE BEST ROCK GROUPS LAST ANY LENGTH OF TIME, AND ALTHOUGH the Byrds have gone through many changes, after five years they're still at the top.

During an interview at the Washington Hilton (where the Byrds played for the University of Maryland's prom), Roger McGuinn, the only original member still with the group, explained its evolution.

"We started in the latter part of 1964 in L.A.," Roger said. "I met Gene Clark (now with a group called Dillard and Clark) at a coffeehouse called the Troubadour. A few days later we got Mike Clark (also currently with Dillard and Clark) and David Crosby (now a member of Crosby, Stills and Nash).

"A little after that, we got Chris Hillman (now a member of the Flying Burrito Brothers) and we formed the Byrds," he said. "Then this guy put up some front money, recorded us, sent the dub (a copy of the record) to various companies and Columbia signed us."

Their first two hits were both Dylan songs, "Mr. Tambourine Man" and "All I Really Want to Do." Now, after a period of folk music, then electronic rock, the Byrds seem to have settled into a country-rock bag.

Besides Roger on guitar, the Byrds are John York, bass; Clarence White, guitar; and Gene Parsons, drums.

The first hint that the Byrds were moving toward country music came with the release of their sixth album, *The Notorious Byrd Brothers*. Their next LP, *Sweetheart of the Rodeo*, released in mid-1968, showed that they were solidly into country music.

Their latest album, *Dr. Byrds and Mr. Hyde*, another venture into the country field, includes songs like Dylan's "This Wheel's on Fire," Nashville West," and "Drugstore Truck Drivin' Man."

When asked about their future recording plans, Roger said, "We're going to cut another album as soon as our current tour is over. It could be an album with just Dylan material. Our producer, Bob Johnston (also Dylan's producer) would like that.

"Or the other thing we might do is a completely acoustic album. We'd like to get back to the roots and do some bluegrass with banjos and all that."

Being a member of a successful group that has gone through so many changes, Roger commented on the status of so-called "supergroups."

"Super-stars like Eric Clapton are always trying to find the ideal group situation," he said. "I think the reason those groups keep breaking up is that when you get so many strong minds together, it's hard to make it go.

"I think it's amazing that the Beatles have done it so long and stayed together," Roger said. "They seem to be so well organized psychologically, it's a great thing."

The Byrds, along with twenty-nine other groups will be playing the Atlantic City Pop Festival at the beginning of August.

# Blind Faith

## *June 21, 1969*

ERIC CLAPTON AND STEVE WINWOOD ALWAYS WISHED THEY COULD GET together in a recording studio. Now their wishes are more than reality. Eric, along with Steve, Ginger Baker, and Rick Grech (formerly of the British group, Family) have formed a new group called Blind Faith. They've already recorded their first album, which should be released sometime in July.

After Cream broke up, Eric and Ginger were looking for other musicians and came up with Steve, who had just left Traffic. The combination was good, but it was still the same triangle Eric and Ginger had found unworkable with Cream.

The answer was Rick Grech, an electric bassist, whose experiments with an electric violin had pushed him into the upper flights of British musicians. They chose the name Blind Faith because, according to their record company, "it is an acknowledgement of the inspiration that they find in each other's music."

The biggest problem once the group was formed was which record company had the rights to them. It was finally settled that in America the group would be on the Atlantic label and in Britain their records would be distributed through Polydor and Island, with Polydor distributing through the rest of the world.

Rick, the least known of the four outside musical circles, is twenty-three. His career began with five years of training as a classical musician which landed him a place in the Leicester Youth Orchestra. Until he joined Blind Faith, he toured with Family, an experimental English group.

Because of previous contractual arrangements the group has two managers, Robert Stigwood and Chris Blackwell. Stigwood heads one of the largest show business empires in Europe, taking in film, television, and stage production in addition to his work as a records producer and manager.

Stigwood's company manages Jack Bruce, the Bee Gees, John Mayall, Rita Tushingham, Georgie Fame, and others. At the time of Brian Epstein's death, Robert Stigwood was his joint managing director at NEMS, and held an option on the purchase of the Beatles management company, which he declined to take in order to devote his time to the Robert Stigwood Organization.

Since then, the company has moved into all areas of show business, including the staging of the London version of *Hair*.

Blackwell owns one of the most successful independent record companies in Britain. He founded Island Records seven years ago primarily as an outlet for West Indian sounds, having an immediate success with Millie Small's "My Boy Lollipop."

Island developed Sue Records to take in American rhythm-and-blues product, and now the company's labels or management cover the talents of Spooky Tooth, Jethro Tull, Fairport Convention, Joe Cocker, and the Rolling Stones' producer Jimmy Miller.

Blind Faith will be making a million-dollar tour of the U.S. in July. One of their stops will be the Baltimore Civic Center.

# Musings . . . Blind Faith Lands on the Moon . . . July 20, 1969

I WAS LOOKING FORWARD TO BLIND FAITH'S JULY 20, 1969, BALTIMORE Civic Center concert. I had just written about the group a month earlier. The only trepidation I had was that American astronauts were scheduled to land on the moon that day or night—and it was going to be televised.

Unlike major concert venues today, concert venues in 1969 generally did not have giant telescreens hanging over the arena floor. "Oh well," I thought, "I'll just have to watch the moon landing on the news." I had been lucky enough to see Clapton and Baker on Cream's farewell tour and Winwood when he was in Traffic. I wasn't going to miss those three along with bassist Ric Grech.

Those of us old enough to remember exactly where we were when the news of JFK's assassination was broadcast were then old enough to remember where we were when the first humans set foot on the moon. I'll never forget it. I was backstage with members of Blind Faith watching the moon landing on a small television in their dressing room. I felt sorry for the crowd in the arena that was kept waiting and wondering why Blind Faith had not started on time. I knew, and I'll never forget.

# Clarence Carter

## *July 5, 1969*

NOT MANY RHYTHM-AND-BLUES FANS REALIZE THAT CLARENCE CARTER, whose recording of "Slip Away" rocketed him to the top of the R & B charts, is blind.

Like Ray Charles and Stevie Wonder, Clarence Carter hasn't let his blindness hinder his musical career. Since "Slip Away" was released, Clarence has stayed on the charts and his latest single, "The Feeling Is Right," is currently No. 31 on *Billboard* magazine's R & B chart.

During a recent interview, Clarence was questioned about his career. "I always wanted to be a singer, but my first plan was to be a teacher," he said. "And then I said whenever the day comes that I retire off the road and hang up my rock-and-roll shoes I was going into a classroom and start teaching.

"In fact, I kind of think I could do a lot of good there, especially in the blind school where I went to school in Talladega, Ala.," he continued. "I think they need somebody that they know of to come back to let them know what this big world is about out there."

When "Slip Away" was first released, the record company was plugging the flip side, "Funky Fever." Clarence thought that "Slip Away" was too good a side to be the "B" side.

"I believed from the day I heard the lyrics and rehearsed it with my band that it was a hit song," Clarence said. "And I went on to prove myself right . . . I even went into clubs before the record was ever released and I would sing the song. I knew it was going to be a hit record."

Clarence, who is thirty-six, is glad that success didn't come at an earlier age.

"I feel that success came at the right time," he said. "I knew that if I got connected with the right people that it was destined to catch up with me after a while.

"Perhaps had it happened when I was younger, I may not have been wise enough to know how to manage it. I might have gotten big-headed and to the point where I couldn't talk to people."

When asked who the biggest influence on his career has been, Clarence said, "Ray Charles. Because, you see, the type of singing that Ray Charles came out with, like "I'm a Fool for You," and those kind of songs, are the kind of tunes that I had in my head to do when I was in the ninth or tenth grade.

"That's the type of singing I was thinking would do well in the market," Clarence said. "Another big influence on me was Otis Redding. When he took me to the Apollo Theater in Harlem with him to perform, I knew that if he thought I was good enough to be there, I could make it."

# Charley Pride

## *July 26, 1969*

ONE OF THE HOTTEST SINGERS IN THE WORLD OF COUNTRY MUSIC IS ALSO one of the few black performers in that field, Charley Pride.

Charley began his country music career before the microphones at the Grand Ole Opry in January 1967. Now, after two-and-a-half years, Charley is one of the biggest attractions on the country nightclub circuit.

Currently, Charley is represented on the country chart in *Billboard*, with a number two single, "All I Have to Offer You Is Me." He also has two RCA albums on the charts.

Charley was born in Sledge, Tennessee, and spent most of his childhood working in the Mississippi cotton fields with his seven brothers and three sisters.

After he heard about Jackie Robinson, Charley decided he wanted to become a baseball player. He left Sledge at seventeen and started playing ball in the Negro American League, with Detroit and the Memphis Red Sox.

He interrupted his baseball career for a two-year stint in the military, during which he married. Returning to baseball, he made it to the majors in 1961 for a brief time, playing outfield and pitching for the LA Angels.

Between baseball seasons, Charley worked as a smelter for Anaconda Mining's zinc complex in Great Falls, Montana, by day and as a nightclub entertainer evenings.

Country singer, Red Sovine, caught Charley's club act in 1963 and suggested that the singing baseball player consider making music his career. Sovine arranged for a recording audition for Charley in Nashville. The session came out so well that Chet Atkins signed Charley to a long-term contract with RCA.

Charley put out his first single, "The Snake Crawls at Night," in 1965. The next year, his recording of "Just Between You and Me" won him a Grammy nomination for the best country and western male vocal performance.

Other most promising male artist awards followed from many of the country music publications during that year, and these honors were capped by an invitation to debut at the Grand Ole Opry, where he was introduced by his longtime idol, Ernest Tubb.

Pride recently taped three appearances for a CBS-TV summer series, *Hee Haw*, and will guest star on ABC's *Johnny Cash Show* during the first week in September. In addition, he recently made a pilot film for 20th Century Fox television.

# David Bowie

## *August 2, 1969*

SINCE OUR SUCCESSFUL LANDING ON THE MOON, A NUMBER OF RECORD companies have released space-oriented records.

Probably the most unusual and controversial of the bunch is "Space Oddity" on the Mercury label. Written and recorded by a twenty-two-year-old Englishman named David Bowie, the song has received mixed reaction at radio stations because of its ending.

On first listening, the song appears to be the story of an astronaut who goes into space and, during a walk away from his capsule, his lifeline is cut, and he floats away, lost forever. It's this misinterpretation, coinciding with America's successful space effort, that has caused a number of stations to ban the record.

When thoughtfully listened to, the lyrics become more than a simple story. The astronaut, Major Tom, realizes that Earth has more problems than he can face. He tells ground control to say good-bye to his wife for him, cuts his own lifeline, and peacefully floats away from his craft.

Although he has been recording for three years, Bowie says, "'Space Oddity' is the first single I ever really wanted to release."

Rock critic Penny Valentine, in the British musical weekly *Disc and Music Echo*, wrote of "Space Oddity," "I listened spellbound throughout, panting to know the outcome of poor Maj. Tom and his trip into the outer hemisphere. Apart from that, and some really clever lyrics, the sound is amazing. Bowie sounds like the Bee Gees on their best record, 'New York Mining Disaster,' and has managed to arrange the backing to sound like a cross between the Moody Blues, Beatles and Simon and Garfunkel."

David's real name is David Robert Jones. Born in London in 1947, he organized his first group at fifteen. By the time he was eighteen, he had become frustrated with amplifiers and turned to the acoustic guitar as a solo performer.

During David's nineteenth and twentieth years, after his first LP was released, he dropped out of music and devoted all his attention to studying Buddhism with the Tibet Society.

Now that "Space Oddity" has been released, David plans to stick to music. Explaining his name change from Jones to Bowie, he says, "I started a local group called 'David Jones and the Lower Third.'

"The group had some success and finally made the London clubs," David says. "A couple of years ago, my manager was in New York, and he sent me a cable telling me to change my name, as it looked as if another David Jones (remember the Monkees?) was going to make it big. We became David Bowie and the Buzz, and I went solo early in 1967."

If radio stations start listening to David's record, "Space Oddity" is bound to become a hit.

# Janis, Little Richard

## *Rock Jersey Festival, Atlantic City, New Jersey, August 4, 1969*

ALL OF ROCK 'N' ROLL'S GLORIOUS MOMENTS WERE CAPTURED LAST NIGHT at the Atlantic City Pop Festival, but it took some time.

Janis Joplin and Little Richard, in their two sets, summed up what all the other acts tried to put across—some successfully and others not so successfully—during the three-day festival at the Atlantic City Race Track.

Janis, who finally has gotten a funky band together since her split with Big Brother and the Holding Company, drove the tens of thousands of fans to a frenzy with her throaty, gutsy versions of such standards as "Ball and Chain" and "Piece of My Heart."

Although the vibrations already were good when Janis came on, the crowd was even more together when she left the stage to make way for the man some consider responsible for starting it all, Little Richard.

Beginning with "Lucille," Richard had the audience standing on their seats through his set which included "Long Tall Sally," "Whole Lotta Shakin' Going On," "Good Golly Miss Molly," and "Roll Over Beethoven."

After seeing Little Richard end the pop festival with his 1956 brand of rock 'n' roll, it is almost impossible to describe what went on before he sauntered onto the stage.

The highlights of the first day of the festival were Doctor John the Night Tripper, Procol Harum, Mother Earth, and the Chambers Brothers.

Doctor John, in his floor-length robe, war-paint, and feathered head dress, cast his Bayou spells on the audience with voodoo oriented tunes such as "I Walk on Gilded Splinters" and "Mama Roo."

Mother Earth, with lead vocals by one of the best female country-blues belters, Tracy Nelson, brought across its Texas-based sound with an extra added punch on numbers like "Down So Low" and "It's a Sad Situation."

Saturday's show featured American Dream, Tim Buckley, the Byrds, Booker T and the MGs, Hugh Masekela, B. B. King, the Butterfield Blues Band, Lighthouse, Creedence Clearwater Revival, and Jefferson Airplane.

Conservative estimates put the crowd at 60,000 that day, and there was no doubt that with their current chart-hit, "Commotion," included in their repertoire, Creedence Clearwater was the top act of the day.

The Sir Douglas Quintet started off yesterday's show with some "honky blues" that led into fine sets by Santana, Three Dog Night, England's Joe Cocker, Canned Heat, Buddy Miles, the Mothers of Invention, Miss Joplin, and Little Richard.

All of the bands equalled or surpassed the sounds they put down on their albums, but there were some noticeable changes in personnel.

Bob Hite, the Canned Heat vocalist, announced that Henry Vestine had quit the group and had been replaced three days ago by guitarist-supreme Harvey Mandel.

Besides all the fine music by the thirty or so top groups, the over-all atmosphere was one that won't soon be forgotten.

The audience was allowed to go as close to the stage as it wanted and there were no police to stop fans from doing what they wanted to do.

The extremely successful festival, which attracted a three-day total of 150,000 to 200,000 will probably go down as the Monterey of the East Coast.

# Musings . . . Atlantic City Pop Festival . . . Getting There and Getting Dosed

AT THE BEGINNING OF JULY 1969, I WAS SCREWING UP THE COURAGE TO ASK my editor if the newspaper would pay for me to attend one of the two major "pop music festivals" taking place in August on the East Coast: the "Woodstock Music and Arts Fair" and the "Atlantic City Pop Festival." I finally decided I would ask and if turned down would just go on my own money. I shouldn't have worried. I asked, and she replied, "Sure. Which one?"

Both events were multiday and had similar lineups of acts. The deciding point for me was that the newspaper would pay for my hotel room in Atlantic City. In Woodstock, I would have to camp out. Hotel or camping? Hotel! Now it seems I might be the only person of my generation who admits he did not attend Woodstock.

Another plus was that my brother, Ron, would be at the Atlantic City festival. Ron was working for Mercury Records at the time, and an act he was helping to promote, the Sir Douglas Quintet, would be performing. I convinced my girlfriend and several of my best friends to attend with me. Somehow I managed to get everyone I traveled with "all-access press passes."

In 1969, there were two ways a reporter could "file a story" when out of town. One was to phone it in and read it to a "dictationist." Dictationists sat at a table with typewriters and headsets. When a reporter called a story in to the paper, the dictationist typed it and, when finished, yelled "Copy," and a copyboy would scurry over, grab the story, and take it to the appropriate editor. The other way was for the reporter to go to a Western Union office, sit at one of their teletype machines, and write the story, which would be transmitted by Western Union to the newspaper.

The festival, held at the Atlantic City racetrack, was everything I had hoped for: great performances, an opportunity to interview a number of acts, and a chance to hang with my friends. For me, there was only one problem, and it happened on the last day of the festival. I was directly in front of the stage when the Sir Douglas Quintet came on to perform. I had become friends with Doug Sahm, lead vocalist, guitarist, and namesake for the group. Someone in the crowd passed me a pitcher of Sangria. I poured myself a cup just as Doug came to the edge of the stage and said, "Hey Miiiikkke, let me have some." I passed him the pitcher, and he gulped some down and passed the pitcher to Joe Cocker (standing offstage). The problem was that someone had "dosed" the pitcher with a psychedelic substance. I grooved, Doug Sahm grooved, Joe Cocker grooved. By the end of the festival, I was still grooving. I had a story to write. I couldn't drive—grooving. I didn't know how I could write—grooving. It was too late in the day to phone the story in—someone had to drive me to the Western Union office. When we arrived, I sat at the teletype machine for an hour—grooving. Finally, I came to my senses and wrote the story.

# The Sir Douglas Quintet

## *August 12, 1969*

A VERY PERMISSIVE CALIFORNIA ENVIRONMENT HAS NURTURED THE CAREERS of many fine musicians and singers who migrated westward from Texas.

Among those who have made the move are Janis Joplin, Steve Miller, Mother Earth, and Doug Sahm of the Sir Douglas Quintet.

Doug left for San Francisco two years ago because he realized that his "extraordinary musical talents and the freedom he would enjoy there would make for a great combination."

The change in atmosphere from small, conservative towns in Texas to the creative San Francisco scene has enabled Doug to get his first hit record since his chart-topper of a few years ago, "She's About a Mover."

Now that the Sir Douglas Quintet is back on the scene with their new single, "Mendocino," and an album of the same title, Doug says that "San Francisco is the least paranoid place you can be. It's the best place in the world for music, and everything else."

Besides Doug, the others in the Quintet are Augie Meyers, Harvey Kagan, John Perez, and Frank Morin. A few months ago, before they released "Mendocino," the group put out an album titled *Sir Douglas Quintet + 2 = Honkey Blues.*

Although that album is far from being commercial, it is probably one of the finest "white blues" LPs. According to Doug, "Honky blues is our form of San Francisco soul music, with the lyrics geared for more far-out ears than for the regular R & B market, while at the same time sticking to our old, Texas-style arrangements. But the lyrics are into what's happening today."

Doug, the group's vocalist and guitarist, boasts that he has the "heaviest musicians that can be found almost anywhere in the world."

Doug credits much of the Quintet's musical ability to the members' upbringing in Texas. "In the Southwest they were exposed to virtually every form of music, especially country and blues," says Doug. "And, too, none of them have been playing for less than five years."

A native of San Antonio, Doug began his musical career at the age of six, when he learned how to play the steel guitar. By the time he was nine, he was a featured performer on the *Louisiana Hayride* country show.

He switched to rock in 1956 "when some of the younger people were getting away from country music," and that's where he's been ever since.

Since arriving in San Francisco, Doug has rarely played live, preferring to spend most of his time perfecting recording techniques. Now, with two LP's on the Smash label out of the way, he's getting back on the personal appearance track.

# Musings ... Doug Sahm ...
# Bill Clinton and More

IN ALL MY YEARS OF WRITING ABOUT, WORKING WITH, AND BEING AROUND great musicians, the one musician I miss the most and had a three-decade friendship with is Doug Sahm.

Doug died in a motel room in Taos, New Mexico, in 1999 at the age of fifty-eight of a heart attack (in his sleep I hope). I first met Doug in 1967. It was the beginning of my six-year stint as a music columnist. Doug was recording for Mercury Records, and my brother, Ron, worked at Mercury. Ron wasn't a guy who hyped acts, but he raved about Doug Sahm to me. I had known of Doug from his time as "Sir Douglas" in the Sir Douglas Quintet. Their 1965 hit record "She's About a Mover" was a favorite of mine: Doug's great vocals and Augie Meyer's infectious Vox Continental organ riffs remain locked in a part of my brain that produces endorphins every time I think of the song.

It wasn't until they made five terrific albums for Mercury records—*Sir Douglas + 2 = Honkey Blues*, *Together after Five*, *The Return of Doug Saldana*, *1 + 1 + 1 = 4*, and their West Coast masterpiece, *Mendocino*—that I realized the abundance of talent and styles that Doug was able to weave into what many think of as the "Texas groove." Doug could do it all, from Tex-Mex to blues to pure unadulterated rock.

Every couple of years, my phone would ring, and I would hear, "Hey Mike, Doug here. Coming to D.C. to play at ..." The "at" sometimes was a college, sometimes a concert venue, and sometimes a club but always turned into a "Doug Sahm Groove." I remember, in particular, one outdoor concert at American University—a huge crowd, mostly students but also kids who had heard there was a free concert at the college.

Before Doug went onstage, he walked out into the audience to greet me. I had been sitting near a guy who showed up at almost every free concert in D.C. Sometimes he was handing out copies of the *Washington Free Press*, sometimes he was selling underground comics, but he was always tripping on acid. On this particular day, he was just mumbling to himself and waiting for the music to start. A guy who looked like a cross between a college football player and a fraternity member ran through the crowd and kicked the "mumbler" in the head. This happened just as Doug was nearing me. Doug and I witnessed this unprovoked act of violence. Doug grabbed the kicker by his collar and in his unmistakable Texas drawl said, "Don't move an inch!" Doug was not a big guy, but the kicker was. The kicker knew that Doug was serious, and he didn't move an inch. Campus security was walking through the crowd toward us. They removed the attacker and checked the victim to make sure he was okay. Doug turned to me and said, "Glad you could make it." Then he walked to the stage and launched into the rollicking song "Mendocino."

Although I saw and hung out with Doug many times after the American University show, it wasn't until 1993 that I had the opportunity to see and hear Doug with his "supergroup," the Texas Tornados. It started with a phone call and that familiar raspy Texas voice on the other end saying, "Hey Mikeeeee . . . I'm bringing the Texas Tornados to D.C. to perform for Bill Clinton's inauguration. I got you all-access passes."

Little Feat, the Texas Tornados, Willie Nelson, Bob Dylan, and dozens of other artists were performing at myriad inaugural balls. This would be my first chance to see Doug front an incredible lineup of players that included Freddy Fender ("Wasted Days and Wasted Nights"), Flaco Jimenez (Norteño, Tex Mex, and Tejano music accordionist and singer from San Antonio, Texas), and Augie Meyers (with his distinctive Vox Continental organ sound that helped make "She's About a Mover" a hit for the Sir Douglas Quintet).

Well, it was a time I'll never forget. There were eleven official inaugural balls in 1993. After hanging with and hearing the Tornados and Willie Nelson and seeing President Clinton dance with Hillary (yes, and Bill played the sax at all the balls he attended), Doug and I went to the Young People's Ball at the Pension Building. Bob Dylan was the headliner there. Dylan and Sahm were old friends. We heard Dylan perform and then went backstage to say hello. The affection that Sahm and Dylan had for each other was obvious.

While they were in town for the inaugural festivities, I took Doug and Augie to my favorite Italian restaurant, Fio's. Fio's was inside an apartment building on 16th Street in D.C. It was a small restaurant and idiosyncratic in its own way. Because the stove in the kitchen had only four burners, even if you were with five or six people, you could order only four different dishes. Chef Fio wanted everyone served at the same time, so four different dishes at the most was the house rule. There were only two waitresses, and they both knew me and always greeted me warmly. When I walked through the restaurant doors with Doug and Augie, we were met with bemused smiles—I don't think they had ever seen anyone who looked like Doug. With his cowboy hat and his almost floor-length duster, Doug didn't look like a typical Washingtonian.

While we were having dinner, I asked Doug why Freddie Fender didn't want to come along. Doug explained that Freddie's wife insisted that Freddie stay in his hotel room and she would call him a couple of times a night to make certain that he did. If Freddie was going to have a "wasted day and wasted night," his wife wanted him to have it alone in his hotel room.

After a wonderful dinner, we drove back to my house. I had recently found a parrot, and for some unknown reason, the parrot liked to scream, "Bring Me a White Boy," which the parrot screamed when Augie approached the bird. Augie's jaw dropped. Augie reached into his jacket pocket and handed me a CD. He said, "Mike, you won't believe this, my new album is called "White Boy."

When I dropped Doug and Augie off at their hotel that night, I had no idea that it would be the last time I would see either of them. Doug's untimely death in 1999 was unsettling. My father used to say to me, "Michael, if you make it to age fifty-seven, you'll live into your eighties." Doug's death at age fifty-eight proved my father's theory to be wrong.

In 2015, I saw the documentary film on the life of Doug Sahm, *Sir Doug and the Genuine Texas Cosmic Groove*. The film filled a lot of holes for me. Doug disappeared from my life for several years when he moved to Scandinavia. There is footage of those Scandinavian years in the documentary. The film also introduced me to Doug's sons, Shawn and Shandon. Shawn reminded me so much of Doug, in particular his machine gun–fast delivery when he spoke.

Doug was one of a kind. I know it's trite to say, but they broke the mold when they made Doug. Sometimes you just have to be trite.

# Ian and Sylvia

## *August 30, 1969*

WHILE THE FOLK SCENE IN AMERICA LONG AGO MERGED WITH ROCK AND various other forms of music, Canadian "folksters" only recently began relying on amplified instruments.

One such Canadian group is Ian and Sylvia and the Great Speckled Bird. Appearing for a week at the Cellar Door, the husband and wife duo did much of their familiar folk material only this time around with an amplified back-up group.

The only American in the group is Bill Keith on pedal steel guitar. The others are Amos Garrett, electric guitar; Ken Kalmusky, electric bass; and Rick Marcus on drums.

Ian and Sylvia Tyson have been singing together for ten years. Over that period, they have worked for two record companies, first Vanguard and now MGM.

During an interview between shows at the Cellar Door, Ian explained why he and Sylvia left Vanguard, one of the strongest folk labels. "First of all, MGM offered us a lot of money. Secondly, Vanguard's album prices in various parts of the country are too high. And, MGM gave us full production control of our product and freedom to record at whichever studio facilities we chose.

"Another reason we signed," said Ian, "was that Bob Dylan was thinking of going with MGM at the time. Of course, as we all know, he re-signed with Columbia."

When asked why the current trend in music is uncomplicated basic rock or country rock, Sylvia said, "Things are swinging around because acid rock got so far removed that people couldn't understand what was being done.

We've been getting tremendous response at the various rock festivals we've played this summer."

Included among the places they played were the Atlanta Pop Festival, the Mississippi Valley Festival, and the Fillmore East. "The show we did at the Fillmore was headlined by Buffy Sainte-Marie, but most of the kids that work there as ushers and on the light show really liked us," said Sylvia. "The audience itself didn't give us a great reaction. As a matter of fact, some of the hippies didn't even know what a steel guitar was.

"Our music is so much more flexible than country rock groups like Poco and the Flying Burrito Brothers," Ian said. "We don't do whole sets of country or whole sets of rock, we mix our material."

One of the strongest musicians in the Speckled Bird will soon be leaving the group. "Bill Keith is being replaced because he's living in Boston and it's hard for him to rehearse with us in Canada. A young steel player named Buddy Cage will be taking his place.

"Bill will probably become the busiest (and highest paid) studio musician in New York," Ian said.

Ian and Sylvia's current album *Full Circle* leans more towards country rock than folk.

# The Hollies

## *September 6, 1969*

AFTER ACHIEVING FIFTEEN CONSECUTIVE TOP TEN HITS IN ENGLAND, THE Hollies lost an integral member of the group, Graham Nash.

In November of 1968, Nash decided to leave the Hollies in order to further his own musical career. On Dec. 8, he and the Hollies parted company following a final concert at the London Palladium.

Now, Graham Nash is a member of one of the hottest recording groups in the industry, Crosby, Stills, Nash and Young. But, what happened to the Hollies?

During the winter after Nash's departure, an extensive search was made to find a replacement who could blend with the group's fine vocal harmonies.

The unanimous choice of all the Hollies was Terry Sylvester, a twenty-three-year-old rhythm guitarist and singer from Liverpool. Terry first met the group in Munich in 1965 while he was with a group called the Escorts. Earlier, Terry had been with the Swinging Blue Jeans ("Hippy Hippy Shake").

After his first live performance with the Hollies, Terry said, "It took a few minutes for me to realize that I was actually on stage with them. After each number I wanted to start applauding. By the third gig it was fine . . . I felt right in with them."

Besides Terry, the other Hollies are Allan Clarke, lead singer; Tony Hicks, lead guitar and vocals; Bobby Elliott, drums; and Bernard Calvert, bass guitar and piano. Their most popular U.S. released singles were "I Can't Let Go," "Look through Any Window," "Bus Stop," "Stop, Stop, Stop," "Dear Eloise," and "Carousel."

After almost a year away from the recording scene, the Hollies have released a new album on the Epic label, *Words and Music by Bob Dylan*.

Allan Clarke was singing professionally long before the creation of the Hollies. He and Graham Nash had been in and out of groups together throughout their school days. They once had their own act called the Two Teens (the youngest act ever to appear at the Cabaret Club in Manchester, England) before joining in with such equally unsuccessful groups as the Deltas, the Guytones, and the Fourtones.

All of the cuts on their current album could make good single material, but the standouts are "All I Really Want to Do" and "Mighty Quinn."

# Ike and Tina Turner

## *September 20, 1969*

IN THE SPRING OF 1966, A SONG CALLED "RIVER DEEP—MOUNTAIN HIGH," by Ike and Tina Turner, shot up the charts in England. It went nowhere in this country.

Now the song has been released again on a new A & M album by Ike and Tina and may receive the acclaim it deserves.

The song was written by Phil Spector, Jeff Barry, and Ellie Greenwich and produced by Spector. Phil has had quite a musical career. He wrote songs like "To Know Him Is to Love Him" and the Righteous Brothers' "You've Lost That Lovin' Feeling." Spector was also in the group the Teddy Bears.

Spector had a small role in the movie *Easy Rider*. He played a gangster type who sold heroin or cocaine to Peter Fonda and Dennis Hopper. (Hopper took the photographs on Ike and Tina's album.)

Besides "River Deep—Mountain High," the album contains Ike and Tina Turner's original hits "A Fool in Love," "I Idolize You," and "It's Gonna Work Out Fine."

Ike was born in Clarksdale, Miss., and started playing piano when he was six. The first band he formed was called the Kings of Rhythm.

"This was the first band I could really call my own," says Ike. "Everybody depended on me to find work, teach them the songs, find them when it was time to go to work, and after they got there, I had to try to stay with them to keep them in line."

The Kings of Rhythm cut a song, "Rocket 88," and when the record made the charts, Jackie Brenston took the group from Ike.

"After that, I went to West Memphis and started playing with Little Junior Parker, Howlin' Wolf, and B.B. King," says Ike. "I wrote thirty-two songs for a record company. At that time, I didn't know you were to get paid for writing and producing.

"All I got was a weekly salary, and it was just that—weakly. On the hit 'Rocket 88,' I received only $40."

In 1956, Ike met Tina, whose real name is Ann[a] Mae Bullock. She was only in the eleventh grade when she joined Ike's group.

Ike and Tina's first hit came about when Ike wrote a song called "Fool in Love" for a male singer.

"In the process of teaching him the song, Tina was living at my home in St. Louis," Ike says. "She would sit up with me while I put songs together.

"The song I wrote for this fellow was a great song, but he never showed up for the recording session," Ike says. "He came to my home the night before the session and borrowed some money and the next day he didn't show at the studio.

"Ann[a] Mae (Tina) asked me if she could sing it and if I found the male singer, I could take her voice off and put his on. I agreed. I was going to have to pay for the studio anyway.

"After I cut the session with her voice, I went to work at the Club Imperial in St. Louis. During intermission I played the tape for the kids and wow—that did it!

"They flipped and demanded I put it out with Tina singing. That's what started Ike and Tina Turner. The song, 'Fool in Love' was released on Sue Records and was a hit."

# Paul McCartney

## *October 25, 1969*

PAUL MCCARTNEY'S "DEATH" AS REPORTED IN THE OCT. 14 ISSUE OF THE University of Michigan newspaper, the *Michigan Daily*, has resulted in detailed studies of Beatles' albums by thousands of fans all over the world.

But, according to Apple's London office, Paul has stated: "I am alive and well and unconcerned about the rumors of my death. But if I were dead, I would be the last to know."

The story of McCartney's "death" originated with a thesis written by John Summer, a student at Ohio Wesleyan University. The *Michigan Daily* elaborated on the thesis and McCartney's demise.

The clues started with the *Sgt. Pepper's Lonely Hearts Club Band* album, which was released in 1967 (Paul's "death," according to the university paper, was in Nov. 1966). On the cover, a hand, symbolic of death is held over McCartney's head. Flowers in the form of a bass guitar are on the grave the Beatles are facing. A doll with the inscription "Welcome to the Rolling Stones" is holding a toy Aston Martin (Paul's "death" car).

Supposedly the Rolling Stones have known about Paul's "death" and hint at it in their *Satanic Majesties Request* album. On the album cover, hidden in the bushes, are the Beatles heads with a casket appearing under Paul's head.

Mysterious album cuts include "Revolution No. 9," which when played backwards contains the phrase "turn me on, dead man" and "Strawberry Fields," when played at 45 r.p.m. has John saying, "I bury Paul." The title of one of their songs, "Glass Onion" is British slang for casket handle.

On the inside cover of *Sgt. Pepper's*, Paul has a patch on his sleeve with the initials O.P.D. In England, O.P.D. means Officially Pronounced Dead.

Many other clues appear on the *Sgt. Pepper's* album, but the *Magical Mystery Tour* LP has even more clues. On that album the song "I Am the Walrus" refers directly to Paul being "dead" (walrus is Greek for corpse and Paul is the walrus). On page 21 of the booklet that comes with the album there is a crash about to occur between an Aston Martin and an MG. On page 23, John, George, and Ringo are wearing red carnations while Paul's is black.

On page 4, all the Beatles are wearing pointed wizard's caps, except for Paul. His cap is crushed. Other clues are too numerous to mention.

Apple and U.S. news media have been flooded with telephone calls, cables, and letters about the "death." On Wednesday, John Lennon was reached, and his only comment was, "It's a lot of nonsense."

Since the "death" story was released, strange rumors have been started all over the country. One of the strangest involves a student from Northwestern University who supposedly deciphered a telephone number from the back of one of the albums. Upon calling the number he was asked questions and when he answered them all correctly, he was invited to Pepperland.

Seven days later he received an envelope in the mail with an invitation and tickets to Pepperland. The invitation instructed the student to lick the stamp after which he became very apathetic and dropped out of school. Shortly after this he told his friends he was going to Pepperland and jumped out a fifth-story window.

Other rumors of people meeting strange deaths after solving the Paul McCartney puzzle have been circulating. So far, none of them have been proven.

Clues over the last three years may not be conclusive, but they weave an interesting story.

The man who is supposed to be taking Paul's place is William Campbell, the winner of a "Paul McCartney Look-Alike Contest." Campbell reportedly had plastic surgery and has been filling in for Paul since 1966.

Disc jockeys all over the country have been spending hours talking about McCartney's "death" and some say that every song the Beatles have done since 1966 has references to Paul.

One idea that has been brought up by students of the Beatles is that Paul's "death" and awaited resurrection will start a new religion that will bring peace to mankind.

# Dillard and Clark

## *November 1, 1969*

THE INFLUENCE THAT COUNTRY AND BLUEGRASS MUSIC HAS HAD ON THE rock scene over the last two years is phenomenal.

Country-rock groups like Poco and the Flying Burrito Brothers have been formed and folk artists like Bob Dylan have jumped on the country bandwagon.

Having been influenced by many different groups, Dillard & Clark and the Expedition is one of the better contemporary country groups.

The seven-member band with two albums on the A&M label to their credit includes: Gene Clark, guitar, mouth harp, and vocals; Doug Dillard, banjo, guitar, and vocals; Bernie Leadon, guitar and vocals; David Jackson, bass guitar and vocals; Donna Washburn, percussion and vocals; Jon Corneal, drums; and Byron Berline, fiddle.

Doug and Gene's careers had criss-crossed in recent years, but it wasn't until 1968 that they formed their group.

Doug move to the West Coast several years ago from Missouri with a famed bluegrass-folk group, the Dillards, for whom he played banjo. Gene move to the West Coast from Kansas and joined the New Christy Minstrels.

After a year with the Minstrels, Gene met Jim McGuinn and David Crosby and together they formed the Byrds, picking up Michael Clarke and Chris Hillman soon after.

In his frustrating two-year stay with the Byrds, Gene exhibited his talents as a songwriter. He wrote one of the Byrds' best songs, "I'll Feel a Whole Lot Better," and he collaborated with McGuinn on "You Showed Me," which became a hit for the Turtles years later.

In 1966, Gene, who was tired of traveling all over the country with the Byrds, left the group. Shortly afterward, the Byrds went on tour with the Dillards and an unknown group, Buffalo Springfield.

Gene ran into Doug when they recorded an album together with Glen Campbell and several members of the Byrds. The album was released in early 1967 as Gene Clark with the Gosdin Brothers.

In the spring of 1968, Doug left the Dillards and as Gene had done, joined the Byrds. After a tour of Europe with the Byrds, he too left the group and came home to form Dillard and Clark and the Expedition.

The group's second album has just been released and with the current country mad music scene working for them, they should do very well.

# Fat City

## *November 29, 1969*

WASHINGTONIANS HAVE WAITED A LONG TIME FOR IT, AND IT HAS FINALLY started to happen.

A bit of the music scene has come to town in the form of a number of local rock groups that have signed or will be signing with major record labels. Love, Cry, Want has signed a contract with Elektra, Claude Jones is negotiating with a number of companies, and Fat City has just released an album on the ABC Probe label.

Unlike MGM's push on the "Boston Sound" of two years ago, Washington groups are making it on their own merit and individuality.

Bill Danoff and Taffy Nivert form the duo that makes up Fat City. Bill has his bachelor's degree in Chinese from Georgetown University and Taffy graduated from O'Connell High in Falls Church, VA and went on to Steubenville College in Ohio.

During a recent interview, Taffy explained how she met Bill. "We got together through a mutual friend who turned me on to Bill's group.

"Bill had already formed Fat City but wasn't totally satisfied with the group," said Taffy. "At the time, the group consisted of three guys and two girls, but it turned out that the combination of my voice and Bill's voice was better than the five voices combined.

"We wanted to do basically a vocal thing," Taffy continued. "But, it's hard to get individuality with five voices. So, now it's just Bill and me and a back-up group."

The cover of Fat City's *Reincarnation* album shows a dozen of their friends here eating watermelons, plastic grapes and drinking wine. Each person's costume refers to a song title. Among the local people featured on the

LP cover is John Hall (a DJ on WHFS-FM's *Spiritus Cheese* show) dressed as a convict. His costume refers to a tune titled "Locked in a Cage."

Bill agrees that things are really looking up in Washington. "What's groovy is that music is happening on its own," he said. "It's not confined to one category like the original San Francisco hard rock-blues scene.

"Another thing is that nobody's ever come to D.C. looking for talent before. Now, record companies are becoming aware of the potential of Washington groups."

When asked how he picked the name Fat City for the group, Bill said, "It's an old cliché—like 'easy street.' You know, like when everything is groovy you're in Fat City."

Fat City will be appearing this week at Emergency in Georgetown and plans on doing a road tour of the East Coast in the near future. They've also released a single that they hope will reach the top ten. The song, "City Cat," was written by Bill and Taffy and taken from their album.

# Musings . . . Fat City, Country Roads, and Then the Starland Vocal Band

In 1971, Bill Danoff and Taffy Nivert began writing "Take Me Home Country Roads." John Denver heard it, helped finish writing it with Bill and Taffy, and the rest is history. Not only did that song become a giant hit for Denver, it has also been covered by hundreds of other artists around the world, has been used in commercials and movies, and is one of those songs that could be called an "ear worm."

In 1972, Bill and Taffy were married.

In the mid-1970s, Bill and Taffy joined with Jon Carroll (keyboards, guitar, and vocals) and Margot Chapman (vocals) to form the Starland Vocal band. The group's debut album was the self-titled *Starland Vocal Band* and included "Afternoon Delight." The song was a U.S. number one hit, and the album also charted. They were nominated for four Grammy Awards in 1977 and won two: Best Arrangement for Voices and Best New Artist. The band hosted a variety show, *The Starland Vocal Band Show*, that ran on CBS for six weeks in the summer of 1977. David Letterman was a writer for and a regular on the show, a blip on Letterman's career in television.

While there is a myth that winning the Grammy for Best New Artist comes with the curse of rapid disintegration of fame, many artists who won that award (think John Legend, Amy Winehouse, Mariah Carey, Cyndi Lauper, Christina Aguilera, and even the Beatles) have proven that the award doesn't curse all. But then think about Milli Vanilli or the Starland Vocal Band, and there is some truth to the curse. In a 2002 interview for VH1's 100 Greatest One Hit Wonders, Starland Vocal Band member Taffy Danoff said, "We got two of the five Grammys—one was Best New Artist. So that was basically the kiss of death and I feel sorry for everyone who's gotten it since."

# Jefferson Airplane

## *December 27, 1969*

ALTHOUGH THEY HAVEN'T HAD A HIT SINGLE SINCE 1967, THE JEFFERSON Airplane is still one of the country's top groups.

Formed in San Francisco in 1965, the Airplane had a two-year wait before they became nationally known. In 1967, the group had two hit singles, "Somebody to Love" and "White Rabbit" and did a tour of the country.

Now, two years later, the Airplane's views have changed, but their music still bears the unmistakeable mark of lead singers Grace Slick and Marty Balin. Caring less about the commercial success of their records and more about artistic satisfaction, the Airplane's sixth LP, *Volunteers*, was held from release by RCA because of a dispute over the lyrics of some of the songs. The Airplane won, the obscene words stayed on the album.

Besides Grace and Marty, the others in the group are Paul Kantner, vocals and rhythm guitar; Jack Cassidy, bass; Jorma Kaukonen, lead guitar; and Spencer Dryden, drums.

During a recent AP interview, Grace talked about the group's stage act. "It's hard for us to get it together because nobody plays the same thing twice.

"You can't just assume the drummer is doing the same thing he did last night," she said. "Some songs are predictable, but most aren't."

Most of what the Airplane does on stage is free-form. "You've got a vague idea of what's supposed to happen, and you play what you feel like playing and you sing what you feel like singing," Paul said. "Sometimes during a jam, Grace or Marty or I will sing somebody else's song, I will pick up somebody else's lyrics, like Grace singing one of Crosby, Stills and Nash's new songs."

Although they've sold a lot of records and made a lot of money from personal appearances, the Airplane doesn't think they made it financially.

"We don't save money, we spend a lot of money," Paul said. "We paid Glen McKay's Head Lights, one of San Francisco's better light shows even though we don't need a light show. We put more work on our album covers, it costs us more money. We carry a lot of equipment and that costs a mint.

When questioned about politics in their music, Paul said, "I don't see us being political in our songs. 'Volunteers' is not political, Outlaws aren't political. That's what the song is about.

"I don't get involved with crazy revolutionaries. They're spending all their time being paranoid when they could be out on the West Coast enjoying themselves."

According to Grace, "Musicians play music, other people impose political or leadership qualities on the musicians. The media decided we're spokesmen for this generation. We're not the ones who decided it. So, when they ask us questions about politics, it's stupid."

In the future, the Airplane would like to go to the Far East and the Iron Curtain countries." But, we don't know about that," said Paul. "We might have trouble from both sides getting in. And our government probably doesn't think we're the best representatives to send abroad."

# Quicksilver Messenger Service

## *January 10, 1970*

"It's easier to know who you are when you're living with the trees."
The above quote from "Shady Grove," the title song from the Quicksilver Messenger Service's new album, just about sums up the group's feelings on life. They all live in and around Mill Valley, California, an area not only lush with foliage, but also with talent.

Because the group is more concerned with what they do than how much they make, they took a year off to rethink their music. The result is their *Shady Grove* LP on the Capitol label.

The members of Quicksilver are David Frieberg, bass violin, viola, and vocals; Greg Elmore, drums; John Cipollina, guitar; and Nicky Hopkins, piano.

Frieberg, thirty-one, started playing violin at age five. "I quit at seventeen so I could play baseball," he says. "I played viola in high school and in my sophomore year I was third chair in the all-state high school orchestra."

After moving to San Francisco in 1960 and getting married, Freiburg drifted into the folk music scene and teamed up with a girl named Michaela, doing traditional folk material.

Although he just joined the group, replacing original member Gary Duncan, Nicky Hopkins has probably done more music than the three other members combined.

Nicky was born in London in 1944 and started playing piano at age three. "I studied at the Royal Academy of Music from 1956 until 1960," he says. "I left school at sixteen to join my first group."

In 1962, Hopkins joined Britain's top rhythm and blues band, Cyril Davies (the name of the leader and the name of the band). In May 1963, after a strenuous tour, Nicky became seriously ill and spent nineteen months in the hospital. During that time, in January 1964, Cyril died at the age of thirty-two from pleurisy.

"I left the hospital on Christmas Eve 1964, and in January 1965, I did my first session as an independent musician. Glyn Johns, the Stones engineer, was at this session and Jimmy Page, Jeff Beck and John Mark were on it.

"From this session, Glyn asked me if I wanted to do more session work. This was an excellent idea to me, because for quite some time I knew I couldn't join a band and go back on the road again, and all recording studios were in London, which only meant local traveling."

For nearly four years, Nicky did sessions for various groups. Among the groups he recorded with are the Rolling Stones, Jefferson Airplane, Steve Miller Band, the Kinks, the Who, the Small Faces, Jeff Beck, Donovan, Dusty Springfield, and the Beatles.

It was while doing some session work on Quicksilver's new album that Nicky was asked to join the group. "By this time, I was beginning to dread returning to England, and by the time "Shady Grove" was finished, I decided to stay on with the group," says Nicky.

So far, Quicksilver has done three albums, *Quicksilver Messenger*, *Happy Trails*, and *Shady Grove*. Their future plans include more recording and possibly a tour.

# Rod Stewart

## *January 17, 1970*

LEADING A DOUBLE LIFE AS THE LEAD SINGER WITH A GROUP AND AS A solo artist can become quite hectic, but Rod Stewart, former vocalist with the Jeff Beck Group enjoys it.

Stewart, who was in town last week to promote his new Mercury LP, *The Rod Stewart Album*, told of his departure from Beck.

"I only left because after my last States' tour, six months ago, Jeff and I were going to join two members of Vanilla Fudge," Rod said. "When I met the two, Carmen and Tim, I really didn't dig them. It was then I decided to leave Jeff and join the Small Faces."

Stewart just completed his first album with the Small Faces for Warner Bros. "My work with the Small Faces will be in a heavier vein than my solo work," he said. "My next solo album will contain material similar to 'Man of Constant Sorrow' (from Stewart's first album). One song that will definitely be included is Dylan's 'Only a Hobo.'"

When asked what he thinks about musicians like Eric Clapton, who are constantly changing groups and forming new "supergroups," Stewart said, "Blind Faith was a complete put-on in America.

"Anything Eric Clapton and Steve Winwood do would sell. Their album wasn't very good. Clapton is now touring with Delaney and Bonnie and probably enjoying it. George Harrison is also doing some gigs with them."

Rumors that Jeff Beck was in an auto accident and will never be able to play guitar again were partially dispelled by Stewart. "Jeff did have a car accident, but he will be able to continue playing guitar," he said.

"Jeff bought a hot rod with racing slicks on it in Boston. He took it back to England where he smashed it up and fractured his skull and pelvis."

Surprisingly, one of Stewart's favorite American groups is the Meters, whose "Cissy Strut" did very well on the rhythm-and-blues charts. "The one problem with the Meters is that you can't find their records in England," Stewart said. "Another of my favorite groups is Cold Blood. The chick singer is like four feet tall with an eight-foot voice."

Stewart describes his own singing as "a cross between Ramblin' Jack Elliot and Sam Cooke, with a drop of David Ruffin thrown in." Besides singing, Rod plays guitar and five-string banjo.

The promotional tour Stewart is on takes him to various major cities where he meets disc jockeys and members of the press. "This tour is especially tiring because I can't perform. I'm not over here on a work visa. But I realize I have to meet as many people as possible in order to get album sales and air play."

The Small Faces, along with Stewart, will be touring this country in March and should be in the Washington area around March or April.

# Musings . . . End of January 1971 . . . My Brother Brings David Bowie to the United States . . . David Becomes Ziggy Stardust

DAVID'S DEATH IN JANUARY 2016 WAS LIKE A PUNCH IN THE GUT TO ME. I first wrote about David in 1969. I had spoken with him on the phone before I wrote my column about him in 1969. It was a brief conversation centered around his song "Space Oddity." My brother had sent me a copy of the single and encouraged me to write about David. David and I were contemporaries, at least in terms of age. We were both born in 1947.

A number of artists I interviewed between 1967 and 1973 had died young—Jim Morrison, Janis Joplin, Jimi Hendrix, and Otis Redding—whether accidental overdose or, as in the case of Otis Redding, a plane crash. If you survived drug abuse and the fast life of rock 'n' roll and made it past age fifty, you had a chance to live another few decades, unless illness or accident befell you.

Cancer took David at age sixty-nine. The gut punch to me was that I knew David personally, as he spent his first day in the United States, in January 1971, with me, my brother, and my parents. My brother, Ron, was director of publicity for Mercury Records (Bowie's American label at the time). David was already a star in Great Britain and Europe, but he hadn't really broken big in the United States. Ron decided to bring David to America to do a promotional tour and meet the press, deejays, and others who could help David's career in the United States.

David flew from London to Dulles Airport in Virginia. Ron had flown in from Chicago (where Mercury Records was headquartered). David had told Ron that he wanted to spend his first day in the United States with an American family. Ron saw that as an opportunity for me and my parents to spend time with David; after all, I had already written about Bowie, and this would give Ron a chance to spend some time with his own family while giving David a chance to spend time with an American family.

So, the Oberman family went to Dulles Airport to pick up David. When David's flight arrived, he was held up in customs for a bit longer than we expected. It might have been his hair or his clothing or maybe just chance that caused the slight delay before he came out of customs. He wasn't upset; in fact, he had a huge smile when he saw my brother and my parents. Ron had previously been to England and spent time with David there. Ron believed in David as an artist and really wanted to see him achieve success in the United States, success that had eluded him in this country so far.

After arriving at my parents' home on Admiralty Drive in Silver Spring, we all sat in the living room to have some refreshments and chat. Conversation flowed smoothly. David already (obviously) knew what Ron and I did for a living. David was curious about my father's work. My father told David about his job as branch manager for National Bohemian Beer, and David was delighted. He asked my father for a business card to have as a memento.

After giving David one of his business cards, my mother stood up with her trusty Instamatic camera and snapped a photo of me, Ron, and David seated on the living room sofa. David has my father's business card in his hand in the photo. The reason I mention this is that the photo has appeared in many publications. It was the second photo taken of David on his first trip to the United States. The first photo was taken at Dulles Airport.

People have e-mailed me, texted me, and messaged me on social media, most saying they thought David had a joint (marijuana) in his hand when, in reality, it was my father's business card.

After an hour or two at my parent's house, we all went to Emerson's Restaurant in Silver Spring (not Hofberg's Deli, as some publications have reported). The hostess at the restaurant seated us in a booth and proceeded to close the curtains on our booth. We all had a good laugh over that.

After dinner, we dropped my parents back home, and David, my brother, and I went to my house in Takoma Park. Besides writing for the *Star*, I also managed a band called Claude Jones and had co-managed a band called Sky Cobb. When we got to my house, the members of Sky Cobb were in my living room passing a bong around. The band didn't even try to communicate with David, something that some of them regret to this day. David had never seen a bong before—and, no, he did not partake of the substance in the bong.

Late that night, David went to his hotel in D.C. and left the next day. An interesting fact for all Bowie fans: David went to Mercury Records headquarters on East Wacker Drive in Chicago. After a meeting in my brother's office, Ron handed David several 45s that were on the Mercury and Smash labels. One of those records was "Paralyzed" by the Legendary Stardust Cowboy. David took a fancy to "Paralyzed," and on that 1971 promotional tour of the United States, David decided to use "Stardust" as part of his new persona, Ziggy Stardust.

To this day, among my brother's many achievements in the music business, his giving David Bowie "Paralyzed" ranks high on the list.

While I wrote a second column on David in 1972, it didn't contain any of the facts of David's 1971 trip to America. Those facts felt too personal to me at the time. Over the years, the photo my mother took of Bowie, me, and my brother sitting on the living room couch has appeared in a number of publications.

Fast-forward to February 2019. I had just received word that Backbeat Books wanted to publish the book you are now reading. A few days later, I heard from a friend in England that Salon Pictures (a U.K. company that produced a number of films, including *Churchill* and *My Weekend with Marilyn*) had announced they were making a film titled *Stardust*. The film was to be an account of Bowie's 1971 trip to the United States and how he adopted the persona of Ziggy Stardust.

I went to my computer, Googled "Salon Pictures and Stardust," and, in fact, Salon was making the movie. As I read more details, I became frustrated. Salon had cast comedian Marc Maron to play my brother. Maron was fifty-five years old. My brother was twenty-seven years old in 1971 when Bowie came to the United States for the first time. Maron was old enough to be my brother's father. I thought, "How else is Salon going to fictionalize the movie?"

I took a chance and sent an e-mail to one of the partners in Salon Pictures, Paul Van Carter. I explained my Bowie connection and told him I was available to give his company facts about David's trip to the United States.

Paul responded with an e-mail saying that he would like to put the screenwriter and director in touch with me.

Paul CC'ed both the screenwriter, Chris Bell, and the film's director, Gabriel Range. Six months went by before I received an e-mail from the film's director, Gabriel Range. Gabriel said that he would love to talk with me and arranged to phone me from London.

So, in August 2019, Gabriel Range phoned me from England. I asked him when the film was going into production. He responded, "Oh, we just wrapped up eighteen days of filming in Hamilton [Canada]." I was shocked. Where did they get the facts for the film? My brother (with dementia) couldn't have told the story to anyone. My parents are dead. I was the only one who could give a firsthand account of David's first day in the United States, and I hadn't been asked by anyone at Salon Pictures to give my account.

Gabriel also told me that the movie was "more of a buddy picture . . . including David and Ron's road trip across the United States." I realized that, since that road trip across the United States never happened, the film was going to be highly fictionalized.

After Gabriel's phone call, I received another e-mail from Paul Van Carter saying that he was happy that Gabriel and I had a chance to chat. I responded to Paul that I was unhappy that Gabriel called me after the filming was completed. I was also unhappy seeing publicity for the film calling my brother a small-time publicist when in fact he was director of publicity for a major record company. I had also read that the film depicts Bowie's road trip across America with my brother. Unfortunately, that road trip never happened.

By the time you read this, the movie *Stardust* will most likely have been released. At the time I am writing this, it has not been released. Perhaps it will be a great movie. I harbor no ill will regarding the film being made. I am curious about the depiction of my brother in the film. I am hoping it will be positive.

One thing is for certain: I know important parts of the true story of how David Bowie became Ziggy Stardust. I hope Salon Pictures' "fictionalized" version of David's trip in 1971 gets at least some of the story right.

Michael Oberman, Ron Oberman and David Bowie . . . Bowie's First Day
in the United States, 1971, Silver Spring, Maryland
OBERMAN FAMILY ARCHIVES

# Musings ... Grateful Dead, Allman Brothers ... Fillmore East ... February 1970

THERE WERE TWO SHOWS THAT NIGHT. I WAS AT THE LATE SHOW. IT started either at 11:30 p.m. or at midnight—the current fog in my brain is nothing like the fog that was in my brain that night. Without going into detail, I have to say it was one of the most incredible concerts I've ever attended. I had arranged to interview the Grateful Dead back at their hotel after the show. I didn't ingest any psychedelics that night; I may have been the only person at the Fillmore who didn't dose that night. I wanted to be fresh for the interview. Walking out into the sunlight after an all-night show was a new experience for me.

To quote from Grateful Dead bass player Phil Lesh, "It's daylight, and snow is falling gently on the streets of New York ... we stand there, our breath steaming, and look east down the crosstown side street. A distended orange sun is rising between the buildings, casting lurid shadows on the fresh snow. I grab Bob and Jerry in a group embrace: this is what it's all about."

When I arrived at the hotel room, Jerry Garcia and some others were sitting around a coffee table. I felt welcome when I entered the room. I was offered a seat and ended up sitting with the coffee table in front of me and Garcia sitting on my right. I had three years of weekly interviews behind me, so I wasn't nervous. However, I wasn't certain who all the people in the room were except for band members. I felt that before I pulled out my notepad and began asking questions, maybe some small talk was needed as an "icebreaker." As I was chatting with the band, I noticed that a fairly large joint had been lit and was being passed around the table. When I saw that, I remembered that I had a small pad of "flash paper" in my pocket. (Flash paper, or nitro-cellulose, is tissue treated with nitric acid so that it will burn instantly with no smoke or ash when touched to a flame. Flash paper is used for creating theatrical special effects and is also employed by magicians.) I had discovered flash paper when I was thirteen. I saw it used at Al's Magic Shop in D.C. and knew I had to have some. Igniting a piece in one's hand sent a small ball of flame up but didn't burn your hand or leave any ash behind.

When Garcia passed me the joint, I dropped ash from the lit end into my hand, where I had a piece of flash paper balled up. A flame shot out of my hand, and before anyone uttered a word (although I think I heard a few "wows" uttered in the room), Garcia picked up a bottle of wine that was on the coffee table and doused my hand with wine, thinking my hand was really on fire. I quickly explained what I had done, and there was "stoned" laughter in the room.

I never pulled out my notepad to do the interview. Garcia wanted to know about flash paper. I explained that it came in all sizes. I told him that illegal bookies often kept notes of bets placed on sheets of flash paper. They would usually have a lit cigar in an ashtray in their office. If police raided the office, the bookie would simply open his desk drawer and flick the cigar ash onto his flash paper betting sheets—a ball of flame, no residue, and no proof of illegal activity. I explained that any big-city magic shop could fill the group in on using flash paper or flash pots. (Basically, a flash pot is a sturdy container that can hold a pyrotechnic powder and is usually wired to fire an igniter. The powder can be standard flash powder, colored flash powder, smoke powder, or flame powder.)

I don't know if I was the impetus for the Dead using "flash pyrotechnics" onstage, but thinking back on that night puts a big smile on my face.

# Redbone

## *March 7, 1970*

TAKE FOUR YOUNG AMERICAN INDIANS, PUT THEM IN A RECORDING STUDIO for four months, and what have you got?

In the case of Redbone, whose first double-album was just released by Epic Records, the answer is not a cacophony of war whoops and tom-toms. Rather, the group has released some of the finest, most unusual and infectious rock to be heard in a long time.

In Washington to perform for a conference of college newspaper editors last week, Redbone put on a fantastic visual and musical show. Sounding at times like a cross between a Native American Sly and the Family Stone and Dr. John the Night Tripper, the group produced a unique sound that could be called Cajun-rock or Indian-rock.

The group consists of Lolly Vegas, lead guitar and vocals; Pat Vegas (Lolly's brother), bass guitar and vocals; Tony Bellamy, rhythm guitar and vocals; and Pete DePoe, drums.

The group's name is a Cajun slang expression for someone who has Indian blood but is not full-blooded. All of the members of the group fit that category and together represent over a dozen Indian tribes.

When asked how the group formed, Tony said, "Pat and Lolly Vegas were playing in L.A. I was working with another group, but I used to sit in with them. It got to be a regular thing and eventually they put me on their payroll."

Pat and Lolly have their own publishing company, Novalene Music and have written over 400 songs including tunes for Aretha Franklin, the Four Tops, Bobbie Gentry, and P.J. Proby. Their biggest hit was "Niki Hoeky" (originally recorded by the Cleftones on the Gee label) which has been recorded by more than sixty artists.

Some of the money the group makes will go "to buy back some of our land for our people," Tony said. He feels that the Indian occupation of Alcatraz is "something that will get people hip to our plight."

"One of our most important concerts will be in conjunction with Earth Week (a week of teach-ins and other events concerning our present environmental crisis) in April," Warren Winston, the group's manager said. "We'll be appearing with a number of other national groups in Philadelphia."

# Allman Brothers

## *March 14, 1970*

AFTER PLAYING LEAD, SLIDE AND ACOUSTIC GUITAR ON OTHER ARTISTS' albums, Duane Allman has finally released his own LP.

Duane, one of the finest studio guitarists, performed on albums by Aretha Franklin, Arthur Conley, Wilson Pickett, the Soul Survivors, Clarence Carter, and John Hammond, before he and his group, the Allman Brothers, were signed to Atlantic Records.

Besides Duane, the Allman Brothers are Greg Allman, organ and vocals; Dickey Betts, guitar; Berry Oakley, bass; Butch Trucks, drums, timbales, and maracas; and Jai Johanny Johanson, drums and congas.

The Allman Brothers is basically a blues group and Duane feels that his task has been made easier by the success of the British blues-rock groups.

"The best thing that happened was that the British intervention on the scene made it possible to play what you wanted to play and do what you wanted to do without having to be relegated to the funky places," Duane says. "It widened the whole thing to the point where we didn't have to be restricted.

"Everyone began to dig the blues and everyone was getting it. At first I didn't like it because they were doing something new," Duane says. "Later I appreciated the Stones. Now everything's run together and melted into one big thing."

In 1965, Duane and his brother Greg formed a four-piece group called the Allman Joys. Recalls Greg, "We did the club circuit down South, and then we broke up around February, 1967. I guess it was about that time that we formed the Hourglass with some musicians from Alabama.

All of the songs on the Allman Brothers first album were written by members of the group, except "Trouble No More," which was written by McKinley Morganfield (Muddy Waters).

"Our next album will be a lot different," says Duane. "There will be more variations in the material. The sound will probably be different, more separated, so that individual patterns will emerge. It will just be a collection, not necessarily a total concept album.

"We'll go off somewhere and jam for two weeks. Out of it will come the basis for new material. But it's always good to keep those old blues cats in mind because they really did it.

"Structurally, you don't even have to stay within the framework to convey the blues idea or feeling," Duane says. "You really can't explain it, it's not something you can hear. You just have to feel it, deep down inside. And, let it all come out naturally."

# Nina Simone

## *April 25, 1970*

"Each year, as Nina Simone gets deeper and deeper into herself and her music, new facets of this remarkable performer come into view. Last year she branched into rock, her own version, of course, for everything she does bears the stamp of her strong personal style."

The above quote comes from a *New York Times* review of a Nina Simone concert at Philharmonic Hall in October of last year. Besides good reviews, another result of the concert was a live album, *Black Gold*.

Among the songs on the album are the traditional "Black Is the Color of My True Love's Hair"; "To Be Young Gifted and Black," a tribute to the late black playwright, Lorraine Hansberry; and "Ain't Got No; I Got Life" from *Hair*.

During a recent interview, Nina talked about the benefits and problems connected with doing a live album. "The particular night we were recording 'Black Gold' was magic," she said, "as a matter of fact, after the album was cut, my husband said to me that it needed very little editing, if any.

"But you can't always capture the feeling that happens," Nina said. "Live performances sometimes are entirely different from when you go into a studio. You may make a live recording of a performance and the people who are recording you don't capture the warmth that's there."

For many years, Nina has been referred to as the High Priestess of Soul. When asked if she likes being labeled, Nina said, "I usually don't, but I don't mind this one. This label is very mystical in character, and if one studies what a high priestess is, I don't mind it at all."

Nina chooses the material for her LPs in various ways. "Lots of songs are sent into the office, hundreds of them weekly," she said. "I go through as many as I can, but most of the time the songs I choose are things that I hear just in an instant somewhere.

"I may hear something on the radio, or I may hear someone humming a tune, or my daughter may be in the mood to improvise a tune and we go from there."

Nina was born Eunice Waymon in Tryon, NC. She learned to play piano by ear and by age seven she had mastered the organ. "By then I had acquired a deep and intense devotion to sound," she said. "Anything musical made me quiver ecstatically, as if my body were a violin and somebody was drawing a bow across it."

One of Nina's most important concerts was at the Westbury (Long Island) Music Fair. The concert took place forty-eight hours after the assassination of Dr. Martin Luther King.

Nina wrote a song, "Why? (The King of Love Is Dead)," especially for that performance. Her recording of it was used recently at the very end of *King . . . A Filmed Record . . . Montgomery to Memphis*, which was shown at 1,000 theaters on March 15th.

# Rick Nelson

## *May 2, 1970*

TEASED HAIR AND HIGH HEELS WERE THE STYLE AT THE CELLAR DOOR two weeks ago when Rick Nelson brought a bit of nostalgia to the Georgetown nightclub.

Most of the people who packed the club remembered Rick as Ricky from the *Ozzie and Harriet* television series and couldn't get into his newer material as much as his old hits like "Poor Little Fool" and "Lonesome Town."

During an interview with Rick after the club was cleared of hordes of over-aged autograph seekers, he explained where he is now. "My new style didn't come about as an abrupt change," he said. "It evolved. I didn't set out to change anything—my taste changed more than anything else."

Rick's change in style is more a change in material than anything else. His new material includes songs by Bob Dylan, Eric Anderson, and songs Rick began writing a year ago.

"Easy to Be Free," Rick's last single, was an original tune. "I really started writing a year ago," he said. "It's a much more personal thing when you write your own material."

Rick is accompanied on the club and concert circuit by a back-up group known as the Stone Canyon Band. Its members are Alan Kemp, lead guitar; Pat Shanahan, drums; Tom Brumley, steel guitar; and Phil Volk (formerly Fang of Paul Revere and the Raiders), bass.

Ozzie and Harriet live in Laguna Beach, California. "They're just taking it easy right now," Rick said. "If the right roles should come along, they might get back into acting.

"As for my brother David, he's making films now. He recently completed a film taken on my tour last summer. It was filmed at the Bitter End in New York, the Troubadour in L.A. and the Cellar Door.

"Dave has people working for him, but he does a lot of the filming himself," Rick said. "As of this time he hasn't sold the film, but a lot of people are interested in it."

When asked how he got started in his musical career, Rick said, "I never had any schooling in music. Carl Perkins was my idol. I used to listen to him for hours.

"I started fooling around with guitar and just learned from playing."

Rick doesn't feel his television image has hampered his present career. "My image really depends on the people at the club I'm appearing at," he said. "When I'm at the Cellar Door, I get an older crowd. They request more of my older material.

"The Troubadour gets a younger crowd. They respond better to my newer material. I never put down my old songs, and I'm never embarrassed by doing them."

Rick's last album on the Decca label was recorded live and if all goes well, he'll be in the studio next week doing another LP.

Decca Records Promo Man Bernie Block with Rick Nelson at Cellar Door Nightclub, Washington, D.C.
PHOTO BY MIKE KLAVANS

# Musings . . . Rick Nelson
## and *Saturday Night Fever*

It wasn't often that I went into an interview awestruck. Usually, the artist I was interviewing was well known from a hit record or had just been signed to a major label deal. Rick Nelson was different. I was in awe. In 1952, I was five years old. Ricky Nelson was twelve years old and starring in the ABC television sitcom *The Adventures of Ozzie and Harriet*. I was glued to the family television (a Motorola with a seven-inch screen) whenever the show was on. The show, which aired until 1966, starred the real-life Nelson family, Ozzie Nelson and his wife, singer Harriet Nelson, and their young sons, David Nelson and Eric Nelson, better known as Ricky Nelson. In 1957, Ricky (who started out learning drums and then switched to guitar) went into the recording studio and recorded the Fats Domino standards "I'm Walkin'" and "A Teenager's Romance."

Both songs became hits and made it to the Top Ten on the *Billboard* charts.

Before the songs were released, Ricky made his singing debut lip-synching "I'm Walkin'" on his television show. I was sold. I had put up long enough with my brother, Ron, listening to WDON (the first real rock station where we lived) on his homemade transistor radio. No speaker in the radio, just a plug-in earpiece. I couldn't hear a note!

Now I had my own rock 'n' roll in the form of Ricky Nelson doing a song at the end of almost every episode of *The Adventures of Ozzie and Harriet*.

Now, with trusty pen and pad in hand, I was going into Rick (no longer Ricky) Nelson's dressing room at the Cellar Door nightclub to interview the guy I grew up idolizing.

Fast-forward to several years after my interview with Rick.

In the late 1970s, I was in the reception area at Epic Records in Los Angeles. I had a demo album of a group I was managing, the Rosslyn

Mountain Boys. I was hoping to get them a major label deal. Ten minutes before my appointment, Rick Nelson walked out of the office I was about to enter. Rick, to my surprise and delight, recognized me and asked what I was doing at Epic. I told him, and he replied, "I hope your album doesn't have pedal steel guitar on it." I said it did and asked him why that would be a problem. "Mike," he said, "Epic just dropped me and the Stone Canyon Band. They don't want anything that sounds country. *Saturday Night Fever* has killed it for us."

It was true, the soundtrack to the John Travolta smash hit movie had launched disco, jump-starting a new era in music with songs like the Bee Gees' "Stayin' Alive." That was the last time I saw Rick. Rick, his girlfriend, and members of his band died in the crash of a small plane in DeKalb, Texas, on New Year's Eve 1985.

# The Doors

## *May 9, 1970*

AFTER A GROUP HAS PRODUCED FIVE STRAIGHT GOLD ALBUMS, ONE BEGINS to wonder how it keeps its popularity up.

In the case of the Doors, their popularity could come from their spontaneity. They try not to pre-plan any of their actions.

During an interview with the group after a concert last week in Philadelphia's Spectrum auditorium, Ray Manzarek, the Doors' keyboard man, said: "We never really know what we're going to do when we go on stage. It's just whatever we feel like at the moment and we try to keep it going as quickly as we can.

"Sometimes we bog down and just don't know what to do. Then somebody calls out a tune and we do it."

The same holds true for recording. The group sometimes doesn't know what material they're going to do until they get into the studio.

When questioned about trouble at rock concerts, Manzarek said: "I don't think there are generally any problems. I think everybody would get along fine if there weren't those men in blue patrolling. Nobody got into trouble at Woodstock. There's no reason for any trouble at all."

Besides Manzarek, the Doors are Jim Morrison, vocals; Robbie Krieger, guitar; and John Densmore, drums.

Morrison prefers indoor concerts to large outdoor shows. "For our music, I think whatever magic there is turns out better in an indoor place," he said. "Outdoors it gets dissipated. It's more like a crowd phenomenon for the crowd's sake than a musical event. So, we try to steer away from outdoor concerts."

He feels (as do many others) that music won't be very "heavy" in the future. "It looks as if a softer kind of minstrel-troubadour thing is coming back in. It's a refreshing change."

The Doors' latest LP on the Elektra label, *Morrison Hotel*, reflects the change to a softer, more countrified sound than the Doors' earlier hits like "Light My Fire" and "When the Music's Over."

Krieger agreed that a softer sound is coming if not already here. Of their own music, he said, "We're thinking of doing some vocal harmony things and some jazz influenced things."

He attributes the group's longevity to destiny. "I think we were a destined group to happen," he said. "We're the four perfect people for one group, because we all pull in different directions—then the whole thing kind of stabilizes itself.

"We've had a good rapport with our audiences," Krieger said. "The best possible rapport that can happen between a group and an audience is a total mystical happening. This has happened a lot with us for some reason, especially with numbers like 'The End' and 'When the Music's Over.' It's just kind of a total understanding."

Area fans can see the Doors along with Insect Trust and a group called Rig tomorrow night at 8 p.m. at the Baltimore Civic Center.

# The Guess Who

## *May 30, 1970*

THE GUESS WHO MADE THE TOP OF THE CHARTS WITH THEIR FIRST SINgle, "These Eyes," and after four more consecutive hits, they're back in the number one position with "American Woman."

The Canadian quartet consists of Randy Bachman, lead guitar; Burton Cummings, vocals, piano, organ, and rhythm guitar; Jim Kale, bass; and Garry Peterson, drums. Randy and Burton share the songwriting responsibilities.

Besides their hit singles, the Guess Who have three top selling albums to their credit: "Wheatfield Soul," "Canned Wheat Packed by the Guess Who," and "American Woman."

Canada's top music trade publication, *RPM*, recently presented the Guess Who with the Gold Maple Leaf Award, for being the top vocal and instrumental group in that country.

One of the problems a group like the Guess Who faces is the barricade between Top 40 radio and underground or FM radio. But, according to bassist Kale, "Things are changing and are going to keep changing.

"When groups like the Band, Blood, Sweat and Tears and Crosby, Stills, Nash and Young are all making the charts, you know the barriers are about to fall," Kale says. "We've been lucky so far. People listen to us."

Although the Guess Who had a hit with their first RCA single, they weren't an overnight success.

"We were playing our music in Canada for years before we made a hit record," Bachman says.

Garry finds that the years of "paying dues" have finally paid off. "You play hard enough and long enough together, and you find yourself pre-guessing what the next move is," he says. "I can almost tell what we're going to do before it's done. Everything is our very own . . . natural, easy and comfortable."

Burton's main complaint is about the way people label groups in this country. "Scoring on the charts can be a hang-up, you know," he says. "It's really weird over here (the U.S.) the way they make their differentiations. Music is music and the only thing that should count is whether it's good or not.

"I don't like to think of things in terms of classifications. People who get hung up over labels forget to listen."

The group is currently on a two-and-one-half-month tour of the U.S., which was highlighted by their recent debut appearance at the Fillmore East in New York. The Guess Who will spend June in Japan, where they'll be spotlighted at the Canadian Pavilion at the World's Fair in Osaka.

# Fairport Convention

## *June 6, 1970*

Since the formation of Fairport Convention in 1967, the group has gone through many changes and disruptions, yet they've managed to gain a worldwide following and maintain their musical integrity.

Hailing from England, Fairport only has two of its original members, rhythm guitarist Simon Nicol (whose house "Fairport" gave the group its name) and lead guitarist Richard Thompson. Drummer Dave Mattacks became a member of the group in the middle of last year to replace Martin Lamble, the original drummer who was killed in an auto accident.

Around the same time Mattacks joined the group, violinist Dave Swarbrick was added to the lineup. The newest member of the group is bassist Dave Pegg, who replaced Tyger Hutchings. Hutchings formed his own group as did Fairport's female vocalist, Sandy Denny.

Fairport's roots are in traditional British folk music and American country music. They combine the two into their own form of rock.

During a recent interview with the group at radio station WHFS, Simon brushed off the group's troubles by saying, "It would be fair to say we've gone through some changes. Let's leave it at that."

Just before the interview, Fairport played two sets at Emergency in Georgetown. Although their performance was imaginative and well received (they didn't have their own P.A. with them so their vocals were hampered), the Monday night crowd was under fifty people ... scarcely the sellout crowds the group is used to playing for.

Currently on tour to promote their albums on the A & M label, the group's most embarrassing experience so far was in Minneapolis.

According to Fairport's road manager, "Kids were already boycotting concerts in that area." The boycott was a result of high ticket prices for a Crosby, Stills, Nash and Young concert.

"We were on a bill that was headlined by Ike and Tina Turner," the roadie said. "It was to be an all-day affair with a number of groups on the bill.

"The concert was to be held at the Hippodrome, which seats 15,000. Because of the boycott, only seventy people showed up.

"All the groups played full sets and put on a good show. The only problem was the lack of people to absorb the sound caused a lot of echo and delay."

Fairport's latest LP, *Liege & Lief,* is a mixture of traditional British folk material and original tunes written by members of the group.

# The Bonzo Dog Band

## *June 20, 1970*

OFTEN CALLED THE "BRITISH MOTHERS OF INVENTION," THE BONZO Dog Band has broken up, but they've left one final musical offering, an LP, *Keynsham*.

Bonzo was a popular band in Britain before they had ever recorded, because of their zany stage routines.

"Actually, our show was quite ordinary," says Vivian Stanshall, originator of the group. "We each played about a half-dozen instruments, sometimes simultaneously . . . interspersed with what our reviewers and critics called 'insane comedy,' but to us it's just acting naturally.

"We avidly looked forward to recording sessions, so we could utilize some of our more effective musical techniques, such as pants being pressed, and rabbits munching carrots. Now, that's music."

The Bonzo Dog Band was originally called the Bonzo Dog Doo Dah Band when the members were attending art school together. At first, they played for themselves and their close friends, but soon entered the professional world by signing with Imperial Records. Besides *Keynsham*, which was released last week, the group's other American album releases are *Gorilla* and *Urban Spaceman*.

In addition to Stanshall, other members of the Bonzo Dog band were Dennis Cowan, Neil Innes, Larry "Legs" Smith, Roger Ruskin-Spear, and Rodney Slater.

Roger was the inventor in the group, responsible for the wild mechanisms that were part of their act and records.

"My machines are getting down to more what I want to do, relate three-dimensional art to music," Roger says. "I've always wanted to involve the spectator in what I do, and you can if you make things that walk around them, and go out to sit in their laps."

Neil, who describes himself as the "serious" member of the group, looked forward to a successful career as an artist before he became involved with the Bonzos.

"At one time I thought it would be great to have a one-man show in a fancy art gallery, but it doesn't matter anymore," he says. "You find that life isn't the dream world it was at college. It's better working in a commercial medium, it makes you own up more."

Rodney, one of the co-founders of the group, also became very disillusioned with college life. "I swapped art for music when I used to go to college and paint things, and then spend most of my time in the pub," Rodney says.

"I got terribly fed up at college. All those people getting serious and clever in little cliques . . . they missed the point of what's going on outside their little world. I found it very sick."

Some of the best of their adlib comedy has been captured by Imperial Records on *Keynsham*. Included are songs like "You Done My Brain In," "The Bride Stripped Bare by Bachelors," and "Noises for the Leg."

# Flying Burrito Brothers

## *June 27, 1970*

IN A RECENT BOB DYLAN INTERVIEW IN *ROLLING STONE* MAGAZINE, DYLAN says his favorite group is the Flying Burrito Brothers.

After listening to the Burritos' two albums, *Gilded Palace of Sin* and *Burrito Deluxe*, it's easy to see why. The Burritos are one of the few groups to successfully blend country and rock music.

The Burritos are Gram Parsons, vocals and piano; Chris Hillman, vocals, bass, and mandolin; Bernie Leadon, guitar and dobro; "Sneaky" Pete Kleinow, pedal steel guitar; and Michael Clarke, drums. Parsons, Hillman, and Clarke are all former Byrds, while Leadon came to the Burritos via Dillard and Clark.

Sneaky played with various bands, but he had a full-time sideline as a stop motion animator. He stopped and started all kinds of monster movements for TV's *Outer Limits* and movies like *The Wonderful World of the Brothers Grimm*, *Seven Faces of Dr. Lao*, and *The Power*.

Talking about the Burritos' music, Pete says, "It's a mistake to geographically place our music. What we want to do as the Burritos is completely do away with any typing of our music in any form. We don't want to be influenced by any geographic area. We do our own thing with what 'they' call country.

"Okay, how is country defined," Pete says, "it's the simple, earthy form of three or four chord song types with a kind of rural style."

Parsons stresses that "we're playing roots music. Music that's happy and simple. It's a form of love music, a binding type of sound between peoples. Our music is simply saying 'find a way to love.' And, it's emotional because all our music takes all our emotions.

"There are a lot of messed up young people in this country today," Parson says. "Our music is simply saying 'Get out of your rut.' We're playing white soul as opposed to black soul. There is a color chart in soul. There's White, Yellow and Black. And it's been proven that boys in South Carolina can't cut the sitar like boys in Beirut."

Chris Hillman feels his music is humanizing rock. "Rock has always had it bad side," he says. "Too much nursing, idiocy and ignorance. The record industry has even aligned itself with the established order even though the industry execs are wearing hippie clothing. I call it 'crime in the conference room.'

"What could kill the essence of rock? Media! It can submerge rock, stifle it, smother it. We've got to fight the dehumanizing process in all art forms."

The Burritos' latest LP, *Burrito Deluxe*, contains a number of original songs, but the highlight of the album is "Wild Horses," penned by Mick Jagger and Keith Richards.

# Grand Funk Railroad

## *July 4, 1970*

WHILE MORE AND MORE GROUPS ARE BECOMING INFLUENCED BY COUNTRY music and turning to acoustic instruments, there are still a few hold-outs for a "heavier" sound.

One of these hold-outs is Grand Funk Railroad. Although the group has had two LP's on the charts and a third *Closer to Home*, recently released, they rely heavily on publicity gimmicks to promote their music.

The members of the group, all from Michigan, are Mark Farner, Don Brewer, and Mel Schacher. They recently rented one of the largest billboards in New York to promote their new album.

The press release sent out by the group's record company doesn't tell too much about Grand Funk's music, instead it gives out unimpressive facts like: "To belong to Grand Funk Railroad, you must be willing to spend over $10,000 a month on commercial and charter jet travel (they have logged over 150,000 air travel miles in the last year alone) and pay $300 a day for hotels and food."

When asked why Grand Funk plays extremely loud and what he thinks about "softer" groups, Mark said, "A lot of songs in soft-rock are meaningful and you can get into the words, but I like to express myself through my guitar.

"I like to scream when I feel like it," he said. "With just three pieces, if I played without distortion and feedback, it wouldn't be as effective. The distortion and feedback is controlled, and it fills. It makes the sound a lot bigger. The louder it is, the bigger it is."

Some of the group's songs were inspired by their upbringing in Michigan (home of other overly loud groups like MC5 and Frost).

"Where we come from, Flint, Michigan, there were a lot of greasers, a lot of factories, a lot to put up with, but something to really protest in our music," Mark said. "Our music is like switchblade music.

"There were a lot of fights. I protest against people who are down on me because of my hair. I really got beat up bad by some straight people at this motorcycle race. I was the only one there with long hair. No one else even had sideburns. They pulled out handfuls of hair and kicked me in my ribs and face. The ambulance had to take me away. It was really a terrible experience. I thought I was going to die. That inspired me to write certain songs."

The musicianship of Grand Funk is above average, but they need to forget about the violence they grew up with before their material will equal their musicianship.

# Poco

## *July 11, 1970*

MOST NATIONAL ROCK GROUPS THAT APPEAR IN WASHINGTON FLY IN THE day of their concert and fly out the next morning. Not Poco.

The West Coast–based group spent over a week in Washington promoting their second album. The original purpose of their visit was to appear at the now defunct Ark in Alexandria. While they were in town, they visited various radio stations and gave a free concert at American University's amphitheater.

Poco, whose forte is blending country and rock, consists of Richie Furay, rhythm guitar and vocals; Jim Messina, lead guitar and vocals; George Grantham, drums and vocals; Tim Schmit, bass; and Rusty Young, steel guitar.

Richie and Jim played together in Buffalo Springfield before forming Poco. During a recent interview on the *Steve Walker Show* on WHFS, Richie talked about Buffalo Springfield's final days.

"Steve and Neil (Steve Stills and Neil Young) didn't really get along," Richie said. "They felt like they wanted to make the artistic and business decisions. There never was much trust for a manager.

"The major conflicts were between Steve and Neil. I see the guys in Poco a lot more than I saw the guys in Buffalo Springfield. I don't know why, we just never got together.

"Jim went on the road with the Springfield for their last tour," Richie said. "We already knew that Neil was going to leave after the tour."

Poco, like the Springfield, has no manager. Instead they have what they refer to as a tour coordinator. The tour coordinator for the group is Larry Heller, a 1963 graduate of Montgomery Blair High School in Silver Spring, MD.

After Larry left high school, he went to the West Coast where he eventually became agent for the Chambers Brothers. Poco makes all its own business decisions, but Larry gives his opinion on everything. As tour coordinator, he does exactly what his title implies—arranges all aspects of their tours and enables them to concentrate on their music.

All of the songs on Poco's first LP for Epic Records were average length (around three minutes each). "The first time we went to San Francisco we were hassled a lot about doing three-minute songs," Richie said. "They were uptight that we didn't play long songs.

"We decided to do a long instrumental and put it on our second album at the end of 'Nobody's Fool.'" That instrumental is the highlight of the album, with Rusty doing an incredible pedal steel guitar solo—with the use of a rotoverb making the steel guitar sound more like an organ.

Poco's songs are of a non-political nature. "The thing we're contributing is a very up trip," Richie said. "It's happy. It's the way we feel.

"It's us or it wouldn't be our music. We express 'us' through our music."

# Cat Stevens

## *August 15, 1970*

A FEW YEARS AGO, AN ENGLISH POP SINGER, CAT STEVENS, RELEASED A string of hits in his home country, rose to pop stardom, and then disappeared.

Now Cat Stevens is back with one of the best albums released in recent months. The LP, *Mona Bone Jakon*, is not (except for a couple of cuts) commercially oriented as were his previous records.

Stevens stopped performing shortly after two of his songs, "Matthew and Son" and "I Love My Dog," reached the top of the British charts. In September, 1968, Stevens entered a hospital where he stayed for three months.

"That was the result of the pressures of my life then," he says. "I was too hung up on what I was doing to worry about my health, and I just let it get to a head, and it got to a stage where another four weeks in the state I was in and I would have copped it."

After he got out of the hospital, Cat decided to change his way of life. The most dissatisfying thing about his old way of life, he says, "was the whole process I went through, being with a big anonymous company like Decca who are into the Top 20 thing . . . very pop conscious. There are a lot of very heavy pressures in that kind of setup, all in a very fickle direction.

"Then there were the heavy agency figures who really didn't know me. The minute I said I wanted to develop, that the stuff I was doing really wasn't me or what I wanted to do, that didn't interest them. What did interest them was how much I was getting that night and making sure they got half the bread before."

"Matthew and Son" and "I Love My Dog" were heavily orchestrated. The personnel on Cat's new album has been kept to a minimum, with Cat on guitar, piano, and vocals; Alun Davies, guitar; Harvey Burns, percussion; and Peter Gabriel, flute.

"What we did was to record the songs simply, then discuss with Del Newman, the arranger, how they could be improved," Cat says. "We were lucky because he was into what we were doing.

"That was one of the things that got out of hand before. Because it was all done on the session with these clockwork players who just read the music, sat down, and played it. They didn't feel it or care about it.

"Sessions in the old days used to scare me," he says. "I used to get all knotted up days before, just being scared about it. And you just can't work in that frame of mind. So we just hit it from the roots with this album. Basically, just me and guitar and piano. It's the only way, really."

Cat's future plans include writing film scores. "I was supposed to be writing for a movie last year, but it was one of the things the studio cancelled when that money panic happened in Hollywood," he says.

One of the songs on *Mona Bone Jakon*, a cut titled "Lady D'Arbanville," is now No. 5 in England. If the fact that Cat Stevens is relatively unknown in this country doesn't hamper him and if A & M Records promoted the album, we should be hearing a lot more from him in the future.

# James Taylor

## *August 29, 1970*

WHETHER PERFORMING HIS OWN SONGS OR DOING SOMEONE ELSE'S TUNES, James Taylor is one of the finest talents to come along in a long time.

Taylor, who recently played to sold out houses at the Cellar Door and Shady Grove Music Fair, was born on March 12, 1948, at Boston's General Hospital, where his father, Isaac, was studying medicine.

"My mother, Gertrude," Taylor says, "had four children . . . Alexander, Kate, Livingston (who has a solo album out on Atlantic), and myself . . . in Boston, and one more, Hugh, in the town of Chapel Hill, NC."

Taylor's father joined the staff of the University of North Carolina Medical School, where he is currently dean.

When he was fourteen, Taylor moved to Milton, Mass., where his parents lived at the time of his birth. "I went to a private boarding school in that town for more or less five years," he says. "It seemed to please my parents.

"In the fall of 1965, I entered a state of what must have been intense adolescence and spent nine months of voluntary commitment at McLean Psychiatric Hospital in Mass.

"I split that place in the summer of 1966 and left for New York to form a musical group, the Flying Machine, with three friends."

Taylor went to London where he met Peter Asher and landed a contract with Apple Records. Asher, now Taylor's producer and manager, helped James with his first album, which was overly produced and didn't show off all of Taylor's talents.

James is now recording for Warner Bros. and his second LP, *Sweet Baby James*, emphasizes his vocals and acoustic guitar work, as well as his songwriting talents.

"As far as music is concerned, it simply seems to have happened," James says. "When I was younger, I played the cello and took some music theory in school, but formal studies never agreed with me, and for whatever reason, I took up guitar on my own."

James plans to continue recording and doing concerts, but he has twenty-seven acres of land on Martha's Vineyard, where he hopes to build a home and settle down in the not too distant future.

# Gordon Lightfoot

## *September 5, 1970*

WHILE THE FOLK SCENE HAS BECOME AMPLIFIED IN THIS COUNTRY, CANada has clung to its acoustic roots with singers like Joni Mitchell, Ian and Sylvia, and Gordon Lightfoot.

Lightfoot was born and raised in Orillia, a small town eighty miles north of Toronto. "I finished high school there," he says, "and had to choose between going to a university or going on to some kind of professional thing, which I wasn't quite ready for."

Instead, Gordon went to Los Angeles where he attended a now defunct music school, Westlake College. "At that time the music scene was totally up in the air, and not having any direction to go in, I just more or less decided to become an arranger.

"Then in 1960," Gordon says, "I started to listen to some people like Pete Seeger and Bob Gibson. That's when I got interested in folk music and that's when I started to play guitar.

"Ian and Sylvia were friends of mine from before and we used to hang out at the folk clubs and coffee houses. I used to get up on stage and play and sing like everybody else."

Gordon's first Canadian hit, "Remember Me," was a country tune he describes as a "Jim Reeves kind of song." All the while, Gordon was writing songs and his first big break came when Ian and Sylvia incorporated two of his songs, "For Lovin' Me" and "Early Morning Rain," into their repertoire.

Ian and Sylvia were managed by Albert Grossman, who after being introduced to Lightfoot, took over his management. Another of Grossman's groups, Peter, Paul and Mary, recorded "Early Morning Rain" and released it as a single.

"It wasn't a big hit," Gordon says, "but it was a hit. It made the Top 10 in the U.S. and that was a foot in the door."

In 1965, Gordon was signed to United Artists Records, which released a new Lightfoot LP about every ten months until he changed labels in 1969 and signed with Reprise Records. His first album with Reprise is "Sit Down Young Stranger."

Gordon's songs are some of the most meaningful in the folk genre. "I used to keep writing all the time," he says. "Writing almost became an obsession. Then, sometime around 1967, I discovered a new method and went to England.

"I just got on a plane and said, 'Goodbye, I'll see you later,' and I sat in a hotel room on Oxford Street and in six or seven days I came up with fifteen songs, most of which are on my fourth album (*Back Here on Earth*).

"So now that's my method. I find it's much easier on the brain to just really get at it by closeting myself in. I make notes if I think of interesting lines or phrases, ideas, or subject matter. Then, when I get the time, I just go somewhere. I can go anywhere."

Gordon has had four hit singles in Canada since his first. All of his albums have sold well in Canada and the U.S. and he has begun to make an impression in England, where he has also performed.

# Joe Cocker

## *September 12, 1970*

After one tour with the now legendary Mad Dogs and Englishmen, Joe Cocker leaves one wondering what he could possibly do as a follow-up.

Cocker's association with the Mad Dogs and Englishmen came about after he flew into Los Angeles to recuperate from a long road tour and form a new band.

He was contacted by his management agency and told that a seven-week tour had been set up to begin eight days later in Detroit. Since Cocker had split with his backup group (the Grease Band) and hadn't had time to form his new band yet, he found himself faced with the possibility of being barred from performing in America again.

Leon Russell, a guitarist, pianist, singer, and songwriter who had previously toured with Delaney and Bonnie and Friends, offered his services in forming and playing in a band for Cocker to take with him on the tour.

In one day, Russell lined up ten musicians and started a series of marathon rehearsals. Four days later, Cocker and his new group recorded "The Letter" and "Space Captain."

By the time his tour began, Cocker's musical entourage numbered forty-eight and became known as the Mad Dogs and Englishmen. On March 27 and 28, A & M Records recorded four performances of Joe Cocker, the Mad Dogs and Englishmen at the Fillmore East. The double set LP that was the result of the Fillmore appearance is better than most live albums but can't quite capture the thrill of seeing the group perform.

Cocker was born May 20, 1944, in Sheffield, England. "When we were kids we were constantly bored," Cocker says. "All there was to do was walk up and down the street. Then skiffle music came along, Lonnie Donegan ("Does Your Chewing Gum Lose Its Flavor on the Bedpost Overnight?") and that stuff.

"So, when I was about thirteen, I bought a cheap drum kit and began messing about with some kids who'd bought guitars," he says. "Eventually when skiffle started to fade, only those who were strongest stayed with music.

"At this time, I was into Little Richard and Gene Vincent and the other rock 'n' rollers, but I was especially attracted to the blues, which seemed to have a great honesty compared to all the junk English pop amounted to then."

In 1967, with the release of the Beatles' *Sgt. Pepper* LP, Cocker found himself "caught up in the acid centered frenzy of the times." He got together with longtime friend, Chris Stainton, and Procol Harum's producer, Denny Cordell, and recorded an original tune, "Marjorine."

Cocker's next studio venture was a slowed down version of "With a Little Help from My Friends," which led to the release of an album with the same title. That album was followed up by an LP that included two Beatles songs written especially for Joe: George Harrison's "Something" and Paul McCartney's "She Came in Through the Bathroom Window."

Cocker's twitching fingers and windmill arm movements when he performs leaves audiences wondering if he is serious.

"I've always done me little theatrically bit of throwing me arms about with the music," he says. "Some people think it's just a bit too much. Like when I was on *Ed Sullivan*, they surrounded me with thousands of dancers to keep me hidden. But, you know, it's not contrived. Why would anyone want to contrive a stage routine that turned so many people off?"

# Lee Michaels

## *October 10, 1970*

WEEKS OR MONTHS OF HARD WORK IN THE RECORDING STUDIO ARE GENerally required to complete an album.

But, every so often a best-selling album is completed in less time. Lee Michaels' third album for A & M Records, simply titled *Lee Michaels*, was completed in six hours and forty-five minutes. The album consisted solely of Lee on organ and vocals and his drummer, Frosty.

Lee's latest album, *Barrel*, has one additional musician, guitarist Drake Levin (formerly with Paul Revere and the Raiders).

When Michaels first signed with A & M, he was working with guitar, bass, drums, and organ. "That group, that sound of months ago, was not me," he says. "We were playing my tunes, but I was strangely absent.

"Close friends would come to my house and I would play my tunes on the piano. They'd tell me, 'Wow, that's so much better than all those guitars and things on your album. It's just too bad people can't hear you.'"

Lee tried to remedy the situation by concentrating more on the piano, but knowing the limitations of the instrument, he decided to switch to the organ.

"I had all these amplifiers around which companies had given me for promotional purposes," says Michaels. "So, I hooked them up to my organ, and the effect was interesting, if not a little startling.

"I began jamming with a bunch of people over at A & M, and it started sounding real for the first time in months. I realized then that for two years I had been sidetracked in my music. I realized that what I had been playing and singing in the beginning wasn't me. Guitars? Guitars weren't Lee Michaels."

Lee, a native Californian, started his first group in the fourth grade. He describes it as "a kid with a drum, and my buddy and I who played accordions. We played at this theater in Northern California between showings of Mexican movies. We got a buck apiece for this action."

Lee went to college in Fresno, where he majored in music but "but soon quit because I was drugged with the music department. It was like taking band in primary school all over again."

After finishing his academic pursuits, Michaels joined a band called the Sentinels and went to Canada with them.

"In Canada, everybody in the group got draft notices except me and the drummer, John Barbata," says Lee. "John joined a group called Joel Scott Hill and I split for San Francisco where I began working pizza parlors playing organ.

"John eventually looked me up and asked me to join Hill. I did and was with them for nine months. Then John split and joined the Turtles."

It was while watching a performance of the Jefferson Airplane in San Jose that Lee decided to quit Hill and form his own group. "The Airplane freaked me out so much with their originality," Lee says.

Lee signed with A & M as an individual artist and now has four LP's to his credit: *Carnival of Life*, *Recital*, *Lee Michaels*, and *Barrel*.

# Seals and Crofts

## *October 31, 1970*

A BAHA'I IS A FOLLOWER OF BAHA-U-LLAH WHO IN 1863 BECAME HEAD OF the sect. Baha'is emphasize the spiritual unity of mankind, advocate universal peace, and reveal a mild Oriental mysticism.

Jim Seals and Dash Crofts, two young men who appeared with John Hartford at the Cellar Door last week, are both Baha'is. All the music they write and even their stage presence reflects their "religious" feelings.

Jim, who plays guitar and violin, and Dash, who plays mandolin, have known each other for eighteen years, but only formed a duo two years ago.

"At the time we decided to play together, we switched instruments," Dash said during a break at the Cellar Door. "I had been playing drums and Jim was playing tenor sax. I saw a mandolin hanging on a wall, picked it up, and haven't put it down since."

Seals and Crofts have recorded two albums for David Susskind's new label, TA Records. The newest LP, *Down Home*, was produced by John Simon (producer for the Band and Simon and Garfunkel among others).

"The good thing about our label is that there aren't very many artists on it," Jim said. "They're going to try to keep it at eight or ten artists for a year or so."

John Simon entered the picture after Seals and Crofts did a concert with Delaney and Bonnie at the Fillmore East in N.Y.

"Delaney and Bonnie recorded our set on a cassette recorder," Dash said. "They were driving up to Woodstock with John Simon and the cassette was the only music they had with them. John heard it and said he'd like to produce us."

According to Dash, becoming a Baha'i changed his life and music completely. "The faith has enabled me to discover melodies and ideas I never had before," Dash said.

"All of our songs are taken from Baha'i phrases or ideas," he said. "But, we're very subtle about our faith in our music. People don't come to hear about religion, they come to hear music.

"The faith has made it possible for people to like the material more. Part of the charm of the songs is the charm of Baha'i itself."

Seals and Crofts are currently on a tour that has taken them to Boston University, the Baltimore Civic Center (with Chicago), and the Cellar Door.

While on tour, they use only one accompanist to implement their guitar, violin, mandolin combination, Bob Lightig on electric bass.

*Down Home*, which contains songs like "Gabriel Go on Home," "Tin Town," and "Cotton Mouth," makes use of John Simon on piano; John Hall, electric guitar; Greg Thomas, drums; Paul Harris, organ; and Harvey Brooks, Jim Rolleston, and Eddie Rich, bass.

# May Blitz

## *November 21, 1970*

WHEN THE JEFF BECK GROUP BROKE UP LAST YEAR, PIANIST NICKY HOP-kins joined the Quicksilver Messenger Service, bassist Ron Wood and vocalist Rod Stewart helped re-form the Small Faces, and drummer Tony Newman formed a group called May Blitz.

May Blitz is unknown in this country, although they have quite a fol-lowing in England. Their first album (on the Paramount label) simply titled *May Blitz* was just released and is a fine effort for a debut album.

Besides Tony, who is from England, the others in the group are Cana-dians Jimmy Black on guitar and Reid Hudson on bass.

"We've progressed so much since we first started," says Tony, "to the extent that almost every gig is different. We used to be slightly regimented musically, but now we're much more free.

"When we play, we know what's good and what the audience thinks is good. We're a young band and we can't afford to be self-indulgent. We give the audiences what they want, but it's really gratifying that it's exactly what we want, too."

One of the biggest obstacles facing a rock group is putting a realistic sound down on record. "You can have the best engineer in the world, but if you can't communicate with him, you end up accepting something only half as good," Tony says. "Our engineer, Barry Ainsworth, knew exactly what we wanted as soon as we asked for it."

A fourth member of the group is a 300-pound ape-like female cartoon character that was the subject of a weekly cartoon strip in England. The character, also called May Blitz, was originally inserted in magazines to get the group's name out nationally. The character became so popular that it's still running in England as a piece of editorial.

Unlike a lot of British groups, May Blitz's music is not of eardrum shattering volume. "We hit the right tempo every time, which is something English musicians don't always do," Tony says.

"What we want to do is offer something new. People are sick of the very clever programmed groups and the ridiculously hard blues groups. Music doesn't have to be loud and frantic all the time. Contrasts in music are just as effective."

Even though they have a following in England, there aren't many places in that country for May Blitz to play.

"There are very few places here where you have real head audiences who really get into the music," Tony says. "In the States they will listen to your music without comparing you with anyone else."

A tour of the U.S. and another LP are next on the group's agenda.

# Emitt Rhodes

## *November 28, 1970*

ONE-MAN BANDS ARE VERY RARE THESE DAYS, BUT TWENTY-YEAR-OLD Emitt Rhodes partially fills the bill.

The young Californian, in town for a concert at Northern Virginia Community College, explained during an interview how he put together an entire album by himself.

The album, simply titled *Emitt Rhodes*, was nine months in the making and was done in a shed attached to Emitt's parents' home.

"I had four songs when I started," Emitt said. "I wrote the rest of the songs while I was recording the album."

Emitt's recording equipment consisted of a four-track Ampex Recorder, three microphones, microphone mixers, and some amps.

Because I only had a four-track machine, I finished the basic instrumental tracks first," Emitt said. "Then I transferred it to an eight-track machine that I had rented and brought home. The last things to be recorded were the vocals."

After Emitt finished writing a song, he would record the beat with a metronome to keep a steady tempo.

"Then I would put down the basic instrument of the song like piano or guitar," Emmett said. "After that I would just keep adding on."

Emitt has been writing music for five years and playing drums for ten years. On his new album, Emitt plays guitar, bass, drums, harmonium (an organ like instrument), and does all the vocals.

"The first songs I wrote were terrible," Emitt said. "But the only way you can learn is by writing bad songs."

Three years ago, Emitt was in a group called the Merry-Go-Round on A&M Records.

"After Merry-Go-Round broke up, I did a solo LP for A&M, with a producer, arranger, and studio musicians," he said.

"But," Emitt said, "I didn't get what I wanted. I wasn't satisfied with it at all. So I figured the only way to get what I wanted was to do it at home by myself."

Dunhill Records people heard some of Emitt's preliminary work on the album, liked what they heard, and signed him to the label. Emitt's favorite cut on the album is "Ever Find Yourself Running?"

"I believe I said something on that cut that I honestly felt and that's what I was striving for," Emitt said.

When asked how he gets ideas for songs, Emitt said, "It takes a while. The original ideas for the songs just come to me. After that I just have to put them together."

The main criticism of the album is that it sounds similar to Paul McCartney's solo album. But, even with the similarity to McCartney's album, Emitt's creativity shows through.

Emitt Rhodes Backstage, Washington, D.C.
PHOTO BY MIKE KLAVANS

# Linda Ronstadt

## *December 12, 1970*

NOT EVEN A STREP THROAT CAN KEEP A COUNTRY GIRL DOWN.

Linda Ronstadt (appearing at the Cellar Door through tonight) walked on stage opening night with a strep throat and proceeded to do a fine country-rock set.

Linda is being accompanied on her current tour by Swamp Water, a group that consists of lead guitar, bass guitar, rhythm guitar, fiddle, and drums.

Her illness Monday night didn't stop Linda from talking about her career during an interview between sets. Linda started her first group, the New Union Ramblers, in her hometown, Tucson, Ariz.

"The New Union Ramblers," Linda said, "consisted of my brother, my sister and myself. They wanted to stay at home with their families and not go on the road, so the group broke up. I think they made a wise decision."

At age seventeen, Linda left Tucson for Hollywood where she eventually became vocalist for the Stone Poneys. Linda and the group signed with Capitol and released "Different Drum," which became a hit single.

After the Stone Poneys broke up, Linda went out on her own and at various times was backed by musicians from the Nitty Gritty Dirt Band, Kaleidoscope, Dillard and Clark, the Flying Burrito Brothers, and the Byrds.

Linda's roots are in the Tex-Mex sound that abounded in the area around where she was raised and in Mexican country music.

"I grew up with Mexican music," Linda said. "It has fantastic rhythms, but up to now they haven't exploited the rhythm to the fullest.

"When I was a kid, I used to spend every spare moment in Mexico. We lived near the border, so that's my ethnic background.

"One time my father had to go to Mexico on a business trip and he took me along. We were in a bar and my father started singing with the mariachi band and a group of tourists took up a collection for him. They didn't realize that he was an American businessman."

Linda only goes home to California for one-week periods. The rest of the time she's on the road. "There's no way to describe how bad you feel in a club where people sit around and don't pick up on your situation," she said.

"We just played a club like that in Boston. The people there were gangster types with greaser girlfriends who would just stare at me while I was on stage. The Cellar Door is one of the best clubs I've played. The people who work there are friendly and the audiences are into the music."

One thing Linda can't put up with is authority. "Unfortunately, I went to a Catholic school," she said. "It was the grimmest, bleakest place I've ever been in. Now, I can't deal with authority.

"That's hurt me a lot. I have to deal with producers and managers. You have to adjust yourself to authority.

"Luckily, my manager, Herb Cohen (Frank Zappa's partner in Straight Records) is an honest guy," Linda said. "He's the only authoritative figure I can deal with. Herb looks a lot like Pan. When he takes his boots off, I expect to see cloven hooves."

Linda's latest album, *Silk Purse*, is currently number 126 on *Billboard*'s album chart. Linda isn't sure of her future recording plans. "I'm having a hard time finding songs to record," she said. "It's hard finding songs that express ideas you can identify with."

# Eric Burdon and War

## *December 19, 1970*

ERIC BURDON HAS GONE THROUGH A LOT OF CHANGES SINCE HE LEFT THE Animals ("House of the Rising Sun") a couple of years ago.

"I broke the Animals up because I was just completely dissatisfied, both musically and business-wise," Burdon says. "I didn't have the knowledge or ability to get out of it myself. The only thing I could do was to stop what I was doing."

And stop is what Burdon did. He disappeared from the music scene for almost two years. "During that time, I wrote four movie tunes and rode a lot of motorcycles," he says. "I got to know Southern California more than I thought I did.

"I saw it from the bottom end as well as the top end. So those two years I was out of the music business weren't really useless. I learned a lot.

"I was going to the Whiskey (a rock club in L.A.) from time to time and seeing groups that were getting large sums of money from record companies to form, reform and to be exploited.

"There was a lot of money going into them, but no substance. So, I just said well, if that's all everybody's got to offer, maybe it's about time I got back in."

That's when Burdon decided to form his current group, War.

"There's much more of a meeting of heads in War and in War's music," Burdon says. "Everybody has a say and everybody has an influence."

Besides Burdon, who is lead vocalist for the group, the members are Harold Brown, drums; "Papa" Dee Allen, congas and percussion; Bee Bee Dickerson, bass; Howard Scott, guitar; Lonnie Leroy Jordan, organ; Lee Oskar, harmonica; and Charles Miller, sax and flute.

Eric and War signed with MGM, went into the studio, and a few months later released their first LP, *Eric Burdon Declares War*. Their second studio effort, a double album package, *The Black Man's Burdon*, was released this month.

War's music, according to Burdon, is supposed to be a reflection of the times. "Like one of the numbers we do now, which has affected me is Jagger/Richards' 'Paint It Black.' We use it for a different statement than the one of dissatisfaction that Jagger made with it.

"It's a graphic trip of taking cause, taking basically the color black, with the black hands of the musicians. From the color black evolves other colors, and you start to see them grow. And that's the message to the audience.

"I was listening to a tape of it recently and it really struck me that it sounds ugly," Burdon says. "And it made me, personally, realize that all I've been involved with in the past has been ugly. The side of rock that I was involved in . . . punch-ups in the audience, punch-ups on stage. And the group and myself were basically ugly people to look at. But there's beauty coming out of it."

# Alice Cooper

## *December 26, 1970*

ALICE COOPER MUST BE SEEN TO BE UNDERSTOOD.

Alice Cooper, a young man from Phoenix, Ariz., brought his rock group of the same name (more like a theatrical troupe) to town last weekend and won a number of new admirers.

Visual aids and dynamism that are lacking in the group's records made for one of the liveliest rock shows to play the area in recent months.

Alice, with his shaggy, shoulder-length hair, eye makeup, and leotards, does most of the vocals and theatrics for the group. As a climax to the group's act, Alice sings from a "psychedelically" lit electric chair and throws chicken feathers into the audience.

Besides Alice, those in the group are Glen Buxton, lead guitar; Mike Bruce, rhythm guitar, piano, organ, and vocals; Dennis Dunnaway, bass and vocals; and Neil Smith, drums.

During an interview at the Holiday Inn in Fairfax, after a show at the Northern Virginia Community College, Alice talked about the origin of the group. "We started in high school in Phoenix back when the Beatles started . . . except our hair wasn't as long.

"We all went to college together and eventually moved to L.A., but it fell apart," he said. "I mean, there were only two clubs in the city where we could play. If we'd had to wait our turn to get into those clubs, we never would have made a living."

Alice Cooper now lives on a farm in Pontiac, Mich., and hates it. "There's more work in the Midwest than anywhere else in the country, but I hate living on the farm," Alice said. "I'm a city person. I have to get into Detroit a couple of times a week."

Various rumors have circulated about the group, including one that they decapitated live chickens on stage and threw the bloody bodies into the audience.

"There's no truth to that rumor at all," Alice said. "We never killed any chickens. We'd throw live chickens into the audience and sometimes people would accidentally step on them. Now we use feather pillows instead."

Alice and the boys have released two albums, *Pretties for You* and *Easy Action* for Frank Zappa's Bizarre/Straight label and just finished a third for Warner Brothers.

"The new album is more of a rock musical thing," Alice said. "It's more theatrical in a musical way. Our music will really be appreciated when we get into video cassettes and cartridges."

Alice Cooper can currently be seen in the movie, *Diary of a Mad Housewife*. They do one number where they throw kitchen oil, feathers, and mannequin parts into the crowd during the scene they're in.

Cooper won't tell what his given name was. He legally changed his name to Alice Cooper in Detroit.

Alice Cooper, Baltimore, Maryland
PHOTO BY MIKE KLAVANS

# Joan Baez

## *January 9, 1971*

Since her professional debut in 1959 at the Newport Folk Festival, Joan Baez consistently has proved her skills as a songwriter, singer, and musician.

Now, Vanguard Records has released the best of Baez in an LP entitled *The First Ten Years.*

Joan was born on Jan. 9, 1941 on Staten Island. Her mother, of English-Scottish parentage, was the daughter of an Episcopal minister. Her father was born in Mexico and also was a minister's child.

Joan discovered racism at an early age. She went to school in Redlands, Calif., where the Mexican children had to play in separate groups from the white children.

While attending high school in Palo Alto, Joan bought a cheap guitar and joined the school choir, although she had no ambition to make music her career.

After high school, Joan and her family moved to Boston, where she started performing at Tulia's Coffee Grinder, a place where amateurs could come and perform. Joan soon became a regular there, and in the summer of 1959, a folksinger friend of hers invited her to the first Newport Folk Festival.

Her first audience consisted of 13,000 people, including representatives from all of the major record companies.

Joan eventually signed with Vanguard and has recorded over a dozen albums for that label. Robert Shelton of the *New York Times* acclaimed her voice as one which "sends one scurrying to the thesaurus for superlatives ... stunning tone, clear as glass sound, sometimes shimmering with a glint of reflected sunlight, then darkening a bit with a passing lowering cloud."

Folklore and vocal techniques never interested Joan. "I don't care very much about where a song came from or why, or even what it says," she says. "All I care about is how it sounds and the feeling in it."

On March 26, 1968, Joan married David Harris, a former student leader at Stanford University and now in federal prison for draft resistance. One of Joan's albums is a collection of songs dedicated to her husband, entitled *David's Album*.

Unlike many of her contemporaries, Joan doesn't like the idea of the public paying a lot of money to see her perform. When asked how much time during the year she would like to devote to singing for money, she replied, "As little as possible." At times she has refused to perform if admission tickets were priced more than $2.

Ralph Gleason, writing for the *San Francisco Chronicle*, gave one of the best appraisals of Joan when he wrote: "She is natural and real, and the way she is on stage is the way she is at breakfast.

"It is this utter reality, plus the glowing humanity of her personality, and the remarkable gift for vocal communication she possesses, that makes her appeal so incredibly strong."

# Jimmy Webb

## *January 16, 1971*

HAVING MORE THAN PROVED HIMSELF AS A SONGWRITER, TWENTY-FOUR-year-old Jimmy Webb is now trying to make it as a performer.

Jimmy, who recently appeared at the Cellar Door, has only been touring for five weeks. Although he is a fine interpreter of his own songs, his voice did not hold out toward the end of his week-long engagement.

Born in Elk City, Okla., the son of a Baptist minister, Jimmy and his family (three brothers and three sisters) moved to Southern California when he was eighteen. Jimmy majored in music, but didn't do too well in his courses.

"A sympathetic counselor told me I failed most of my courses and suggested that if I didn't enjoy college I should get out and do things I was better at," Jimmy said during an interview en route to WHMC, where he was a guest on the Barry Richards show.

"I left school and moved to L.A. I made some tapes of my material on a home machine and ended up working for Jobete Music, Motown's publishing wing."

At Jobete, Jimmy wrote "Christmas Tree," which was recorded by the Supremes on a Christmas LP and tunes for Brenda Holloway and Billy Eckstine, some of which were never released.

Jimmy eventually signed with another publishing company, Madelon Music. While he was working for Madelon, he wrote "By the Time I Get to Phoenix." The tune was showed to Johnny Rivers, who bought Webb's contract from Madelon.

Besides Glen Campbell's successful versions of Jimmy's "By the Time I Get to Phoenix," "Galveston," and "Wichita Lineman," various artists have had hits with his songs like "Up, Up and Away," "MacArthur Park," and "The Worst That Could Happen."

After spending a year working on his own solo album, *Jimmy L. Webb: Words and Music*, Jimmy's songs have developed into less commercial but more mature vehicles.

Some of the better tunes on his album are "Songseller," "P.F. Sloan," and "Jerusalem." The latter contains the warning "you'd better get out of L.A."

Jimmy's noticeable absence from the music world came about because, "I was holding back my songs in case three film projects I was working on came through."

One major obstacle stands in Jimmy's path to becoming a successful performer. He's got to win the respect of his peers.

"The artists who have been successful with my songs have mainly appealed to older audiences," he said. "I'm no longer writing for Top 40 radio. My music has been associated with the older world of entertainment for long enough."

Jimmy's album, on the Reprise label, is good, but not great. None of the songs were performed for an audience before they were recorded. They lack the drive that is so noticeable when Jimmy and his band perform them live.

"The people I want to hear my album aren't hearing it," he said. "They simply aren't taking it out of the jacket."

# Moody Blues

## *January 23, 1971*

In 1965, the Moody Blues, at that time a little-known British group, released "Go Now," a single that became a world-wide hit.

Then, after a few unsuccessful records, the group seemed to disappear. Musical styles changed, and in the autumn of 1967, the Moody Blues recorded an album titled *Days of Future Passed*. The album was a moderately successful attempt to fuse rock and classical music.

Since *Days of Future Passed*, the group has recorded four orchestrated albums, the latest called *A Question of Balance*.

The Moody Blues, a quintet, consists of Justin Hayward, vocals and lead guitar; Graeme Edge, drums; Mike Pinder, mellotron; Ray Thomas, flute; and John Lodge, bass guitar.

According to Ray, the group's longevity stems from its closeness. "There is nobody on a superstar kick at all," Ray says. "If I come up with a song, everybody else will help towards polishing it.

"It's down to individual effort with the 'family' working it out together . . . and it is a "family," a 'family' in which I have been able to choose my own brothers.

"It's gone way past a friendship thing," says Ray. "We know everything there is to know about each other."

The Moody Blues now have their own record company, Threshold Records, distributed by London Records. All their albums since *Days of Future Passed*, have been on the Threshold label and have been produced by Tony Clarke.

"Since we started Threshold," John says, "the amount of scope is limitless. There is a sense of unity but at the same time you feel free and no one ever says, 'You can't do that.'"

One of the most frequently heard criticisms of the Moody Blues is that they can't take an orchestra on tour with them, therefore they can't produce on stage what is heard on their albums.

Fortunately, the group puts on an excellent concert act and the orchestration is rarely missed and probably not necessary.

"The basis of the Moody Blues is that there is a sense of individual expression within the group," John says. "Playing live is part of the Moody's secret, as it gives you an identity as a band. Luckily, we all like playing before live audiences, so there are no hang-ups."

The individual members of the group are starting to branch out into other areas of music. "A lot of things I write don't fit in with the Moody Blues," says Graeme. "Sometimes I get a little too bitter and cynical which doesn't suit the group. Mike gets a little occult and he wouldn't want to do that with the group either, so Mike and I are doing an electronic album together."

# Ry Cooder

## *February 6, 1971*

AFTER SEVERAL YEARS OF RECORDING BOTTLENECK GUITAR AND MANDOLIN for artists like Taj Mahal, Captain Beefheart, and the Rolling Stones, Ry Cooder has recorded his own album.

Ry, whose album is on the Reprise label, was in town last week for a concert with Captain Beefheart (also a Reprise artist).

Born in L.A. on March 15, 1947, Ry began playing guitar when he was three. "I didn't go out of the house much," he says. "I got right into listening to records and playing along with them. My parents bought me a Josh White album when I was eight. That was the first blues I ever heard. I learned all his runs, spent hours with him."

At age ten, Ry's father gave him a six-string Martin Guitar and sent him to take lessons. The lessons didn't last long and a few years later Ry started hanging around the Ash Grove, a Los Angeles folk music club.

"Whenever there was a good guitar player there, I'd sit in the front row and watch," Ry says. "I got pretty good at remembering stuff."

"If someone like Gary Davis was in town, I'd talk to him, go to where he was staying, and give him $5 and get him to play as much as he could while I watched. About a month later, I'd find that I'd start to remember how he did things."

Eventually, Ry learned various country guitar runs from friends, learned banjo, and met John Fahey, who introduced him to bottleneck guitar playing.

"Sometime around 1964 or '65, Taj Mahal showed up in L.A.," says Cooder. "He was real raggedy, so we got together and went to the Teenage Fair in Hollywood and sat in a booth for Martin guitars and just played Delta blues.

"It was hard, and it was good. There were sequined bands with saxophones on either side of us and the Byrds were the big thing, so it was different, blues at the Teenage Fair, it was far out. That attracted attention, and all of a sudden we had a rock group, a blues band, a terrible band."

The band, called the Rising Sons, dissolved before its debut album. In the meantime, Ry met Don Van Vliet, also known as Captain Beefheart. They became friends and Ry worked on Beefheart's first LP, *Safe as Milk*.

That album led to a lot of session work for Ry. "Through the studio work I met Jack Nitzsche, who helped me a lot and got me more work, playing blues," he says. "Specialization was coming in, and bottleneck guitar, mandolin and other things started to make a difference.

"That led to my working on the film score to 'Candy' with Jack. After that, he and I went to England and worked with the Rolling Stones on 'Let It Bleed.'"

Although he spent hours with the Stones in the studio, they never used any of his guitar playing on the album, just his mandolin work on "Love in Vain."

After he returned from England, Ry worked on records by Harpers Bizarre, Sal Valentino, the Everly Brothers, and others. Late in 1969, Ry signed to Reprise Records and his first album, simply titled *Ry Cooder* was released in October 1970.

"I don't write, really," Ry says. "I just take these old tunes and rework them. It's more like arranging. You take some primitive tune and work it up somehow, develop it, make it more accessible to people. I can never play as good as Robert Johnson, I don't think, but I can develop his music."

# Kris Kristofferson

## *April 10, 1971*

THIS YEAR'S COUNTRY MUSIC ASSOCIATION AWARD FOR SONG OF THE YEAR went to a Rhodes Scholar with shoulder length hair . . . not exactly the typical Nashville songwriter.

His name is Kris Kristofferson and the song that won him the award is "Sunday Mornin' Comin' Down." Kris' first album, simply titled "Kristofferson" (on Monument Records) is a collection of songs that seem more like short stories or film scripts.

Kris recently did the film score for Dennis Hopper's *The Last Movie* and Hopper is basing his next film on another Kristofferson song, "Me and Bobby McGee."

Kris' career as a singer and composer has taken some strange twists and turns. "My family moved from Brownsville, Tex., to California when I was in high school," he says. "At the time, country music wasn't as popular out there as it is now. I was buying Hank Williams records and I was really considered a square.

"I started making up songs when I was eleven, but the first one I had published was in '58. I don't even know what happened to it. The guy was some kind of crook."

While Kris was in England studying literature at Oxford, he was "discovered" by a British promoter who tried to turn him into a rock-and-roll star.

"I was trying to do something I wasn't equipped to do," Kris says. "I wasn't a rock-and-roll singer. They renamed me Kris Carson and my friends were calling me the Golden Throated Thrush. I got so embarrassed about the whole darn thing I said to myself, 'I'll never get into the music business again.'"

Kris received his degree from Oxford and his scholarship was extended another year so he could work on a novel.

"I got to feeling guilty about taking their money and I didn't want to become a perpetual student so when I went back to the U.S. for Christmas vacation I split. I bailed out, got married, and went into the Army.

"While I was stationed in Germany, I got into music again. I started writing satirical songs about the Army and playing country music in NCO clubs."

Kris volunteered for Vietnam, but his application was turned down and he was sent to West Point to teach English literature. On weekends and leaves, he went to Nashville to sell his songs. "I got so excited, I wrote ten songs the first week," Kris says.

After his military hitch was up in the summer of 1965, Kris took various jobs, sweeping floors in recording studios, tending bar, and flying helicopters to offshore oil rigs in the Gulf of Mexico. During that time, Kris got divorced and ran into monetary difficulties.

"The oil company wanted to send me to South America or the North Slope of Alaska, so I had to quit or else get out of the music business. It panicked me because I had a monthly child support bill and the remainder of a $10,000 medical bill.

"In the meantime," says Kris, "I got with Combine Music, which started paying me more money than my previous music publisher and Fred Foster wanted to record me on Monument Records. So, I quit flying helicopters.

"Fred said they'd pay me enough to pay my bills. He bailed me out and paid all my bills."

Now, Kris doesn't have to worry about bills. He's the hottest property in country music at the moment. He'll be making his second appearance the week of July 12 at the Cellar Door.

# Emerson, Lake and Palmer

## *April 17, 1971*

NOT WANTING TO BE LABELED A "SUPER-GROUP," EMERSON, LAKE AND Palmer, an aggregation of British musicians culled from three top groups have established their popularity as a new group in a hurry.

The group consists of Keith Emerson (formerly with the Nice), Greg Lake (King Crimson), and Carl Palmer (Atomic Rooster). ELP was formed after King Crimson and the Nice toured the United States last year. Talk about forming a new group started in New York and came to a head in San Francisco two months later.

Keith and Greg finished the tour with their respective groups and then started looking for a drummer. "We didn't realize it would be so hard," says Keith. "We went through all the name drummers and that was a joke and they were a joke."

Finally, they came up with Carl, drummer for Atomic Rooster, a group whose popularity didn't extend to the United States.

The group's instrumentation includes acoustic guitar, bass guitar, piano, organ, and Moog synthesizer. The Moog was built especially for live performances but limits the group to playing large halls.

"The Moog has twelve programs to be preset before you go on with the Moog. "The Moog cost four grand and it kept going out of tune," says Carl. "We worked hard rehearsing for months before we were ready to play for an audience."

The group's single, "Lucky Man," is currently number fifty in the country and their album, *Emerson, Lake and Palmer* is number twenty-five.

Their repertoire includes rock, jazz, and country fused with classical elements. Keith has a classical background and his organ work lifted the Nice out of categorization as a rock group.

Keith's reason for leaving the Nice was "because each member in this band has something new to offer. I am quite satisfied and so is everybody else with the freedom we have in a three-piece band.

"Greg," says Keith, "has a similar sort of background in music to mine. He's very interested in jazz and classical. We are both very broadminded toward music."

The group seems to center around Emerson but isn't an extension of the Nice, he claims. "In the past, the image of the Nice was mainly an instrumental group," says Keith. "The new band will include everything. We've got a good singer who can play acoustic guitar as well and a good drummer. I hope people look upon us as a new group."

Emerson, Lake and Palmer will be appearing at the Alexandria Roller Rink on May 9. Tentatively scheduled as a second act is another British group, Mott the Hoople.

# Elton John

## *May 1, 1971*

REG DWIGHT HAS BEEN PLAYING PIANO SINCE THE AGE OF THREE. NOW, AT age twenty-four, he has three albums in the Top 50.

For those not familiar with the name Reg Dwight, his stage name is Elton John. Elton, as he'd rather be called, studied for five years at England's Royal Academy of Music.

At eighteen, Elton joined a group called Bluesology, a back-up group for one of England's top blues singers, Long John Baldry. Finding no challenge to the work, he soon left.

His real break came after he answered an ad for musical talent in one of Britain's top weeklies. Answering the same ad was Bernie Taupin, a lyricist from a farm in the County of Lincolnshire.

The two met and began working together, but didn't meet the requirements of those who placed the ad. A music publisher, Dick James, saw the potential of the two and advised them not to concentrate on writing hit songs, but instead on music they liked.

Following James' advice led to their first album, *Empty Sky*—yet to be released in this country.

Since then, three albums have been released in this country, *Elton John*, *Tumbleweed Connection*, and the film soundtrack *Friends*—all three currently on the charts.

Bernie generally writes the lyrics first and takes four or five songs to Elton who sets them to music.

"Reg has never failed to come up with a melody to my lyrics," says Bernie. "There are some that we decide later not to use but all come out as finished songs. It's amazing, you know, because Reg always writes a melody that's just perfect."

Elton is backed on stage by Nigel Olsson (formerly with Uriah Heep) on drums and Dee Murray (from the Spencer Davis Group) on bass.

"When he's performing, Elton's music comes off differently than on record. He'll come on stage in purple tights, red jumpsuit, velvet cape, and stovepipe hat and launch into a twenty-minute rock-and-roll medley surrounding one of his LP cuts, "Burn Down the Mission."

Asked about the difference between his recorded and stage presentations, he says, "Well, we're talking about two different things. In the studio you're playing music not performing.

"Why do I come on stage in a cape as opposed to dirty denims and a T-shirt? That's part of the fun. I've always been hunting around for something outrageous to wear.

"I came on stage one night in Mickey Mouse ears and sang 'Your Song' and they couldn't believe it," Elton says. "The thing is never take yourself too seriously. We're always sending each other up and that's the whole thing about it—just be natural and have a laugh."

# J. Geils Band

## *May 8, 1971*

THERE'S ONLY ONE WAY TO DESCRIBE THE J. GEILS BAND: ROCK 'N' ROLL personified.

The sextet came together in Boston where they played for a long time before deciding to record. Their first album, simply titled *The J. Geils Band*, is one of the best rock albums to be released in recent months.

"One of the things we always liked about rock 'n' roll was that it was a very spontaneous means of expression," says Peter Wolf, lead singer for the group.

"In this first album we've just tried to get the roots together, to show where we start from and what we're trying to do.

"When we recorded the album," Peter says, "we started with three weeks of studio time and at the end of the third day we were finished. We did everything live.

"Simplicity is so deceiving because you can listen to a song or watch a dancer and think that's so simple and easy. It's not. But it is pure energy and it is alive."

Besides Peter, the others in the band are J. Geils, lead guitar; Magic Dick, mouth harp; Danny Klein, bass; Steve Blass, drums and vocals; and Seth Justman, keyboards.

Twenty-year-old Justman graduated from Washington D.C.'s Hawthorne School and lived in Greenbelt, Md. While living in this area, he played organ for the Open Road (the remnants of which, with a few additions are now called Sky Cobb and are still playing in the area).

One of the main reasons the J. Geils Band has stayed in the Boston area is the abundance of colleges in the area.

"In Boston there are people graduating all the time from the different schools and then there are new people coming in and they're game for anything," says Wolf. "We supported ourselves in Boston for a long time without an album.

"If I were just starting out in a band now and I was in New York, I think it would terrify me. In Boston it's a whole lot easier, because there are a lot of small clubs so it's easier to get the whole thing together."

The group recently played at American University to a capacity audience. Although their music was exceptionally tight and their stage performance was enjoyable, the group lost a lot of the audience because their volume was ear-splitting.

Wolf feels the musical scene should drift back to singles and away from albums.

"I really like singles," he says. "I think the same thing happened to the supermarket industry. There once was a time when you could go in and buy an orange. But today you have to go in and buy six oranges. And if I like a song or two, I have to buy a whole album to hear that song."

Besides playing small clubs and colleges in the Boston area, the group has performed at the Fillmore East in New York and the Fillmore West in San Francisco.

"We want to make music that isn't pretentious, that we would enjoy playing," Wolf says. "We may not have any really new music to offer folks, but we know they'll have a good time."

J. Geils Thank You Note to Mike Oberman (1971)
OBERMAN FAMILY ARCHIVES

Dear Mike,                                    July 21, 1971

    Although your article on our band
appeared quite a while back, I only found
out about it a couple of weeks ago. The
article was really fantastic. Can't possibly
thank you enough.

    What have you been up to during the
past year or so? It's been quite a while
since I've seen you. Please let me know
what's been happening.

              Thanks again.        BEST—
                                    Seth

J. Geils Band's Seth Justman Thank You to Mike Oberman (1971)
OBERMAN FAMILY ARCHIVES

# Richie Havens

## *May 15, 1971*

"WHEN I SING," SAYS RICHIE HAVENS, "MY MIND IS BUSY LOOKING AT THE pictures the writer created. My body has something to do, which is play the guitar. And my spirit is feeling the song's sensations all over again. I sing from what I see. It goes out and then it comes back to me."

Richie's singing has been going out since 1962, when at the height of the folk music revival he turned to music.

Richie was born Jan. 21, 1941, in Bedford-Stuyvesant, Brooklyn. His father was a pianist who earned his living as an electroplater and his mother worked in a bookbinding factory.

The oldest of nine children, Richie organized a group called the McCrea Gospel Singers when he was fourteen. The group was formed just for fun. "I really thought I'd be a surgeon," he says.

Although he was a better than average student, Richie dropped out of high school shortly before graduation. "I loved school," Richie says. "I mean, here was this one big building with a lot of people in it. But we used to laugh a lot and they'd never let us laugh.

"I liked learning, but I couldn't see any reason why I had to go over something I already knew. You know, we'd go over a lesson a week and then on Friday, the teacher would say, 'It's time for review.' I said, 'Why?' I already knew it.

"So, I quit. It was just time to go, I guess. I've always known when it was time."

Richie left home at seventeen and moved to Greenwich Village, supporting himself by doing portraits of tourists.

In 1962, after hanging around Village clubs, Richie began his musical career. "It was at the Gaslight and Café Wha," he says. "I began hearing people like Len Chandler and Dino Valenti. They inspired me to try singing."

Richie began singing in the Village, living off contributions from a passed basket. His first album, *Mixed Bag*, on the Verve-Folkways label, really launched his career.

Since that time, Richie has released a number of albums and has formed his own record company, Stormy Forest. He has appeared at every important rock and folk club in the country and is a frequent television guest.

Richie's latest single, "Here Comes the Sun," is currently number seventeen in the nation and his most recent LP, *Alarm Clock*, is number forty on the charts.

"I found out," says Richie, "there are just two places to be. Happy and unhappy. Everything I do is looking at that one big question—what are we doing here, why and how?

"That's part of what I have to say in my music. I want everybody to discover it because this is the time for finding out."

Richie Havens Preparing to Play at WHMC in Gaithersburg, Maryland
PHOTO BY MIKE KLAVANS

# Mick Jagger

## *May 29, 1971*

WITH THE FORMATION OF THEIR OWN RECORD COMPANY; A NUMBER ONE album, *Sticky Fingers*; a number one single, "Brown Sugar"; a move en masse to France; and the marriage of Mick Jagger, the Rolling Stones are back to their headline-making days.

The Stones company, Rolling Stones Records, distributed in the United States by Atco, marks the second successful record company to be formed by a British group (the first of course was Apple formed by the Beatles). All of the Stones' previous records were on the London label.

Twenty-eight-year-old Jagger married Bianca Perez Morena de Macias, the twenty-six-year-old daughter of a Nicaraguan diplomat in a civil ceremony on Saints Tropez on May 12.

Jagger was interviewed by American disc jockey Tom Donahue in April. The interview was recorded and sent to radio stations and writers all over the country. The following are excerpts from that interview.

Questioned about concerts and the general state of rock music, Jagger said, "The whole thing about concerts is that the music has a certain set nature. In a club where there's no room to move I would just sing. Not all that sort of dancing around. You could just get on with the music." About American audiences, Jagger said, "I don't know, I think American audiences get very involved. You only have to listen to that Madison Square Garden concert.

"Dancing is the participation of rock 'n' roll. Dancing to the music. Sitting down to the music is a real drag. I like to see people dance."

One major complaint about the Stones has been that their ticket prices for concerts ($10 and up) have been too high. "If you're going to do one night, the transportation for two groups plus the Rolling Stones plus the lighting plus any sound facilities, well, the last English tour and the European tour we didn't make any money at all," Jagger said. "We lost money on the European tour."

The Stones definitely don't want the record company to go the same route as Apple records. I always sort of looked at Apple and got the feeling that it was a new company with new ideas running through the old structure and it was going to be an important record label," Jagger said.

"They ran ads every week saying 'You Can Be a Millionaire Like Paul McCartney' if you come to Apple with your songs. This company isn't like that. We're not going to try to make some big corporate image and try to build a skyscraper on the corner of Savile Row.

"It would be nice," Jagger said, "if we could have another act on the label. We've got these very nice people working and we don't give them enough product to keep them busy. if anyone comes along with a great sort of thing, it would be great if we could have it and we'd make sure that they get paid, that's all."

When it was made known that the Stones contract with London was running out and they weren't interested in re-signing, every major label started negotiating for the distribution rights to their product.

"Everyone had their own line about their own particular company," said Jagger. "I suppose they were true, some of them, but they were so funny.

"After about the first four, I started cracking up, laughing. Some people would say, 'ours is the best company because we have all the racks,' and the next one would say 'ours is the best because all our profits are going to go to the revolution.' There is nobody doing anything really different."

The Stones finally chose Atlantic because, Jagger said, "I thought Atlantic was the most sympathetic musically, quite honestly. They didn't offer us the most money, but I thought they do the best job. The thing with Atlantic is that the people at the top are still producing music and can talk about it.

"Like the Beatles, the Stones plan to do some recording on an individual basis. I think Mick Taylor wants to make an album on his own," Jagger said. "There are a few things I'd like to do . . . certain kinds of folk music I personally like.

"With the exception of three songs, all of the music on *Sticky Fingers* was recorded in England. We did three tracks in Muscle Shoals, Alabama a long time ago, 'Brown Sugar,' 'Wild Horses,' and 'You Got to Move.' We just save them."

Although some of the songs on the new LP deal with drugs, Jagger doesn't think it will hurt the amount of air play the album will get.

"None of our songs encourage drug use," he said. "I don't particularly want to encourage drug use. You can write about it, but you don't have to encourage it."

# Ian Matthews

## *June 5, 1971*

After a successful career with two groups, Fairport Convention and Matthews' Southern Comfort, Ian Matthews is going it alone.

His first solo album, "If You Saw thro' My Eyes," has just been released on the Vertigo label (distributed in this country by Mercury Records). Of the twelve cuts on the LP, nine were written by Matthews.

Matthews' vocals are as accomplished as his lyrics. Although electric instruments are used, the basic sound of the album is acoustic and very listenable.

Ian, in town last week to promote his album, talked about how his career as a professional singer started. "I started with a band in London in 1966 called Pyramid," he said.

"If you can believe it, we did Curtis Mayfield songs with a surfing feel. I stayed with them for a year."

Ian became involved with Fairport Convention through Tony Hall, label manager for Deram Records. "Tony knew some of the people in Fairport," Ian said. "They were looking for a singer.

"I was supposed to do a month's probation period with them. It went on for two years."

Ian left Fairport because of musical differences. "They wanted to do different things," he said. "Sandy (Denny) had joined the band. Our vocals were different. She had a lot to offer. Sandy's direction was the obvious choice."

After leaving Fairport, Ian didn't do much for the next ten months. He was looking for management and when he found it, he started work on an album. The title of the album probably would have been *Ian Matthews*, but he liked an Ian and Sylvia album titled *Southern Comfort*," so he changed the title to *Matthews' Southern Comfort*.

"The band of the same name came about as a natural extension of the album," Ian said.

Ian's group had a hit with their version of Joni Mitchell's "Woodstock."

"I picked up 'Woodstock' as a stage number," Ian said. "But it got such a good response after I did it on a radio show, that we released it as a single.

"For three months it didn't do anything. Then a friend of mine got Tony Blackburn (an influential British disc jockey) to play it. With the kind of influence he's got, it took off."

On Ian's new solo album, he's backed by a number of fine musicians, including Sandy Denny. The title cut, "If You Saw thro' My Eyes," contains the lines

I take the blame for where I've been.

On all the ones I've had to lean.

When asked about that song, Ian said, "The whole song is posing a musical question. I find it hard to explain my songs. I take the blame for where I've been.

"I've never been happy with anything I've done. It's no one else's fault. But, I really am satisfied with this album. I find I like listening to it.

"Each time I hear it," he said, "I feel more satisfied with it. Maybe it's because it's just me. I'm not relying on anyone else."

Ian has already started work on his next album. "I like it even better than this one," he said. "It's a little more funky. More electric guitars."

Ian will be touring this country starting Aug. 1 in Columbus, Ohio. The tour will take him to clubs like the Troubadour in L.A. and the Bitter End in N.Y.

If his album is any indication of what his live performance is like, let's hope he'll also be doing a week at the Cellar Door.

# Musings . . . Reconnecting With
# Iain Matthews in 2019

As I began writing this book, I thought I would try to get in touch with some of the artists I had interviewed in the 1960s and 1970s. Facebook seemed like a good starting point. Just type in a name and hopefully find the person you're looking for. When I interviewed Ian (now Iain) Matthews in 1971, I felt that we became more than an interviewer and subject. I had always liked Iain's work when he was in Fairport Convention and later as the driving force in Matthew's Southern Comfort.

Iain had heard some of the songs recorded by a group I was managing in 1971, Claude Jones. He particularly liked "Lesson to Learn." Coincidentally, years later, "Lesson to Learn" (written by Joe Triplett and Peter Blachly of Claude Jones) was recorded by Rod Stewart. The song was released as the flip side to "Love Touch" from the movie *Legal Eagles*.

I located Iain on Facebook and messaged him. He responded that he remembered me but confused me with my brother, as he knew both of us. I explained that he and I had met when I interviewed him and that he knew my brother when my brother worked at Columbia Records.

Coincidentally, Iain said that he was playing a "house party" in Hillsboro, Virginia, on the following Friday. He said that it seemed Hillsboro was only an hour away from my home, and he invited me to be his guest.

I was free that evening in April 2019 and drove to Hillsboro (it was more like a two-hour drive). The house party was in the beautiful old home owned by a woman named Cynthia Elliot and her husband. Iain hadn't arrived yet, but I was graciously invited into Cynthia's home. I explained that I was a friend of Iain's and that he had put me on the guest list. "My name is Michael Oberman," I said to Cynthia. She responded, "I know you. I follow your photography on Facebook. We're friends on Facebook." Small world.

When Iain arrived, we caught up. Over the years, our musical paths had crossed. We knew many of the same people. Iain's performance that night was perfect. An intimate setting, great acoustics, Iain in fine voice, and a friendly group of forty to fifty people enjoying the song-filled evening. I also learned from Iain that he had written a memoir that was published (I believe in 2018) titled *Thro' My Eyes: A Memoir*. Now, Iain is in my memoir.

Iain Matthews at House Party Concert in Hillsboro, VA, 2019
PHOTO BY MICHAEL OBERMAN

# Alex Taylor and Kate Taylor

## *July 10, 1971*

UNLIKE THEIR BROTHERS, JAMES AND LIVINGSTON, WHO RELY ON A SOFT, folk style, Alex Taylor and Kate Taylor have different roots.

"I got my musical background listening to John Lee Hooker and Mississippi John Hurt from when I was eleven-years-old," Alex says. "I also listened to Ray Charles and that was rock 'n' roll."

Kate also tends to lean towards rock. "I wanted to do 'Mohair Sam' and a rock version of 'I'm a Woman' and 'I'm a Hog for You Baby.'" Although she didn't record any of those songs, Kate's first album does include rockers like "Handbags and Gladrags," "Ballad of a Well-Known Gun," and "Look at Granny Run, Run."

Kate, not blessed with the writing talent of her brothers, has to rely on other people's songs.

"Other people say it for me," she says. "If people write songs that I like to do, then I don't see why I shouldn't do them. I think it's valid to write your own songs but if you find people who express what you feel then it's the same thing."

Alex has been writing songs for a while, but none of them appeared on his first album. "I was almost at a loss for the first album because I was green," he says. "No experience at all. I'm very proud of the new LP that we're starting now. I'm going to be writing more songs for it and it's a much more 'up' album. This one's really going to be rock 'n' roll."

Now that Alex has achieved some of his goals as a singer, he spends some of his spare time in the South and the rest at Martha's Vineyard.

"Macon and Martha's Vineyard are both sunny and quiet," he says." I really tend to like to be around that kind of place. I lived in Atlanta for a year and before that in Wilmington North Carolina. I like places where I can just lie out in back. Of course, on Martha's Vineyard, James and Kate are both around, and occasionally Livingston and my brother Hugh. It's nice to be together.

"I've always wanted to sing," says Alex. "I do that better than anything else. Now I want to get rich so I can buy me some land and build a house where Sweet Baby James, my son, can play ball and fish and stuff. That's what I call living.

Kate is managed by Peter Asher (remember Peter and Gordon?) and Jack Oliver. I listen to them and let them plan it (her career) out," she says. "But I don't think about it too much.

"They want me to be secure and stuff before I do bigger concerts, because first of all on a business level, there's all those reviewers who could put me uptight and write things that could hurt my feelings.

"But I'm as ready as ever," she says. "I can only do what I can do on stage and whatever it is you know it's mainly honest. They want me to grow a little bit, you know. I have a tendency to ramble and stuff on stage. I do a lot of dancing too."

All the singing Taylor's have performed at the Cellar Door and should be appearing again in Washington. Kate's performance was cut short because of a strep throat, but chances are she'll be back at the Georgetown nitery before too long.

# The Band

## *July 24, 1971*

On Aug. 22, 1970, the following review appeared in *Cashbox* maga-zine (a weekly musical trade paper):

"Stage Fright," the Band, Capitol SW-425: "In haughty and homespun majesty the third Band album now floats within range of hands and ears. Close your eyes and you're back 100 years in clear Colorado with a bunch of dusty cowboys sitting around the campfire after a day of cowpunching. Try "All La Glory" and see if it doesn't happen. Or the jolly "Just Another Whistle Stop" with its changing rhythms. Or the Dylan-tinged "Strawberry Wine." The mind fairly boggles at the musicianship and composing abilities of the group. This is an album of incredible beauty and warmth."

That was a year ago and the Band's long awaited third album still hasn't been released. At a recent concert at Merriweather Post Pavilion, the Band didn't include any new material, much to the dismay of the audience (although it didn't detract from the concert).

The Band's first two albums were *Music from Big Pink*," which included "The Weight," and *The Band*. Both combined their original country sound with good old rock 'n' roll.

Canada is the birthplace of four members of the group: Robbie Rob-ertson, Rick Danko, Garth Hudson, and Richard Manuel. The fifth, Levon Helm, is from Arkansas.

The Band, together over ten years, toured the Canadian north as Ron-nie Hawkins' back-up group, the Hawks, before coming across the border to the U.S.

"We started out doing a fantastic amount of traveling in Canada and the South," says Robertson. "We played six or seven nights a week for maybe five or six years. Really, we never stopped."

All the arduous roadwork they did in this country had its benefits. "It was better driving all those roads and playing all those joints than just walking from a hotel on 42nd St. in New York to a gig on 48th St. every night," Robertson says.

"It was good for our lyrics, seeing things on the roadsides, seeing town names, signs, names of people, trees with funny names. And people really come to hear you play . . . not just little kids, but everybody. They're brought up on good blues."

In 1965, Bob Dylan asked the Band to back him and their grueling schedule slowed down. "Meeting Bob meant we didn't have to play those joints anymore to stay alive," Robertson says.

When the group's association with Dylan ended, they decided to strike out on their own. The Band's music deals with America. Not politically, but rather with the land and its people.

Like "Old Jawbone" who says, "I'm a thief and I dig it," the grandpappy in "When You Awake," the weather-worn sailor in "Rockin' Chair," and "The Unfaithful Servant" who's fired for messing around with the lady of the house.

The pictures the Band paints are vivid, like the opening lines to "Across the Great Divide": "Standing by your window in pain, pistol in hand. I beg you Molly, girl, understand your man, the best you can."

One can only hope that the Band or their record company, Capitol, or whoever is responsible for the delay in the release of their new album, sees fit to release it as soon as humanly possible.

# The Holy Modal Rounders

## *August 14, 1971*

GOOD TASTE IS TIMELESS, THE TITLE OF THE NEWEST ALBUM BY THE HOLY Modal Rounders, definitely applies to their music.

Some of their music isn't suitable for AM airplay (the lyrics to a couple of their songs might be objectionable to some people), but their songs combine taste with humor and a flair for unusual instrumentation.

The musicians and instruments are: Richard Tyler, piano and organ; John Wesley Annas, bass, kazoo, jug, growls, and vocals; Michael McCarthy, drums, sandpaper, tambourine, cow bell, party sounds, and background vocals; Steve Weber, guitar oscillator, pig squeals, and background vocals; Peter Stampfel, violin, banjo, caterwauling, and vocals; and Robin Remally, mandolin, violin, rhythm guitar, clarinet, acoustic guitar, animal sounds, and vocals.

Stampfel, thirty-two, is the co-founder of the Rounders. He doesn't say much about his childhood, except that he "wrote funny articles for the high school newspaper and got kicked off the staff for holding a copy of *Mad* comics up in the junior class picture."

Before he and Steve Weber went to New York and joined a rock group (whose members have included Tuli Kupferberg and Ed Sanders but whose name isn't proper to mention in a daily paper), Peter "got kicked out of college for low grades and wearing my ROTC uniform inside out with saddle shoes."

Richard was born in Baltimore and studied at the Peabody Conservatory until he "discovered folk music."

He went to college "for lack of anything better to do" and was also a disc jockey on WJTV-FM. "I ran a good show," he says, "but one night I got into playing the . . . (the group that wasn't mentioned earlier), and they didn't even wait for the show to end to fire me."

With the escapade behind him, he left for New York, where he met Stampfel and joined the Rounders.

Robin started playing the oboe when he was "seven or nine" and played it until he was "thirteen or fourteen." Eventually he met Weber and another musician, Mike Hurley.

McCarthy was born in Oklahoma, where his musical career consisted of playing in local bars every night. It was in Oklahoma that he met John Annas, who already was in the Rounders.

*Good Taste Is Timeless* is their first album for Metromedia Records. The group previously was with Elektra.

# The Beach Boys

## *August 28, 1971*

IT ALL STARTED IN 1961, WHEN THE WILSON BROTHERS, BRIAN, NINETEEN, Dennis, seventeen, and Carl, fifteen, got together with their cousin Mike Love, twenty, and an old friend Al Jardine, nineteen, and decided to form a band that would play music dealing with the favorite Southern California sport of surfing.

A short time after the band (the Beach Boys, of course) started practicing, Brian and Mike wrote a song called "Surfin'." It was recorded and released on the Candix label and became a local hit.

With the Wilsons' father, Murry, acting as their agent, the Beach Boys signed a contract with Capitol Records and the rest is history.

Between 1963 and 1965, they recorded hits like "I Get Around," "Surfer Girl," "Little Deuce Coupe," "Surfin' U.S.A.," "California Girls," and "Help Me Rhonda."

In 1965, Brian decided to stop performing and concentrate on writing and producing. He was temporarily replaced by a studio musician named Glen Campbell. Campbell stayed with them until April, 1965, when he was replaced by Bruce Johnston, who became a permanent Beach Boy.

At a cost of $16,000, the Beach Boys produced their first million-selling single in 1966. The song, "Good Vibrations," has become a rock classic.

That same year, strange things began to happen to the Beach Boys. They wrote a four-part suite called "The Elements," one part of which was titled "Fire Music."

Jules Siegel, a writer for the *Saturday Evening Post*, describing "Fire Music" in a story he was writing on Brian, said, "A gigantic fire howled out of the massive studio speakers in a pounding crush of pictorial music that summoned up visions of roaring, wind-storm flames, falling timbers, mournful sirens and sweaty firemen, building up to a peak and crackling off into fading embers as a single drum turned into a collapsing wall and the fire engine cellos dissolved and disappeared."

Unfortunately, that description is all that is left of "Fire Music." A few days later, the building across the street from the studio burned to the ground. Brian decided to check out fire statistics for the city and found that there had been an abnormally high incidence of fires that past week. Brian deliberately destroyed every tape of "Fire Music."

In 1970, after releasing a number of albums on their own label, Brother Records, the Beach Boys signed a distribution deal with Reprise and released another LP, *Sunflower*.

Which brings us to the present. A new album, titled *Surf's Up*, has been released and should gain the group a number of new listeners.

The album utilizes the Moog Synthesizer on every cut and is one of the best LP's they have released to date. After ten years of ups and downs, it looks like surf's up for the Beach Boys again.

# Fanny

## *September 4, 1971*

Could they be a front for women's lib? Do they really know how to play their instruments?

Those questions were posed when word first got out that Reprise Records had signed an all-female rock group called Fanny.

Their first album, simply titled *Fanny*, was disappointing and left doubts as to whether Reprise had made a wise decision. Then, several months later, their second LP, *Charity Ball*, was released and changed a lot of minds.

The album is mostly original material, with a good deal of hard rock and tight harmonies. The only non-original piece is Stephen Stills' "Special Care."

Last Monday, Fanny performed for radio and newspaper personnel at the Cellar Door, and all four girls showed amazing stamina and instrumental and vocal prowess.

The girls, all of whom sing, are Nickey Barclay, piano and organ; Jean Millington, bass; June Millington, guitar; and Alice de Buhr, drums. Nickey is from D.C., sisters Jean and June from Manila, and Alice from Iowa.

When asked how they got the name Fanny, Alice said, "We wanted to have a name that would be a person's name, like one single entity. That's the one that stuck out."

Jean and June got their start in music in high school by hanging around guys who played in bands and taking their places during breaks.

"We lived right outside San Francisco," June said, "and we got swept up in that scene. Alice started playing drums in grade school and had an all-girl group in Iowa.

Nickey decided to take piano lessons when she was a young girl. "I lasted for three weeks," she said. "I gave it up for eight years. I've been singing ever since I could talk. I used to play clubs and a lot of bars on 14th Street under assumed names."

Their recording contract came about when June, Jean, Alice, and a guitarist who is no longer with the group went to Los Angeles two years ago.

"We went there specifically to try and get a record contract," June said. "Richard Perry, our producer (also Barbra Streisand's producer), heard and auditioned us."

He got us signed to Reprise and we moved to L.A. Then we decided it would be better to find a keyboard player, and we let the other guitarist go. It took us nine months to find Nickey and another six months for us all to click."

Fanny's future plans include playing The Bitter End in New York and the Stonehenge in Boston and doing a tour of England in October and November. They also plan to record the third album while in England.

# Gene Clark

## *September 18, 1971*

GENE CLARK STARTED OUT ON HIS OWN ON THE SMALL CLUB FOLK CIRcuit; graduated to membership in the New Christy Minstrels, the Byrds and the Dillard and Clark Expedition, and now, after seven years, is back on his own with a solo album on A & M Records, *White Light*.

Gene was born and raised in Missouri, where he developed his interest in music by playing in various high school rock bands.

"We had surf bands," Gene said, "which is pretty funny when you notice that Missouri is about as far from the ocean as you can get in the U.S. The only surfing is maybe wake surfing on the big rivers."

After school, Gene started playing the folk circuit in Kansas and Missouri. It was there that he was seen by members of the New Christy Minstrels, who asked him to play twelve-string guitar and sing for them.

Gene played with the Minstrels on two of their albums and their hit single, "Green, Green," before leaving the group in L.A. He was tired of commercial folk music and wanted something more challenging.

It was at Hollywood's Troubadour that he met Jim McGuinn and David Crosby and formed the nucleus for the Byrds.

After a year-and-a-half with the Byrds, Gene split with the group. "I don't like to fly in airplanes," he said. "To be a Byrd you had to be able to fly all the time, and the pressure got to me. It had nothing to do with musical hassles."

Gene tried unsuccessfully to rejoin the Byrds on two separate occasions, but found that he would have to sacrifice his artistic freedom.

In 1966, Gene recorded a little-known album for Columbia, *Gene Clark with the Gosdin Brothers*. Accompanying Gene on the album were the Byrds,

Leon Russell, Glen Campbell, Larry Marks, and Gary Usher. It was the first step back toward country music for Gene.

The next step was the formation, with his friend Doug Dillard, of the Dillard and Clark Expedition. The country-bluegrass-oriented band recorded two albums for A & M before trouble began to set in. Although the albums were good, they failed to sell. What with personnel changes and worrying about directions, the band broke up.

Moving to the woods north of San Francisco, Gene decided to settle back and write songs for a year and then do a solo album. The result of his year alone is titled *White Light*. It contains mostly original songs with the exception of his version of "Tears of Rage."

The album, produced by Jesse Edwin Davis (who also does some fine guitar work on it), is low-keyed and poetic. His songs are easy to listen to and show the maturity his music has developed over the last seven years.

# Van Morrison

## *October 23, 1971*

SINCE HIS CHILDHOOD IN BELFAST, IRELAND, VAN MORRISON HAS BEEN A fan of American rhythm-and-blues and blues.

Although when speaking he has a heavy Irish accent, Van's singing voice sounds American—probably because he practiced imitating Ray Charles, Bobby Bland, John Lee Hooker, and Muddy Waters.

When he was sixteen, Van formed his first group, the Monarchs. "In those days you had to be crazy to be a musician," Van said. "Anybody who thought about being a musician was thought to be a maniac, a nut or something.

"It was hard work. We did seven sets a night, seven days a week, with matinees on weekends—and if you didn't do twenty encores of 'What I Say,' you were lucky to get out of there alive.

"One time," he said, "we went for a job to this place in London. We had been sleeping in the park 'cause we didn't get much money in those days, and after two weeks of sleeping in the park, we finally got an audition at this place.

"So, when we showed up, everybody in the band was wearing something different. One had long hair, one had a brown sweater, one had sneakers.

"We played about six numbers and the cat said, 'You're really fantastic, one of the best things I've ever heard, but you're a scruffy pack and if you get some suits, you can get the job.' So we got some suits and played there. There was nothing else we could do."

In 1964, Van became lead singer for an English group, "Them." An American producer, Bert Berns, heard some of their tapes and went to England to produce the group.

Them had hit singles with "Here Comes the Night," "Mystic Eyes," and "Gloria" (penned by Morrison). Them's records were especially well received in America. In 1966, the group toured this country and shortly after broke up.

Van went back to England to write poetry and get into other kinds of music besides rhythm-and-blues. In 1967, Bert Berns formed his own record company, Bang Records, and asked Van to record for him. Van accepted and moved to America.

His first single for Bang, "Brown Eyed Girl," was a hit. In 1968, Berns died and Van signed with Warner Brothers. His first LP was *Astral Weeks*.

The eight songs on the album "are thematically related through the same characters and places," Van said. With the release of *Astral Weeks*, he picked up what was almost a cult following. The lyrics from the record have been studied and debated.

"One time a guy came up to me and said that *Astral Weeks* had kept his family together," Van said. "Most of the things have seven meanings anyway, so I'm not surprised that people are always finding new things in it."

In 1969, Van released *Moondance*, his first LP to be accepted by a mass audience. One of the songs on the album, "Come Running," was a Top 40 hit. Soon after, Van moved to Woodstock, where he became friends with some of that town's best musicians including the Band. Van co-authored one of the songs on the Band's latest album (*Cahoots*) and sings on the cut.

Van's third album, *His Band and Street Choir*, released in 1970, also contained a Top 40 hit, "Domino." His fourth effort for Warner Brothers, *Tupelo Honey*, was released this week.

Van no longer thinks he can work with just one group of musicians as he did with Them. "For me the concept of a group doesn't work because you're limited to those four or five guys," he said. "Somebody's gonna say something you don't like. With Them, I'd see a lot of stuff they wouldn't pick up on. They'd want to go and hang out in a club or something.

"I was conscientious. I can't rely on four or five guys to make decisions for me."

# Musings . . . Van Morrison, Kurt Vonnegut, and Roman Polanski

In 1974, I was working for WEA (Warner/Elektra/Atlantic) in their branch office in Maryland. I had left the *Washington Star* in 1973 to take the WEA job. While we were not in New York or Los Angeles, we were often invited by the individual labels to attend conferences or events around the country and beyond: Paris for a week for Atlantic Records' twenty-fifth anniversary, a dude ranch in Arizona for an Elektra Records conference, and a Carnegie Hall concert headlined by Van Morrison.

I had attended hundreds of great concerts as a writer and was really looking forward to the party that was being thrown for Van after the concert. The party was being held at the home of a legendary music executive, Mary Martin. Mary encouraged Bob Dylan to work with the Band, signed Leonard Cohen to his first management deal, signed Emmylou Harris to her first record deal at Warner Bros., negotiated and secured Vince Gill's first solo recording contract, and managed Van Morrison and Rodney Crowell.

I had taken an early morning train from D.C. to New York. By the time the party began, I had been awake for more than twenty hours. Mary's house in Chelsea was packed with music business types, celebrities, and others. After a couple of drinks, I wandered upstairs and found a vacant bedroom. Hoping to just chill out for a bit, I went into the bedroom, closed the door, and sat down on the bed. I ended up nodding off and was awakened to the door opening and two men walking toward the bed. I soon realized the two men were Kurt Vonnegut and Roman Polanski. I had read every Vonnegut book and was a big fan of Polanski's films. I was speechless. They both looked at me, acknowledged my presence with polite nods of their heads, and proceeded to sit on the bed with me. Polanski reached for the remote control for the television and turned on the last few minutes of the *Tonight*

*Show.* Johnny Carson was interviewing Polish author (and friend of Polanski and Vonnegut) Jerzy Kosinski.

When the show was over, the three of us walked back downstairs. Van Morrison had been at the party while we were watching television. He had already left. That was okay, as my magical moment that day was being in bed with Vonnegut and Polanski (and I wasn't dreaming).

# John Stewart

## *October 30, 1971*

JOHN STEWART, JOHN DENVER, PAUL STOOKEY, AND MARY TRAVERS ALL have one thing in common—they left highly successful folk groups to embark on solo careers.

Denver ("Country Roads"), formerly with the Mitchell Trio, and Paul and Mary (formerly of Peter, Paul and Mary) have made chart albums since leaving their respective groups. Now, Stewart has released his first solo effort, a Warner Brothers LP titled *The Lonesome Picker Rides Again.*

Describing, with a touch of humor, his start in music, Stewart said, "I bought a ukulele when I was in Pasadena. I would listen to Sons of the Pioneers records. Tex Ritter really turned me on to music. 'I Love My Rooster' was top ten as far as I was concerned. I'd sing those songs and play them on my uke.

"Then," John said, "I left music in search of my own identity as a fat little kid. I went out for football, which was good because I was short and fat. I worked at it all summer, lost twenty pounds, grew six inches, and lost all my coordination, which I never regained. Coaches drew me aside and said I'd never make it as a football player."

After a brief fling at comedy with a friend ("We were the Handkerchief Brothers—we won the Sears amateur contest"), John formed a rock band.

"I found some guys who played guitar; we went into a garage, they turned up (their amps) to ten, and I never heard my voice for the first month," he said.

"We made a record for Vita Records in Pasadena, a song called 'Rocking Anna,' written by the lady who paid for the session. I wrote the B side. We were John Stewart and the Furies.

The record didn't do too well, so John decided to switch to folk music. "I was getting to really like folk music and Burl Ives," he said. "Then I heard the Kingston Trio and freaked. I got a folk group together.

"I was always the leader, very obnoxious. There were three, naturally, mostly because $30 was the going rate, $10 apiece. We played at a lodge called Seven Oaks. I would wash dishes and then the owner would signal me and I would take my apron off and put on my cowboy shirt and do the show. But I was the star, because I played six-string guitar and the others played four-strings."

Eventually John broke loose from the local scene and got the Kingston Trio to record some of his songs, including "Molly Dee." The Trio's manager, Frank Werber, told him that Roulette Records wanted a folk group, so John formed one with his old choir teacher from Pomona and a fellow named John Montgomery.

When Dave Guard left the Kingston Trio, John received a call from them. "My group was going nowhere, and I saw myself easily fitting into the No. 1 group in the world. I was fearless. I could sing and tell jokes and play banjo and guitar.

"I flew out at my own expense, auditioned in Bob Shane's basement, got the job, and immediately lost any identity I might have conjured."

So, he made up his mind he was going to leave.

"I wanted to be back in the Village or just playing clubs," John said. "It took three years to finally sink in. I left the Trio in 1967 after seven years."

After leaving the Trio, he teamed up with Buffy Ford and recorded an LP, *Signals through the Glass.*

"It was one of the great disasters on Capitol Records," Steward said. "We played the Troubadour, using color slides while we were singing. It was just impossible singing with a girl."

John decided to go off on his own. "I went to Nashville and recorded 'California Bloodlines' with Nick Venet," he said. "It was the most fun I ever had recording."

One more album for Capitol and John switched labels. Now he hopes Warner Brothers will be his home for the rest of his recording career.

# John Hartford

## *November 6, 1971*

"It's hard to believe he's the same person who used to be on the Smothers Brothers Show" was one comment heard the last time John Hartford appeared at the Cellar Door.

John "Gentle on My Mind" Hartford now sports a full beard and shoulder-length hair, but his country music roots haven't changed much. "I'm a long-hair and fairly liberal," he said, "but I was just thinking the other day that my music is a combination. Like bluegrass and rock, so maybe it's grass-rock or something."

Born in New York, John was raised in St. Louis. At age eight he was given his first musical instrument . . . an old Washburn mandolin.

Although he took lessons, John couldn't get the hang of the mandolin. So, when he was ten, his mother gave him a beat-up banjo (without a head) and John learned to play that. He also took up fiddle, dobro, and guitar.

Despite evident musical talent, John took an assortment of jobs, commercial artist, riverboat deckhand on the Mississippi, railroader, and disc jockey in Nashville.

His job in Nashville took him into the recording studios there, and he soon began playing banjo on other artists' sessions. Soon he cut his first of eight albums for RCA.

Tom Smothers heard one of his albums and asked John to come to Hollywood to write songs and dialogue and perform for the *Smothers Brothers Comedy Hour*, which evolved into the *Summer Brothers Smothers Show*.

John's first hit song was "Gentle on My Mind," recorded by Glen Campbell. More than 200 people have recorded "Gentle," and more than

15 million copies have been sold world-wide. The song won three Grammy awards and for two years in a row was the most recorded song in the world.

One of the biggest influences on his banjo-picking style was Earl Scruggs. And, just as a certain amount of humor can be heard in Scruggs' playing, John's songs are laced with wit.

His new album (his first for Warner Brothers) is called *Aero-Plain*, and contains songs such as "Presbyterian Guitar," "Symphony Hall Rag," and "With a Vamp in the Middle."

John's band is a masterful one. It includes Norman Blake, a guitarist who has recorded with Johnny Cash, Bob Dylan, Joan Baez, and Kris Kristofferson; Vassar Clements, a violinist as good as anyone in the business; and Tut Taylor on dobro and mandolin.

A bit of Nashville will be brought to town again when John opens a week's stay at the Cellar Door on Nov. 15.

# T. Rex

*November 13, 1971*

When Tyrannosaurus Rex was formed in 1967, there was a lot of talk about it in the British music press, but until recently the group was unheard of in this country.

T. Rex, as the members call themselves now, started out with Marc Bolan handling all the writing chores, playing guitar, and singing. Steve Peregin Took did additional vocals and percussion.

The group had a small but fanatical following in England. Then, in September 1969, Took left and was replaced by Mickey Finn, the other half of the present group.

When Mickey joined Marc, T. Rex shed its acoustic trappings and became more electric. The new group's first album, *Bead of Stars*, did quite well in England.

In October 1970, T. Rex had its first commercial hit, "Ride a White Swan," successful in both England and the United States. It was then that Marc and Mickey decided to sign with an American record company (Reprise), and more people were turned on to the group.

Marc has been into rock since an early age. "The first record that I had," he said, "was 'Ballad of Davy Crockett' by Bill Hayes. Remember that?

"I played that all the time until my dad came home one day and said, 'I've got this new Bill Hayes record for you' and I thought, 'Great.' I looked at the cover and there was this guy jumping around with a guitar.

"I said, 'But dad, this isn't Bill Hayes, this is Bill Haley.' It was a real downer. But I played it . . . 'Rock around the Clock' and 'See You Later Alligator' . . . and I thought, 'Wow! What's this?' Bill Hayes got thrown out of the window."

From 1965 to '67, Marc was a solo artist and sang with a group called John's Children. Then came T. Rex.

Before getting into music, Mickey was a painter. He painted two boutiques in England, the Beatles' Apple Shop and Granny Takes a Trip.

Mickey was also part of Hapshah and the Coloured Coat, "a floating band that made two albums and even played a gig, a bizarre affair in Amsterdam."

The group's current LP, simply called *T. Rex*, contains 11 original songs with titles like "Mambo Sun," "Bang a Gong (Get It On)," "Planet Queen," and "Rip Off." The album also boasts back-up vocals by Howard Kaylan and Mark Volman (former Turtles and current Mothers).

A recent single of theirs, "Hot Love," stayed at the top of the British charts for six weeks. That was a far cry from the days when they had a cult-like following and the mainstream rock audience had no idea who they were.

# Stardom Isn't Cheap Anymore

## *November 28, 1971*

"JUST BUY YOURSELF A GIT-TAR SON. I'M GONNA MAKE YOU A STAR."

Those days (with a few exceptions) are over. Becoming a rock-and-roll star (or any kind of star for that matter) is difficult. The competition is keen.

The rewards for success can make the going a little easier, but there are also obstacles like lawsuits, equipment problems, and drug abuse to contend with.

Top groups command $10,000 and up a night for personal appearances. Record royalties and publishing royalties (if a group writes its own material) can set an artist up for life.

In order to understand what makes a successful rock group click, certain areas must be looked into:

MUSICIANS: No matter what the instrumentation, the musicians must be compatible. One of the major reasons for groups breaking up is the individual egos of the members. Ego problems must be resolved early and the group must take on a collective ego. The musicians must be prepared to travel and not mind tight schedules. When not traveling or recording, the group must have a place to rehearse—preferably one where friends can't just drop in.

EQUIPMENT: A successful touring group must be prepared to invest thousands and sometimes even tens of thousands of dollars to enable them to reproduce their recorded sounds at live concerts. Sometimes musical equipment manufacturers will outfit a group free of charge just so the public sees their equipment being used and the group endorses the equipment. The speakers, amplifiers, microphones, mixers, and monitors used must be able to accommodate rooms with seating capacities from 200 to 20,000. Most groups that play large civic arenas and outdoor concerts rely on the concert promoter to hire a P.A. company for the event.

ROADIES: Hauling a group's equipment is not an easy job. It takes a lot of muscle and responsibility to set up a group in time for a concert. The equipment men get to the auditorium well ahead of the group (which is difficult when you're playing in L.A. one night and Chicago the next). Equipment men often have to double as electricians—at any time, emergency soldering or rewiring might need to be done.

ROAD MANAGER: When traveling, it's the duty of the road manager to make sure plane and hotel reservations are made, equipment is set up, a sound check is done, and the group arrives at the concert on time. He must also act as liaison between the concert promoter and the group and collect money owed for the performances.

MANAGER: The main job of a manager is to make sure the group stays together and supports itself. In seeing to that, he must play many different roles—mediator, babysitter, father figure, and tyrant among others. Negotiations for recording contracts and publishing advances are handled by the manager (often alongside an attorney). Managers are equally loved and hated by the people they deal with. They often must use legal methods to make sure record royalties and performance fees are paid. Just as in any other business where one person takes care of all financial matters, a system of checks and balances needs be used to prevent the mishandling of funds.

BOOKING AGENCY: Most jobs taken by rock groups come through booking agencies. For contacting promoters, clubs, and colleges and obtaining jobs, the agency is paid a fee that varies from 10 to 15 percent of the gross worth of the job.

RECORD COMPANY: In order to be more than a local success, a band needs to have its music heard by as wide an audience as possible. That's where a record company comes into the picture. After a group has been signed to a contract (usually one album plus options for additional albums), the record company must advertise the product, make sure it gets airplay, and set up radio, TV, and newspaper interviews. An average group is usually paid a royalty rate of about 5 percent of the retail price of an album for every album sold.

The above-mentioned areas have been greatly simplified—each one could be the subject of a full-length book. The one thing that remains a mystery is: Why aren't more new groups making it?

Most of the groups that have albums on the charts have been around for a number of years: Jefferson Airplane, Grateful Dead, John Lennon, Paul McCartney, etc. One reason may be that record companies are being more selective in the groups they sign.

But it seems that there just isn't any more room at the top. Groups that have been around for years have filled most of the top positions in the charts and until they stop recording, the chances for a new group making it are slim.

# Neil Diamond

## *December 18, 1971*

IN THREE YEARS, NEIL DIAMOND HAS SEEN FOUR OF HIS ALBUMS AND ALL of his singles make it to the Top 10.

Born in Coney Island, N.Y., Neil moved with his family to Cheyenne, Wyoming when he was only four. By the time he was sixteen and living in New York again, Neil had attended nine schools.

"What I remember most about my childhood was the constant changing of schools," Neil said. "My father was barely able to make ends meet and we moved quite a number of times to be near each shop he owned.

"Making and keeping friends was difficult under those circumstances and I was for the most part an outsider in each new school. Yet I was sustained by two things: a fantasy world I created and the sounds of music which filled my house. These things were my company when I was alone and became a major part of my life."

Neil started playing guitar and writing songs when he was sixteen. He eventually formed a team, Neil and Jack, and signed a recording contract with Shell Records.

Shell put out one record by the group. "One violin player came in and overdubbed his part twelve times to give the sound of a string section," Neil said. "Needless to say, the budget was very low. The record received the kind of fate it deserved—obscurity."

After staff writing jobs with five publishing companies (he was fired from them all), Neil decided to try to make it on his own.

"I rented a storage room above Birdland, a jazz nightclub in New York, for $28 a month; bought an old upright piano for $35 from a storage warehouse; had a payphone installed, and for the next year and a half survived on 23-cent hoagies at Woolworth's and the joy of writing music I wanted to write."

Producers Jeff Barry and Ellie Greenwich signed Neil to a small independent label, Bang Records. The first three songs he wrote and recorded were hits: "Solitary Man," "Cherry, Cherry," and "I Got the Feeling."

His first year with Bang, Neil was voted by *Cashbox* magazine as "The Most Promising Male Vocalist." The next year, after seven straight hits, he tied with Frank Sinatra as "Most Popular Male Vocalist."

When his contract with Bang was up, UNI Records offered Neil a chance to break out of the single image and start recording albums. He was given complete creative freedom over his product.

Neil's latest album, *Stones*, his sixth on UNI is number eleven in *Billboard* magazine's top album list. His songs have been recorded by dozens of artists from Elvis to Mantovanni.

Neil is especially proud of a simple song he wrote called "I Am a Man." The lyrics were used as a theme for a strike of sanitation workers in Memphis . . . the same strike during which Martin Luther King was assassinated.

All of his gold records and trophies are stored away, while in his living room hangs a photo of Rev. King leading the march, surrounded by men carrying signs reading: "I Am a Man."

# John Prine

## *January 15, 1972*

AN ARTIST'S FIRST ALBUM USUALLY CONTAINS A FEW GOOD CUTS AND THE rest filler material, but John Prine's first LP is an exception.

The album, on Atlantic Records, contains thirteen original songs, all sensitive but not without humor.

Prine was "discovered" by Kris Kristofferson in a small club in Chicago. He was introduced to Jerry Wexler of Atlantic and was immediately signed.

John was born in Maywood, Illinois, on Oct. 10, 1946. Talking about his start in music, he said, "My grandfather used to play guitar with Ike Everly and Merle Travis. He taught me to play."

His family was into country music and John and his brother learned tunes from their father. "The first time I ever wrote a song," John said, "it took me a couple of hours and I was really excited about it.

"I played it for my mother and suddenly she started humming 'Will the Circle Be Unbroken'. . . so I found out I wrote somebody else's tune."

The most emotional song on John's album, "Sam Stone," is the story of a man who comes home from the war addicted to heroin. The lyrics describe his family's plight:

> *"There's a hole in Daddy's arm*
> *Where all the money goes.*

"In my songs," Prine said, "I try to look through someone else's eyes, and I want to give the audience a feeling more than a message."

His professional debut didn't come until 1970 at the Fifth Peg in Chicago. "I heard about these hoots where anybody could get up and perform, so I figured if anybody could, I would give it a try.

"They ended up giving me a gig on Sunday nights," he said. "I played for about four people and I had to collect the cover charge myself. Sometimes they'd come up in groups of six or seven and say they only had $1.80 between them. With an audience that small, you'd end up knowing them by the time the night was over, and you'd hate to charge them anything."

Word of mouth enlarged the crowds at the club and finally, "this movie critic from the *Chicago Sun-Times*, Roger Ebert, stopped by and he was really excited. Instead of doing a movie, he reviewed my show. So, they gave me a gig on weekends about the same time his column came out."

For those who can't wait to get John's album, Kris Kristofferson is currently at the Cellar Door and usually includes Prine material in his show.

# David Bowie

## *January 22, 1972*

BORN IN LONDON, DAVID ROBERT JONES "NEVER WANTED AND NEVER went hungry. But I saw people deprived all around and I wanted them to have better."

David decided that Bromley Technical High School wasn't the answer, so he quit to study tenor sax and Buddhism. He also decided to change his name from Jones (because of Davy Jones of the Monkees) to Bowie.

After working as an artist for a commercial advertising firm, David formed a progressive blues group. The amplification needed for the group didn't meet with David's liking, so he took off and recorded his first solo album, "Love You 'till Tuesday" (on the Deram label).

Having completed his first album, David renewed his interest in Buddhism and also joined the Lindsay Kemp mime group as an actor, writer, and producer.

David signed with Mercury Records and recorded two critically acclaimed albums. Unfortunately, neither *David Bowie* or *The Man Who Sold the World* sold very well.

Now, on RCA he has recorded an LP, *Hunky Dory*, which has been called the "album of the year" by a couple of rock publications.

Talking about the self-penned songs on his album and his debut as a sax player on record (he usually plays guitar), David said, "'Changes' is a song about, well, changes. And it is my record debut as a sax player. King Curtis was my idol as a sax man, but I'm not King Curtis."

Another of his songs, "Life on Mars," bears a slight resemblance to Frank Sinatra's "My Life."

"I've never heard such rubbish in my life as to hear that man (Sinatra) talk about how great it is to be an old soak," David said. "The general thing is him saying that I'm getting out now, and I'll tell you how I made it . . . and he's told us how he made it.

"I just parody it and, actually, it's what he said, about how nice it is. I especially like Mick Ronson's guitar break on it. I use the same chords that Sinatra uses in 'My Life.'"

"Eight Line Poem" talks about city life versus country living. "It's a realization that the city (in this case, New York) is a kind of a wart on the backside of the prairie, rather than the city being a thing all its own," David said. "It's not, it's just a blister on the country."

The only song on the album that wasn't written by David is "Fill Your Heart."

"This is a number by Biff Rose that I've been doing on stage for two or three years, so I felt that I'd better put it down on record," he said.

"I don't know why I like his songs so much, but I think they're very funny. He takes himself very lightly and things around him very lightly. I enjoy doing that one."

David and his wife, Angela and son Zowie live in a Victorian home in Kent, England. Hopefully, this album will bring him to the U.S. for more than an occasional promotional tour.

# America

## *February 12, 1972*

AMERICA IS ALIVE AND WELL IN ENGLAND.

America, a trio of sons of service families who emigrated to England six years ago, currently have the number one record on the British charts, "Horse with No Name."

Appearing at the Cellar Door with the Everly Brothers recently, the group talked about their first album for Warner Brothers, *America.*

"It's got a real simple thing about it," said Dewey Bunnell, who along with Gerry Buxley and Dan Peek, plays acoustic guitar and shares vocals. "There's no over-production or anything."

"We could have put strings and orchestration on a lot of songs, like 'I Need You.' Our producer said that for the first album it's much better in the long run to present the group as basically as you possibly can."

Because they were mismanaged for a while, the group almost missed out on a recording contract.

"The guy who was handling us when we were looking for a contract was being a little bit uncool with the companies by playing them against each other," Gerry said.

"We were doing tapes for Atlantic in the morning, Liberty in the afternoon, and Dick James in the evening—the same songs and that wasn't cool at all. All the companies were paying for studio time. We were just dumb. We didn't know what was happening.

"If a company is going to go as far as to put out money for you to do demos," Gerry stressed, "the courtesy is to go along with the negotiations until things go wrong."

A major problem occurred when Atlantic and Warner Brothers, both owned by the same company, Kinney Systems, got together and Atlantic said, "We're recording this group called America" and Warner Brothers said, "No, we are."

"We called a halt to everything for a few weeks, just to figure out where we were and what we were doing," Dan said. "It boiled down to Warner Brothers willing to take us, but they weren't going to take the guy who was handling us at the time."

So, the group was picked up by a new manager, Jeff Dexter, who has been an immense help to them since.

Jeff did all the festivals and things like that," Dewey said. "He's the only guy in England that could get the Who to play for free."

Besides handling America, Jeff is a DJ in England (not the same as an American DJ). "We have DJ's in England that aren't necessarily on the radio," Jeff said. "Like, with every live concert there's always a DJ—like you have an MC here."

"But the MC over in England is also a DJ," he said. "He plays records at all the venues. That's what I've been doing for ten or eleven years in England."

Their hit single, "Horse with No Name," is not on the British version of their album, and was sort of an afterthought for the group.

"We thought they were just going to take something off the album," Dewey said. "But, over there it's a good idea to have a separate single.

"So, we worked up about four new songs and recorded demos and Warner Brothers chose that one."

The American version of the album was originally released without the single, but it has been reissued with the song added and nothing deleted.

Working in England made it easier for the group to make it where they are now. "We couldn't have done what we did in England in the U.S.," Gerry said. "It just wouldn't have been possible, because in England, if you have a group, particularly the way we have our group with just guitars, you're very mobile.

"So, just going into London, we could play for every record company in a day. But, the States aren't localized like that. Offices are spread all over the country.

"The only thing we could have done was headed for New York or something and tried to run around the offices there. But it just wouldn't have happened like it did in England."

America will be doing one more date in the Washington area before they head back home. On Feb. 20, they'll be appearing in concert at the Alexandria Roller Rink with Grin and T. Rex.

# Musings ... Why I Never Set Foot in Blues Alley After February 23, 1972

BLUES ALLEY IS A NIGHTCLUB IN THE GEORGETOWN SECTION OF WASHINGton, D.C. First opened in 1965, the club presented performances by top jazz and blues artists from Dizzy Gillespie to Ahmad Jamal, from Sarah Vaughn to Nancy Wilson. While jazz wasn't really my beat as a music journalist, on (a rare) occasion I would interview a jazz artist for my column. I never had a problem getting in the door at Blues Alley until February 23, 1972.

The best way to explain my self-imposed boycott of the club is to quote from Kevin Avery's excellent book *Everything Is an Afterthought: The Life and Writings of Paul Nelson.*

Paul Nelson was a friend and one of the best music journalists I've ever known. His brilliant long-form interviews with Bob Dylan, Leonard Cohen, Neil Young, and many others have stuck in my mind since they first appeared in *Rolling Stone* magazine.

In February 1972, Paul was running the publicity department at Mercury Records in New York City. My brother, Ron, had been director of publicity at Mercury's headquarters in Chicago when he hired Paul for the job in New York. By 1972, Ron had left Mercury to manage a Chicago-based band, Wilderness Road, before taking a job at Columbia Records.

I often found myself in New York, either taking demos to record companies, interviewing artists, or just for the thrill of being in the Big Apple. The first thing I would do after arriving in Manhattan was call Paul Nelson. I knew that he would take me to lunch at the Russian Tea Room. That was his go-to restaurant. All the waiters knew Paul and would automatically bring him the two Coca-Colas he would always order. Wearing his "newsboy" cap and with a Nat Sherman cigaretello hanging from his lips, Paul cut the hippest figure of anyone I knew.

Our conversations over lunch usually veered from music to film (film noir in particular) and novelists (usually Ross McDonald). Paul never hyped me on a musical act he didn't believe in. One Mercury artist Paul thought highly of was Rod Stewart. Paul knew that I had known Rod since he was vocalist in the Jeff Beck Group in 1969. So, while there was very little music talk over lunch, Rod Stewart would occasionally come up in conversation.

Fast-forwarding to February 23, 1972, and an excerpt from Kevin Avery's book (an entry in Paul Nelson's diary):

2-23-72. In Washington, D.C. today for Chuck Mangione at Blue Alley. Turns out to be a disaster, in a funny, disgusting way. All the omens were there: the cabdriver from the airport gets totally lost, a blizzard starts, I get soaking wet, a writer I'm supposed to meet never shows up.

Supper with Mike Oberman and Dawn, his girlfriend. The snow has turned into heavy rain. We walk over to the club to see Chuck. And the owner won't let us in. Why? I ask, since there's absolutely no audience and I can't imagine what's wrong with us. "Because you don't have a coat and tie on," he says, and gives us a lecture on how shitty we look, how he doesn't have to put up with people like us in his place. Chuck comes over with a couple of members of his group and they look worse than we do. "A musician's audience is liable to look like the musician," I try out on the owner, but it doesn't work. "I can put up with him," the owner says, pointing at Chuck, "because he's a musician and in uniform, but I don't have to put up with your kind." Chuck argues with him to no avail. I start to get furious. Tell him I've never had any trouble getting into Carnegie Hall when I've been dressed like this. I wind up out in the street in the rain, listening to the music through the window.

I never went back to Blues Alley. Paul Nelson left the publicity department to join the A & R department at Mercury. Paul eventually left Mercury to become records review editor and writer at *Rolling Stone*. Sadly, after leaving *Rolling Stone*, Paul's life went downhill. He spent a long time working on an unfinished screenplay. A devoted lifelong cinephile with predilections for John Ford's oeuvre and film noir, he was an early adoptee of the video-cassette recorder and enjoyed taping obscure exemplars of classic Hollywood cinema. Throughout much of this period, Nelson was employed as a clerk at Evergreen Video, a now-defunct specialty shop in the Greenwich Village neighborhood of Manhattan.

Nelson was found dead in his sublet apartment on the Upper East Side in July 2006. The office of chief medical examiner of the city of New York ruled that heart disease was the cause of his death. In a 2011 overview, Charlie Finch of Artnet commented on Nelson's lifestyle choices: "Nelson didn't drink or do drugs: what he did do was eat a hamburger and veal picatta for dinner, always with two Cokes, even for breakfast, while smoking Nat Sherman cigarettes, every day of his adult life."

# Badfinger

## *February 26, 1972*

OUT OF ALL THE ACTS THE BEATLES SIGNED TO THEIR APPLE RECORD label four years ago, only Badfinger remains with the company.

James Taylor and Jackie Lomax, original Appleites, switched to Warner Brothers after their first albums for the Beatles' label failed to sell.

Although they are the only non-Beatle act left on Apple, Badfinger is worth its weight in gold. The group has had three hit singles and two hit albums in the last two years.

Badfinger's current hit, "Day after Day," has just been certified a million seller after thirteen weeks on the charts.

The group, half Welsh and half Liverpudlian, is comprised of Joey Molland, guitar; Mike Gibbons, drums; Pete Ham, guitar and piano; and Tom Evans, Bass.

Badfinger's first hit was "Come and Get It," written by Paul McCartney for the soundtrack of *The Magic Christian*. Since they were signed to Apple and doing Beatles' tunes, the group was often compared to their mentors.

"At first we liked being compared to the Beatles, but it's not much fun now," Joey said. "Our music is becoming more individual. You know, you start out doing one thing and the more you find out about it, the more you start doing another thing. That's especially true when we're in the studio.

"Some of the songs we hadn't even finished when we went to record, so we arranged them there. We listened to the Beatles when we started out and we sent a tape to them when they formed Apple. That's how we got in. It was George, mostly. But now the music is becoming mostly us."

Badfinger is currently preparing for their third tour of the U.S., beginning with a March 1 concert at Carnegie Hall.

"The first time we came over, we had a record, you know, and the second time we didn't," Joey said. "But the gigs we've played so far, people called out numbers from our albums. That's nice to hear."

One thing the fellows dread when they come to this country is the food. "The menu," Pete said. "It's the same wherever you go, any city. There must be a thousand restaurants in any city, and it's all the same."

Once they get past the food, Badfinger finds this country a good place for creativity. "I like the speed of it in the States," Pete said. "People just go ahead and do things.

"We get ideas for our songs when we're there. Little things you can store up. Then when we get back home, we can put them together. We try to write wherever we can."

After their current tour, Badfinger hopes to take a vacation. "We stumble onto a plane and say, 'Now we'll have a holiday.' But it hasn't worked out like that so far," Joey said. "There's usually another album to do. We were supposed to have a holiday the last time around but it didn't work out."

# Pink Floyd

## *March 4, 1972*

PINK FLOYD IS NOT WHAT YOU WOULD CALL THE ORDINARY ROCK GROUP. The British quartet, formed in 1964 (originally a trio), concentrates on the use of electronics. At every concert, the group makes use of over three tons of electronic equipment.

Equipment men for the group have the time-consuming chore of setting up 120 speakers around each concert hall, so sound can come from any direction. They also utilize pre-recorded tapes and an Azimuth coordinator, an instrument that allows sound to be run in circles around the listeners' heads.

When the group was formed in 1964, it consisted of Roger Waters, bass; Rick Wright, keyboards; Nick Mason, drums; and songwriter Syd Barrett. In 1968, Barrett left the group and lead guitarist Dave Gilmour joined.

Pink Floyd's albums like *Saucerful of Secrets* and *Atom Heart Mother*, attracted a cult following in this country but turned them into pop stars of sorts in England.

"I think that we're intellectually ahead of what's happening in music, but it's not all down to intellect," Dave Gilmour said during their recent tour of this country. "We've never thought of ourselves as avant-garde. Basically, for us, it's emotional music, that avant-garde thing was something put upon us."

The group's latest LP, *Meddle*, is on the charts and has expanded their audience.

"Audiences throughout the world are getting more and more the same as far as we're concerned," Gilmour said.

"In England, we've got a bigger and more dedicated audiences, and they expect us to do anything we want. We've never been as daring in the States as we've been in England.

"We've set out there," Gilmour said, "to perform an evening without playing anything we've ever done before and only giving ourselves the day of the concert to prepare, and people dig it, no rules, no anything."

In the U.S., the group has stuck pretty much with standard (if what they do could be called standard) cuts from their albums.

"We did a concert tour in England that was about a man on a journey, sort of a storyline, but we avoided calling it a rock opera," Dave said.

"We had a monster who wandered in from the back of the audience. We did that a couple of years ago and people in England still expect us to surprise them."

Although other groups have started to employ electronic and visual effects, no group has succeeded in copying Pink Floyd. When they're on stage, four engineers are needed to run their electronics.

Besides their album and stage performances Pink Floyd supplied the electronic music for Antonioni's film, *Zabriskie Point*.

# Taj Mahal

## *April 1, 1972*

IF ONE HAD TO DESCRIBE A TYPICAL COUNTRY BLUES SINGER, IT WOULD probably be the opposite of Taj Mahal . . . yet singing country blues is what he does best.

Taj was born in New York twenty-nine years ago, raised in Massachusetts and has an Animal Husbandry Associates Degree from the University of Massachusetts. Quite a difference from most grizzled, old Southern country blues singers.

The first blues Taj was introduced to was the big band variety. His father, a jazz arranger and composer, turned him on to artists like Albert Ammons, Cow Cow Davenport, Illinois Jacquet, and Leadbelly.

"This used to be the traffic over my head," Taj said. "I used to hear sounds in my head that I wanted to play on an instrument and things that I put together that I thought would be nice.

"When I first heard the blues, I forgot about school and everything else for a while, and the guitar is where it was at for me."

Taj started collecting blues records and began to search out the early bluesmen. While a university student, he joined the Pioneer Valley Folklore Society and studied the early roots of American black music.

It was at this time, Taj said, that he "got an insight into the relation of blues and black music to American music as a whole."

His self-education in the blues almost became an obsession with Taj. Besides searching out early blues musicians, he talked to their teachers and even their fans.

"There was a whole part of my cultural life and my ancestral culture that was beginning to be pieced together," Taj said. "The country blues filled in a big gap and helped me to understand my own feelings, things I felt or knew or understood and did not seem to have any backlog of information on.

"A great way to discover yourself is to start from the tradition that you came from . . . to find a thing to do for the rest of your life. I decided to play whether I made any money or not because this is just what I really wanted to do."

Besides his singing ability, Taj plays a variety of instruments, including piano, guitar, banjo and fife. Before forming his own ten-piece band (including a four-tuba horn section), Taj worked with the Rising Sons.

His five Columbia LP's are *Taj Mahal*, *The Natch'l Blues*, *Giant Step*, *The Real Thing*, and *Happy to Be Just Like I Am*.

# West, Bruce and Laing

## *May 6, 1972*

BECAUSE OF CONTRACTUAL COMMITMENTS, IT MAY BE AWHILE BEFORE WEST, Bruce and Laing release an album . . . but the wait should be worthwhile.

Leslie West (guitar) and Corky Laing (drums) (both from Mountain) got together with Jack Bruce (bass) (formerly of the John Mayall Group and Cream) in January in London.

It was at that time that Mountain's bass player, Felix Pappalardi, decided that he wanted "to stay off the road and devote more time to outside interests."

It didn't take Leslie and Corky long to decide that Jack would fit the bill. West, Bruce and Laing was born.

"It's the best thing that ever happened for me," Bruce said. "I'm more excited about this band than I've ever been about anything I've ever been in . . . including Cream and everything."

"Usually with these things," Leslie explained, "it's a case of management saying they want to put these guys together or those guys together, but there was none of that with this band . . . that's what makes it so much fun. We were all friends before, and when we got together it just happened, it was so good."

The trio first assembled at Island studios and recorded an eleven-minute version of the Rolling Stones' "Play with Fire." After that, they launched into a jam, which was overheard by the Who. (They were recording in the next studio.)

The Who was so impressed with West, Bruce and Laing, they offered the new group the use of their entire sound system when they go on the road.

Of the three musicians, least has probably been written about Corky Laing. He was born Jan. 28, 1948, in Montreal.

He started playing drums at fifteen, but didn't get his first set until he was seventeen. He was suspended from his high school band four times because he "set up the percussion instruments like a combo drum set."

"Nobody would let me into their band," Corky said, "because I was too weird. So in 1963 I formed my own group called the Starlights.

"We played parties, clubs and made a few local recordings. In 1965, I changed the name of the group to the Souls and made it down to the Peppermint Lounge in N.Y."

In the summer of 1965, he met Leslie and they became friends. In 1969, Felix Pappalardi formed Mountain, taking Corky from a group called Energy and Leslie from the Vagrants.

Until each of the musicians' contractual problems is cleared up, we'll have to settle with listening to old Cream and Mountain LP's . . . but that's not too bad.

# Black Oak Arkansas

## *May 13, 1972*

In 1964, six long-haired youths broke into the high school in Black Oak, Arkansas, and tried to steal the public address system.

Last year, the mayor of that same town presented the youths with a Styrofoam key to the city.

Why? Because since they broke the law in 1964, the sextet, going under the name Black Oak Arkansas, has recorded a hit single and LP and put the town (population 204) on the map.

According to Butch Stone, manager for Black Oak Arkansas, the members of the group met eight years ago. "We had all known each other by reputation but hadn't met," he said. "Black Oak (the town) was the center and we were all rebels, so it was inevitable that we'd get together.

"We were all different from the folks around us, not just our long hair, but the way we thought. So, as time passed we just naturally came together.

"We left our parents and got a house together and scrounged for a living. And then the Beatles came out and we noticed music. We already had the long hair because we didn't believe in wasting food money on getting our hair cut."

The town council wasn't too happy with a bunch of long-hairs (remember this was 1964) living together in their sedate little community.

Finally, the group, with no money to purchase band equipment, made a mistake that almost cost them lengthy prison sentences.

"We didn't have any equipment," Stone said, "so we went to a local high school and tried to lift the p.a. system, but we got caught. Suddenly every crime in the town in the last two years was being pinned on us. They were determined that we would be used as an example.

"They got four of us on enough charges to put us in Tucker Prison Farm for twenty-two years. Luckily, we got suspended sentences."

Realizing their luck, the group decided to split for the Ozarks, where they played in clubs in the French Quarter; the group decided that if they were going to make it musically, they would have to move to L.A.

They arrived in California in Sept. 1969, and were "so poor that we had to sell blood to stay alive." Work finally started coming in at places like the Topanga Corral and the Whiskey-A-Go-Go.

As their reputation built up, Atco Records signed them and they released their first recordings for that label (they had done one other poorly received LP for Stax Records going under the name *Knowbody Else*). A single, "Keep the Faith," taken from their Atco album, became a national hit.

Now, the sheriff's office in Black Oak has another problem: fanatic rock fans are taking all of the town's highway signs for souvenirs.

# Brinsley Schwarz

## *May 27, 1972*

CUTTING ALL TWELVE SONGS LIVE (NO OVERDUBBING) AT THEIR HOME outside London, Brinsley Schwarz has recorded a thoroughly listenable third album, *Silver Pistol.*

The British group, named after their lead guitarist, decided to record their latest album at home in order to get the most down-to-earth sound possible.

"The idea was to get more than enough songs for an album and then record it at home and select what came off best," said Ian Gomm, one of the guitarists in the group.

Besides Schwarz and Gomm, others in the group are Bob Andrews, keyboards, accordion, guitar, bass, and vocals; Nick Lowe, bass, guitar, banjo, and vocals; and Bill Rankin, drums. Nick also handles most of the writing chores.

*Silver Pistol* started out as an experimental album. "Some of these numbers we'd been playing for months and to just come down and play them in your front room and record them was a bit weird," Ian said. "Some of the tracks, like 'Nightingale,' worked particularly well because it was just the feeling we had in the house at the time."

According to Dave Robinson, manager and producer for Brinsley Schwarz, "We tried to do an anti-album, with none of the things you normally expect. *Silver Pistol* was the result. A live album now might be groovy, but only if the whole thing is geared towards the gig and the recording is a secondary effect."

"The thing is," Nick interjected, "it's not that important for a group to have its own material in (an LP) anymore because it's all been written anyway. Someone somewhere has already done it and it's frustrating to hear a record from 1962 that's so immaculate.

"So, we really prefer to get into playing and if it happens to be our numbers then that's great, but we groove on playing just about anything."

The group, roadies, wives, and children all live together in a detached house in Northwood, Middlesex. Now, they're looking for a place farther away from London.

"Living together as a group, things are getting narrower and narrower," Nick said. "It's like we don't have a musical policy at all now. We are getting into playing anything that anyone in the band happens to like."

Everyone in Brinsley Schwarz feels an affinity to America's Band ("Music from Big Pink," etc.). "It's like the Band," Nick said. "The thing we have got from them is that they have been together for eleven or twelve years now, and they have only just emerged. That is a thing we have seen and we want to do that as well.

"It can happen in America because a band can go along for a long time under their own steam before they make it."

Recording the album in their living room "was something we felt we had to do," said Brinsley. "Everything we do pointed to recording an album at home. If we had gone into the studio to record this album, it would have been a lie. The fact that it worked is something that makes us pleased."

"We thought this is how it has to be," added Nick. "We recorded the album at home to try and create a feeling, but we found that we were so relaxed that some of the songs didn't really begin or end."

# David Bromberg

## *June 3, 1972*

EVEN THOUGH GUITARIST/SINGER DAVID BROMBERG WAS BILLED SECOND to Cheech and Chong at the Cellar Door a few weeks back, he's no newcomer to music or Washington.

Bromberg has been doing studio work and touring with some of the best musicians (Dylan, Jerry Jeff Walker, etc.) for a number of years.

He played with Jerry Jeff ("Mr. Bojangles") Walker for three years, including a week as second act at the Cellar Door around two years ago.

"Jerry Jeff was really unhappy with the Cellar Door," David said during a recent interview. "We were second act and the other act did hour-and-a-half sets which left Jerry with 15- to twenty-minute sets.

"The minute we finished the gig, we went straight to the airport to catch the first plane out—which didn't leave until six the next morning. We were ready to take the first plane anywhere. We really wanted to leave.

"We ended up staying up all night playing with toys," he said.

David's feelings about the club have changed since his recent appearance there. "It's one of the most comfortable clubs I've played in," he said.

Bromberg was backed up at the Cellar Door by the Fabulous Torpedoes—Steve Berg, bass, guitar, and vocals, and Andy Statton, mandolin and saxophone.

They played tunes like "The Holdup," co-authored by Bromberg and George Harrison and taken from David's Columbia LP and some newer material that should be released soon.

Talking about his first interest in music, David said, "The first thing I was knocked out by . . . that really got me interested in music was when I heard

Pete Seeger singing on a Weaver's record. From there I became interested in musicians like Lonnie Johnson and Rev. Gary Davis (who recently died).

Besides playing a fine acoustic guitar, David started playing violin around three months ago. From the way he handled it at the Cellar Door, it seemed as though he'd been playing it for much longer than that.

David lives in New York City and loves it there. "Occasionally I'd like to get some trees and sunshine, but I really dig the city," he said.

A lot of musicians, many of them David's friends, have moved to Woodstock, but David wants to stay away from that community. "There's something about that whole scene that has always left a bad taste in my mouth."

David is currently on the road more than he's at home, but he enjoys the traveling. "You can overdose on it sometimes," he said, "but I haven't yet."

# Rolling Stones Concert
# at RFK Stadium (July 4)

## *July 5, 1972*

ONLY ADEQUATE.

The sound system and lighting were exceptional, but, unfortunately, the Rolling Stones were only adequate at last night's RFK Stadium concert.

They played well and Mick Jagger did his usual rooster strut across the serpent bedecked stage, but the concert was very predictable.

Other than playing new material and touring with three additional musicians, the Stones haven't changed since they last played in this country in 1969.

Their stage presence and musicianship is still exciting but held no surprises for those who had seen them before.

Opening their fifteen-song set with "Brown Sugar," the Stones went on to numbers from their current LP, *Exile on Main Street*, mixed with some older material.

All came across loud and clear thanks to the thirty Tychobrahe P.A. cabinets that lined both sides of the stage.

It was refreshing to hear Keith Richards help Jagger out on the vocals on "Happy" and to hear acoustic guitars miked properly (Mick Taylor and Richards switched from electric to acoustic instruments for "Sweet Virginia").

Accompanying Jagger, Taylor, Richards, Charlie Watts, and Bill Wyman on their American tour are Nicky Hopkins on piano, Bobby Keys on sax, and Jim Price on trombone and trumpet.

Only once during the evening did Jagger take on the demonic glow that so many have associated with him—in "Midnight Rambler." With the stage

345

lit in red, Jagger got down on bended knees, slapping the platform with a thick leather belt while he was "talkin' about the Boston strangler."

The Stones' last two songs, "Jumpin' Jack Flash" and "Street Fighting Man," were played with the stadium lights on and the crowd gyrating madly, causing the massive stadium to tremble.

With the last bars of "Street Fighting Man," the Stones disappeared as quickly as they had come on stage and didn't come back for an encore.

Preceding the Stones, Stevie Wonder played a forty-five-minute set that was genuinely appreciated by the mainly white rock crowd.

Backed by eight musicians and three female vocalists, Wonder played keyboards, harmonica, synthesizer, and drums. His style has clearly changed, crossing the line from soul into jazz-influenced rock.

# Bill Withers

## *July 8, 1972*

IN JUST OVER A YEAR, BILL WITHERS HAS GONE FROM MANUFACTURING toilets for airplanes to writing and singing hit songs like "Ain't No Sunshine" and "Lean on Me."

Withers was in town recently, performing to packed houses at the Cellar Door. The thirty-four-year-old West Virginian, backed by the rhythm section from the Watts 103rd Street Band, leisurely mixed anecdotes about his life with his easy-to-identify-with songs.

During a recent interview, Withers talked a little about his early life. "I come from an area in West Virginia where there were no towns," he said. "They were coal mining communities, not towns. The coal companies owned all the houses and the community store.

"A lot of people never saw any money, they just dealt in scrip through the store. Remember the song 'Sixteen Tons'? That was the real thing."

Withers, who spent nine years in the Navy and only a year ago decided to become an entertainer, doesn't think formal musical training is necessary.

"I've never had any musical training," he said. "I don't think musical training can really give you any creativity.

"All the time it would take now for me to learn how to write music would be just hanging me up. What I mean is to write symbols. I can compose melodies and write lyrics."

Bill's second album, from which his hit single, "Lean on Me" was taken, was self-produced. "My record company, Sussex, assigned me a producer for my first album. I didn't mind it then. They gave me Booker T. and I like him.

"But," Withers said, "the second time around I didn't want a producer. If I'm going to write all the music and make the concepts myself, the only thing a producer could do is get on my nerves, telling me what to do."

347

His sudden rise to the top of the record charts hasn't changed Withers' way of thinking. "I feel like this is a big bonus in my life," he said. "Nobody deserves anything they get from entertaining.

"I was only in music for six months last year. I earned more money for entertaining in that small period of time than I earned in nine years in the Navy. That's a little unfair. That doesn't mean I'm going to give any of it back, but the value structures are upside down."

Bill's back-up musicians also record with him and comprise one of the tightest bands around. He's much happier recording with them than being trendy and using name studio musicians, he said.

"I really liked the way they worked with each other and asked them to join me," he said. "You can get together a lot of great musicians—fly them in from all over the country—and they can't play together.

"I liked working with these guys better than working with Booker T. and Steve Stills and Al Jackson and all those cats. My band's understanding about which direction I want to go is much better."

Knowing they're working with a Grammy winner and the writer of a number one record, it's doubtful Bill's back-up group will be looking for a new employer for quite some time.

Bill Withers (l) in Dressing Room, Washington, D.C.
PHOTO BY MIKE KLAVANS

# Arthur Lee

## *July 15, 1972*

IN 1971, LOVE DECIDED TO TAKE A BREAK.

The Los Angeles based group had recorded seven albums for two labels before taking an extended and possibly permanent vacation.

Now, Arthur Lee, vocalist and songwriter for Love, has recorded a solo album, "Vindicator," for A & M Records.

Lee, the motivating force behind Love, formed an early partnership with Jimi Hendrix. "We wrote a song called 'My Diary,'" Lee said. "It was a small hit by Rosalie Brooks, but I never saw a penny from it."

In 1965, Lee, John Echols, Alban Phisterer, Bryan Maclean, and Ken Forssi formed Love and became one of the first L.A. groups to sign with Elektra Records.

"I was really into Motown, the Rolling Stones, the Beatles, and Paul Jones from the old Manfred Mann," Lee recalled. "The music we did began like folk music and went from there.

Love went to jazz ("Da Capo"), classical ("Forever Changes"), and various combinations with hard rock and rhythm-and-blues.

"When the musicians in the group couldn't take the changes," Lee said, "they left and I found new ones who could cut it."

One of the things Lee feels held them back was that they didn't want to become superstars. "We always did what we liked, and if that meant being a bit weird on stage and not doing too many gigs, that's the way it went. A lot of people are like that now."

Lee's voice had a lot to do with Love's success and should assure his success as a solo artist. "I have a certain kind of voice that I can use any way I want," he said. "That's how I can do all the different types of music. I couldn't very well have used a rhythm-and-blues voice all the time, though it would have been natural."

Arthur sees the possibility of Love getting back together. But in the meantime, he wants to make "Arthur Lee music."

He has spent the last year "observing life and writing a whole lot.

"I write like a letter," he said. "When I perish, I think you'll be able to take my lyrics and read them without hearing the music and make sense out of them—like poetry.

"I write about people. If you understand yourself at all, you can project it outward. If you have your head together at home, you can play in the streets.

"Humans," he continued, "are one big spirit separated into different bodies wandering around a hunk of mud called Earth, and all beings are basically reflections of each other.

"That's what my songs are about. I hope they can communicate enough to help people recognize the unity and the reflections."

# Black Sabbath

## *July 29, 1972*

THE INVERTED STEEL CROSSES THE MEMBERS OF BLACK SABBATH WEAR on stage aren't (as some might think) worn as symbols of an affiliation with the devil.

Vocalist Ozzy Osbourne's father presented the group with the crosses "to protect the lads from Satanists who were incensed with the name Black Sabbath."

All the members of the group were raised in Ashton, a rough section of Birmingham, England. Their factory life upbringing seemed to be leading them down a dead-end street until they decided to form a band.

"If I hadn't got with a band, I probably would be in prison now," Ozzie said.

Besides Ozzy, others in the group are Tony Iommi, guitar and flute; Geezer Butler, bass; and Bill Ward, drums. They formed the band, originally called Earth, in January 1969.

Because a number of other bands were using the name Earth, they decided to become Black Sabbath. The name was taken from a British horror film starring Boris Karloff.

Originally, the group wanted no involvement with black magic and witchcraft. All they wanted was for their name to draw attention. And with a large number of people being interested in the occult, the name did help.

After they were together awhile, they decided to add some theatrics to their stage act. "We've never been into black magic," Ozzy said, "but just to get a break, we decided to do a thing because it had never been done before—with crosses and all that."

Incorporating the black mass into their act, the group soon gained a reputation that wasn't deserved. Their music is loud and hard and lends itself to some of the violent connotations of witchcraft, but that's as close as their monicker comes to the real thing.

During a recent tour of the U.S., the group went back to their hotel after a concert and heard a lot of footsteps in the hall. When he opened his door, Ozzy said, he saw "a lot of weird people with black candles walking up and down and drawing crosses on the doors."

In order to bring some sanity to the situation, the group ran into the hall, blew out the candles, and sang "Happy Birthday" to their "witchy" followers.

With three successful albums behind them, the group hopes their darker side has been left behind and people will concentrate on their music.

Black Sabbath and Black Oak Arkansas will be in concert tonight at the University of Maryland.

# Leon Russell

## *August 5, 1972*

IN 1968, A CRITICALLY ACCLAIMED ALBUM, *ASYLUM CHOIR* WAS RELEASED but met with poor sales.

That didn't deter either of the two musicians who created the album concept and made all of the music on it. The Asylum Choir, Leon Russell and Marc Benno, is no longer together, but individually they're making some fine music.

Benno has released two albums for A & M Records and Russell owns his own label and studio, Shelter Records. Leon was born in Oklahoma and started playing piano (both his parents played the instrument) at the tender age of three.

He studied classical piano for ten years, but when he began high school, he decided to give it up. "I didn't really have the hands for classical stuff," he said, "and my teachers discouraged me from making up my own music."

Leon took up trumpet and at fourteen had his own band, lying about his age to get work in Tulsa nightclubs. Among the musicians who sat in with him were Ronnie Hawkins and Jerry Lee Lewis.

At seventeen, Russell moved to L.A. "I wasn't even supposed to be out at night in Los Angeles, let alone working in clubs," he said. "I'd borrow a friend's ID to get a job, then I'd return the card and work until I was stopped by the police for being under-age and out after curfew.

Within a few years, Leon was one of the most sought-after studio musicians in L.A. After five years of studio work, he built his own recording studio in his home in the Hollywood Hills. It was there that he and Marc Benno recorded two Asylum Choir LPs, the first released on the Smash label and the second on Shelter.

In 1969, Russell joined forces with Delaney and Bonnie which led to his meeting English producer Denny Cordell. Cordell introduced Leon to Joe Cocker and a musical alliance was soon formed.

Russell was given the job of putting together the musicians and the music for Cocker's Mad Dogs and Englishmen tour. Out of the assignment came a highly successful tour, a movie, an album, and the Russell penned song "Delta Lady."

Since that time, Leon has recorded three albums of his own for Shelter, playing guitar, piano, and drums. He was also a featured performer at the now historic "Concert for Bangladesh."

Leon now lives in Oklahoma on a sprawling farm complete with its own lake. On the farm is also a new recording studio (where half of his latest album, *Carney*, was recorded) and houses for visiting friends and musicians.

# Seldom Scene

## *August 19, 1972*

WARNING: Do not go to the Red Fox Inn in Bethesda after 8 p.m. any Tuesday unless you mind standing up for four hours of the best bluegrass music in town.

The five men who have been packing the club once a week since November are known collectively as the Seldom Scene. Because they generally limit their engagements to one night a week and occasional weekend performances, their name is apt.

The group's self-imposed limitations are for good reasons ... they all hold good jobs and have family ties. The members of the band are John Starling, thirty-two, a surgeon in residence at Walter Reed, guitar and vocals; Mike Auldridge, thirty-three, a commercial artist, dobro and vocals; John Duffey, thirty-eight, a fretted instrument repairman, mandolin and vocals; Ben Eldridge, thirty-four, a mathematician, banjo and vocals; and Tom Gray, thirty-one, a cartographer, bass and vocals.

The Seldom Scene currently record for Rebel Records. Their first album contains songs like Steve Goodman's "City of New Orleans," "Raised by the Railroad Line," and "Darling Cory"—all done in the group's inimitable bluegrass/pop style.

To see the group, one would think that when they weren't performing for audiences, they were practicing. But, that's not the case.

"The only time we practice anymore is when we have some new material we want to work up," Starling said during a recent interview. "Most bluegrass musicians have a common repertoire of the old stuff."

For the first time, bluegrass is appealing to mass and diverse audiences. One problem that's keeping the music just out of reach for some people is that not many bluegrass bands are writing new material.

"There are very few bluegrass groups around that do much original stuff," Starling said. "I think that bluegrass is wide open for that right now. "Bill Monroe has written a lot, but all his new material sounds old. It's all in the traditional vein. Bluegrass would gain more popularity if a group were to come along that played basically bluegrass with unamplified instruments and did their own original material, songs that were more relevant."

According to John, a group's first album is the easiest to do. "You've usually been playing that material for quite a while and really have it down when you go into the studio."

Mike and John differ in their views on how popular they would like bluegrass to become. Mike would like to see it be "the music," while John would be content driving 200 miles to see a group.

"To me it's a pleasure to talk to almost anybody and they know what bluegrass is," Mike said. "I feel it's earned it. The only thing I don't want to see is the festivals get so big that they have the same problems the rock festivals have."

The feelings generated at a bluegrass festival or in a club where bluegrass is played are generally friendly.

"There's a strange chemistry," John said. "Bluegrass sort of brings the freaks and the more country types together and they've always gotten along very well. I think both groups look at each other in amusement.

"I just hope it stays that way. But the bigger the crowds get, the less interested they are in the music and the more likely they are to get into trouble."

Although the rest of the band is happy to keep its popularity local, Mike would like to see some national prominence. Mike's first solo dobro album (all instrumental except for two cuts) should be released any day now. He recorded it for John Fahey's Takoma label and some of the sidemen on it include the Country Gentlemen, David Bromberg on guitar and Vassar Clements on fiddle.

If you can't make it by the Red Fox, the Seldom Scene will be appearing tomorrow in Gettysburg and at 8 tonight at a free concert at 4th and P St. S.W. In case of rain the performance will be at the Department of Interior Auditorium, 19th and C Sts. N.W.

# Musings . . . "Long Time, Seldom Scene"

I WAS IN THE AUDIENCE AT THE 2013 NATIONAL ENDOWMENT FOR THE Arts Heritage Fellowships Concert when I ran into Pete Reiniger, who was there to mix sound. Before the show started, I said hello to Pete, and he told me that he had recently produced and engineered a new CD of the Seldom Scene for Smithsonian Folkways. "Would you be interested in photographing the group for the CD cover and the booklet that will come with the CD?" Pete asked. "Absolutely," I responded.

I had some history with the Seldom Scene. Of the 300 interviews I did for my weekly column in the *Washington Star*, only one was with a bluegrass group: the Seldom Scene. Additionally, the group's original dobro player, Mike Auldridge, worked as a graphic artist at the *Washington Star*. If that wasn't enough, a band I managed, the Rosslyn Mountain Boys, played every Wednesday night at the Birchmere, and the Seldom Scene played every Thursday night at the same club. Four decades had now passed, and I was looking forward to the photo session.

Two of the original members of the band were deceased. John Duffey died in 1996. His mandolin playing, vocals, and sense of humor should stick in the minds of anyone who saw the original group, whether at the Birchmere, the Red Fox Inn, or a multitude of other places. Mike Auldridge, dobro player extraordinaire, passed away in 2012. John Starling and Tom Gray were no longer with the group. The only original member still in the group was Ben Eldridge on banjo.

After negotiating with Smithsonian Folkways, it was decided that I would retain copyright on all the photos in return for cutting my fee by 30 percent. The shoot was going to be at an antebellum mansion in Prince George's County. When I arrived, Pete Reiniger was there with the band and the couple who owned the mansion. Where, I wondered, was the art director for the shoot? Well, it turned out there wasn't one. It was up to me to figure out the best way to photograph the group. I had to keep in mind that a CD cover is only five inches by five inches. In addition to five guys with their instruments, graphics had to fit on the cover.

I did the entire shoot without a tripod and using only natural light. We shot some fun poses outdoors, but it was the main staircase in the house that intrigued me. So, I asked the fivesome to stand on the stairs and play a song. They did, and I shot.

I spent the entire next day postprocessing my photos. I knew the staircase photos were the best for the cover, and a number of other shots could be used for the booklet. I did twelve different versions of the "staircase cover" shot, including a high-dynamic-range color shot that I then converted to black and white with a slight sepia tinge to make it slightly "old-timey."

The CD was released in 2014 to very good reviews. It was a delightful surprise to me when the reviewer at *Bluegrass Today* wrote, "Everything about this CD is a winner, including the detail-rich liner notes, spectacular photography by Michael Oberman, the production and, of course, the music. Intentional or not, the sixteen songs presented here trace the arc of the band, from its informal start in a Bethesda, MD, basement to the current lineup, which has itself been together for eighteen years."

It's not often that the photographer of a CD cover is mentioned in a review, but that meant more to me than the money I was paid. (As a postscript, sadly, original Seldom Scene member John Starling passed away this year, following in death John Duffey, who died in 1996, and Mike Auldridge, who passed away in 2012.)

eldom Scene Album Cover, 2014
(OVER PHOTO BY MICHAEL OBERMAN)

# Chuck Mangione

## *August 26, 1972*

FUSING JAZZ AND ROCK WITH A SYMPHONY ORCHESTRA IS NOT AN EASY TASK. Chuck Mangione, leading the Rochester Philharmonic, accomplished it with a flair on his two-album set, *Friends and Love . . . A Chuck Mangione Concert*, released last year.

Since then, Mangione, who plays flugelhorn, has recorded another LP, *Together*, which doesn't come off as well as *Friends and Love*.

Chuck currently teaches improvisation at the Eastman School of Music and heads the jazz ensemble there. He is well known and admired by musicians all over the world.

Lew Soloff, trumpet player for Blood, Sweat and Tears, recently said of Chuck, "When I went to the Eastman School of Music ten years ago, everyone was talking about Chuck, who was a sophomore at that time. Before I got to the school, I knew his name because of the recordings he had done with his brother Gap under the name the Jazz Brothers."

Shortly after the Chuck Mangione Quartet was formed in Rochester, Chuck got the idea of writing music for a philharmonic orchestra to complement the basic quartet.

Chuck wrote a concert, "Kaleidoscope," financed it himself, and publicized it. "It was a musical success and a financial disaster," he said.

But that concert led to a request from the Rochester Philharmonic for Chuck to be a guest conductor. Instead of guest conducting, Chuck wrote the entire concert and handled the publicity again.

This time it was a musical and financial success. The concert, "Friends and Love," was recorded for a small label owned by Chuck's brother, Gap. Mercury Records heard it, signed Chuck, and re-released the concert album.

One of the cuts on the album, "Hill Where the Lord Hides," made the charts in a number of cities around the country and the album climbed high on the national charts.

The performance was also videotaped and shown nationally on the NET network. His second album, *Together*, originated in concert form and also was taped for a ninety-minute special scheduled for national broadcast.

At age thirty, Chuck remains humble amidst success. "I believe in the universality of music," he said. "That's what I have striven to achieve through my work.

"But it is hard for me to comprehend that I have achieved some of it. I am amazed that I am involved with something with such a universal appeal."

# Yes

## *September 23, 1972*

Originality is the key to Yes' popularity.

Each of the British quintet's albums has been different, yet totally original and bearing the unmistakable Yes sound.

The group has been around for a long time, but it wasn't until the release of *The Yes Album* that they were recognized outside of Britain.

Three original members of Yes are still in the line-up. They are Jon Anderson, vocals; Chris Squire, bass; and Bill Bruford, percussion. The other members are Steve Howe, who replaced Peter Banks on guitar, and Rick Wakeman who took over keyboard chores from Tony Kaye.

Rick, who attended the Royal College of Music in London, was originally with the Strawbs. "I think it got to the point with the Strawbs where we just weren't right for each other," he said.

"We ended up lacking challenge. Complacency set in and for the last couple of months we just weren't working. I went back to doing a lot of session work and then Steve Howe phoned and asked me if I'd like to go along and play a bit with Yes and see how we all got on."

Rick played mellotron on David Bowie's classic "Space Oddity" and did sessions for Ralph McTell, Cat Stevens, and T. Rex. He could have joined any number of bands, but he chose Yes.

"I think they are moving into what I can only describe as orchestral rock," Rick said. "You've had the heavy bands such as Cream and Who, now we are trying to move on, one stage further into orchestral rock.

"I think we have the same excitement that heavy rock generated, but what Yes is doing is a hell of a lot more complicated and musically refined."

While the group was working on *The Yes Album*, they realized that their music was not ordinary.

"Making it, we suddenly realized in the first two weeks that we were producing it ourselves and we got really frightened," Anderson said. "But, three-quarters of the way through, we realized that for the first time we were making something that might possibly last.

"I'm never sure that the things I've written are going to last any kind of time, so much music seems a momentary thing. In the next ten years, rock music could develop into a higher art form.

"It could build up the same way classical music did—into huge works that last and stand the test of time. Rock musicians will make music that will last a lot longer in the future."

# Musings . . . Claire M. . . .
## the Group Yes . . . and a Suicide Threat

IN 2013, I RECEIVED A NUMBER OF E-MAILS FROM FORMER CELLAR DOOR employee Morty Glickstein (a pseudonym for my friend Keith Krokyn). Morty (Keith) worked at the Cellar Door for several years in the 1970s. Each e-mail had a humorous attachment. Most of the attachments were letters written to the Cellar Door—some irate, some mundane, all amusing.

One of the letters intrigued me. It was from a teenage girl named Claire threatening suicide if Cellar Door wouldn't sell her two front-row tickets to see Yes in concert. Part of me (a very small part of me) wondered if she got her tickets or if she committed suicide. I thought that it might be easy to track her down in the Internet age. Her letter included her last name and the address of where she lived in 1976. I redacted those facts from the letter printed below:

May 6, 1976

Dear Cellar Door promoters:

I have kept my ears open for months to hear about a Yes concert. Now, tonight, I heard Surf on WHFS say the tickets are on sale already for a Peter Frampton/Yes concert on June 13. Those are my two favorite groups in the whole world.

I know that promoters have good tickets set aside and I want you to know that I will commit suicide if I can't buy two front row tickets. Or at the very least, tickets in the first few rows. I swear that my friend and I are the biggest Yes freaks in Washington, and we are going to go all over town to get tickets if we have to. But I really think you should sell me two front row seats PLEASE! Right now

I feel like that's the only thing in the world I want. I'm going to KILL myself if I don't get them. Please write me back, I trust you.

Love,

Claire M.

Don't worry. I can get the money to pay for the tickets. PLEASE help me.

The only spelling error in her letter was the name "Surf." The deejay on WHFS spelled/spells his name Cerphe, but one wouldn't know that unless one saw his name in print. Using various databases, including LinkedIn and Google, I found a woman named Claire with the same last name as the letter writer. She was also from Washington, D.C., but living and working in Paris. I wrote her the following e-mail:

Hello Claire,

Please ignore this email if you are not the same Claire M. who loved the British group, Yes. If you are one and the same . . . please let me know. I have a copy of a very funny letter you wrote to Cellar Door Concerts attempting to get front row tickets to their concert in D.C. in 1976.

Kindest regards,

Michael Oberman

Claire responded,

Hey Michael,

Wow, you are really the champion of follow-up!
    Yep, that is me . . . or I should say YES.
    I'd love to have the letter. If you have scanned it, please copy it also to my best friend Melissa with whom I doubtless wanted to attend that concert.

I'd also be delighted to know how you came upon the letter—and figured out how to find me now.

Kindest regards,

Claire M.
Paris, France

I felt that I should respond,

Hi Claire,

Last things first . . . finding you was easy. Just put your name in Google and there you were . . . process of elimination allowed me to hone in on someone who seemed to be the right age and was American. The letter was emailed to a number of us who had worked at Cellar Door Concerts at some point in our lives. For the last year we have been having some fun reading letters from fans of acts . . . mainly pleas for tickets. Out of the current batch . . . your letter stood out. Not many people (with one exception . . . you) said they would commit suicide if they didn't get tickets. Since I found you alive and hopefully well, I assume you got tickets.

If you ever get back to the D.C. area . . . give me a shout.

Michael Oberman

Claire wrote me back that she did not get the tickets. However, she said that she would be visiting her aunt and uncle who lived in Potomac, Maryland, in the future. She did visit them, and I had a delightful dinner with them. We have been friends ever since. She visited again in 2018, and we spent another delightful day together. If anyone is waiting for a fairy-tale ending, there isn't one. Claire is happily married, and I wasn't looking for a romantic encounter. I am happy that I have a friend—and a friend who lives in Paris. Perhaps I can couch surf at some point.

# Bonnie Raitt

## *November 2, 1972*

ONE OF THE STRONGEST SHOWS IN RECENT MONTHS HAS BEEN BOOKED INTO the Cellar Door starting Monday. John Prine and Bonnie Raitt open for one week, and if you don't have reservations by now, you probably won't get any.

A lot has been written in recent months about Prine, so it's time to dwell on Bonnie Raitt.

Born in Burbank, California, Bonnie moved east with her family before she was a year old—so her father, musical comedy star John Raitt, could take a role on Broadway in *Pajama Game.*

Because of her father's occupation, the family was constantly on the go. In 1957, they ended up back in California. "I always hated L.A.," Bonnie recently recalled.

Her interest in music was nurtured at age ten, when she heard an Odetta record. She started learning to play guitar and by age twelve was playing country blues.

Bonnie was influenced by legendary bluesmen like "Mississippi" John Hurt, Robert Johnson, and Son House and contemporary bluesmen like John Hammond, John Koerner, and Willie Murphy, who produced the first of her two albums for Warner Bros.

"It was really far out when I finally got to play with these people after having listened to them for so long," she said.

After high school, Bonnie went to college in Cambridge, Mass., where a folk music scene was blossoming. She started to play in local clubs when she realized "there were some really bad second acts playing. I thought to myself—what the hell, I can do this."

Her popularity grew and she found herself playing at the Main Point in Philadelphia, the Gaslite in New York, the Philadelphia Folk Festival, and various colleges.

"I never really did like folk music," she said. "I dig soul music. But it can be frustrating not to be able to sing the kind of music you like—like the Temptations.

Bonnie's vocals are a mixture of country blues and soul and her bottle-neck guitar and piano playing seem to naturally blend in with the material she chooses.

Her second album, *Give It Up*, features songs like Barbara George's "I Know," Jackson Browne's "Under the Falling Sky," "If You Gotta Make a Fool of Somebody," and the title cut, "Give It Up or Let Me Go."

# Gram Parsons

## *January 13, 1973*

WHEN GRAM PARSONS FORMED THE INTERNATIONAL SUBMARINE BAND (one of the first country-rock bands to surface in an era of rock 'n' roll) in 1966, he didn't realize how popular country-rock was going to become.

Born in Florida and raised in Waycross, Georgia, Gram was brought up on country, gospel, and black spiritual music.

"I listened to whatever stations my parents would have on," Gram said, "as far back as 1954."

After having played piano as a child, Gram picked up guitar in his early teens. "I just wanted to play guitar because Elvis played one," he said.

"I really hated what I heard on the radio at that time: Bobby Vee, Bobby Vinton, and that whole bit. It was negative inspiration.

"On the other hand," Gram said, "local dance promoters used to hire these incredible black R & B bands and book them into dance halls in small towns during the early sixties. They figured to make a killing since kids in these towns hardly ever heard live music played by a real show group.

"These bands had names like, oh, Big Jake and the Soul Twisters and so on, with big robes and turbans and jewels on their foreheads. But it backfired a lot when parents wouldn't let their kids go to 'that' kind of show.

"They either had to stay home," he said, "or sneak over—and only the local musicians were always in the audience. I imagine these bands didn't even get paid if the show bombed. Hundreds of incredible bands like those never got national recognition for various reasons, and they never will."

In 1965, Gram enrolled at Harvard. Although he didn't last long there, it was in Cambridge where he formed the International Submarine band.

"Country music formed the basis for what we played," Gram said, "but we experimented with some noises. It was one of those bands that rehearsed a lot more than it gigged. We moved down to the Bronx and lived in a big old house. There wasn't much of a country scene there either."

The band was encouraged by a number of friends and the late actor, Brandon De Wilde.

"De Wilde encouraged us," recalled Gram, "and got us a job pretending to play in a Peter Fonda movie in Los Angeles. So, we got out of the cold and went to California, next door to Bakersfield and near some good country radio stations."

The ISB broke up in Los Angeles and Gram joined the Byrds and then the Flying Burrito Brothers. Gram left the Burritos because "the group didn't evolve like I'd hoped it would. I was looking for some kind of total thing, almost like a revue, but it didn't grow that way.

"The Burritos were a group of good musicians, but collectively they weren't what I was looking for in the long run."

Linda Ronstadt and Gram Parsons at WDCA-TV in Bethesda, Maryland
PHOTO BY MIKE KLAVANS

In 1970, Gram was in a motorcycle accident and spent the next two years traveling, writing music, and thinking about his goals.

"When the time came, I was lucky enough to get good people to help, like four people from Elvis' band, and my old friend Rik Grech (an ex-member of Family, Blind Faith, and Traffic) and Byron Berline. There's also a great new female singer named Emmylou Harris."

Emmylou isn't new to Washingtonians, as she's graced this city with her songs for quite a while.

The results of Gram's recording efforts can be heard on his fine new album, simply titled *GP*.

# Little Feat

## *February 24, 1973*

EVERY NOW AND THEN A GROUP COMES ALONG THAT CAN MOVE SMOOTHLY from one type of music to another, always producing a joyous feeling in the listener.

Little Feat is that type of group. Whether playing blues, country or just plain old rock 'n' roll, the sextet (until recently a quartet) shines.

Their first two albums were critically acclaimed but failed to set any sales records. Now, their third album, *Dixie Chicken*, has been released and this should be the one to put the group into the charts.

Formed by ex-Mothers of Invention members, Lowell George and Roy Estrada (who recently left the group to join Captain Beefheart's Magic Band) Little Feat was named for Lowell's size-eight feet.

When Roy left Little Feat, Lowell, Richard Hayward, and Bill Payne were joined by guitarist Paul Barrere, bassist Kenny Gradny, and Sammy Clayton (brother of vocalist Merry) on congas.

Lead guitarist George does much of the group singing and contributes heavily to the writing chores. Richard Hayward was originally with the Fraternity of Man, a group best remembered for their classic tune, "Don't Bogart Me" used in the film *Easy Rider*.

Bill Payne was born in Waco, Texas and became proficient at piano by attending Southern Baptist churches, thus his gospel-blues style. Kenny played bass for Delaney & Bonnie and the Shirelles, among other top groups.

Some of Lowell's tunes, like "Willin'," deal with trucks and life on the highway. Lowell says he likes to write about trucks because, "That's all there is. I mean whether you realize it or not, the whole West Coast is going to look just like the East Coast.

"And it's all going to be one huge hamburger stand from San Francisco to Los Angeles within the next ten years unless everybody says, 'please don't do that.' In Mexico the peasants want land. Well. here the peasants have the land, but the peasants, or the great unwashed middle-class don't know the whole situation.

"The upper class," Lowell says, "speculates on land and sells it to a developer who ruins it forever. Forever. Once there's a hamburger stand on a given spot of land, it'll never come down. It's paved, a permanent landmark.

"That's why I have such a thing about truck drivers. Here are these people who are caught, stuck just like you and I are stuck. And here's this guy who enjoys himself, doing what he's doing, driving trucks. He loves it.

Although there aren't any weak cuts on the album, two stand-out tracks are the title cut, "Dixie Chicken" and "Roll Um Easy."

# Jonathan Edwards

## *March 10, 1973*

"As long as people give me the feedback and as long as I get off on the people to make it worth living in hotels, I'll continue to perform," Jonathan Edwards said between shows at the Cellar Door.

Judging from the audience reaction and the high quality of his music, Edwards should be performing for quite a while.

Jonathan, who has two fine albums under his belt ("Jonathan Edwards" and "Honky-Tonk Stardust Cowboy"), lived in Virginia from fourth grade through his first year of high school. While attending Groveton High, he was accused of setting fire to some houses and was sent off to military school.

"I was one of those weird people, you know, an only child," Jonathan said. "Although I didn't particularly care for the military, I really liked military school. When I got there, I met a lot of people my own age who shared my beliefs."

At military school, he began writing poetry and playing guitar. "People wouldn't listen to poetry that much, so I wrote songs so they could listen to what I had to say.

"I had a Kay guitar and my friend had a Stella and the hours of joy we got out of those axes I'm still trying to recapture," Jon said. "We used to sneak out and catch the bluegrass and country bands that came to town for square dances.

"Such incredible spirit and energy. I remember a group called Harry Buttermilk Snyder and the Buttermilk Drinkers. We'd get them to sit down and show us everything they could."

When he lived in this area, Jonathan used to do the hoots at the Cellar Door and perform at the Blue Sparrow coffeehouse. "The guy at the Blue

Sparrow used to let me sleep on the floor. When I was looking for something to do, I could go there. I still appreciate it."

Now, Jonathan plays the top clubs and concert halls around the country. "At this point," he said, "I like to do both concerts and clubs. In a club it's a quality of energy you get back and in a concert, it's a quantity of energy."

Jonathan has been managed for a number of years by a good friend of his, Peter Casperson. "I really don't get off on the business end of things," Jon said. "I explain to Peter not what I want, but how I feel—unlike most relationships."

Jonathan lives on a farm an hour west of Boston. It affords him the privacy he needs and yet is close enough to the city for his gigs. "I work directly to produce things," he said. "Like growing my own food."

Future plans call for another LP, but for now Jonathan is going to take it easy on his farm. "I've got a lot of friends in Boston who write tunes that when I sing, they're as much me as if I wrote them," he said. "I'll do some of those on my next album and I'll probably do some live tunes."

# AFTER LEAVING MUSIC JOURNALISM
## ...FROM 1973 TO 2019

# Musings . . . Warner/Elektra/Atlantic . . .
## A Brief Stay

I LEFT THE *WASHINGTON STAR* TO WORK FOR WARNER/ELEKTRA/ATLANTIC in late 1973. Three record companies that I greatly admired, Warner Brothers, Elektra, and Atlantic, had formed a distribution company known in the industry as WEA. My friend Eddie Kalicka was the Washington/Baltimore promotion man for Warner Brothers. Eddie and I had been friends since 1967, which was the year I began writing a weekly music column for the *Washington Star*. Eddie was one of the only local promotion men who followed my column and sent me new releases from Warner Brothers and Reprise Records.

Eddie approached me about coming to work for WEA in whatever capacity would eventually lead to a permanent job with a record company. The only opening at the time was the position of junior salesman in Baltimore and Washington, D.C. I took the train to Cherry Hill, New Jersey, where the regional WEA office was located. The interview went well, and I was hired. I was assigned to work for a salesman named Geoff Edwards. Basically, the job entailed going to record stores and inventorying the product distributed by WEA. It was a pretty mindless job, but I had my foot in the door. To this day, I can still remember the catalog numbers of many of the albums I inventoried.

Three months after I began working, Geoff Edwards left the company. I was offered his job and accepted and became a full-time salesman for the company. My territory ranged from Baltimore to Hagerstown, Maryland. Now I had a junior salesman doing the grunt inventory work for me. My main job was to get record stores to buy new releases and catalog product that they were running out of.

I never thought that I would be a salesman, but anything to get my foot in the door of the music industry was a plus for me. Although the main office I reported to was in Cherry Hill, our satellite branch was in Maryland. So, in reality, I had two bosses: the branch manager in Maryland and the sales manager in Cherry Hill.

Before I get to the juicy stuff, let me digress a bit. There were a number of perks working for WEA: free albums, concert tickets, and most importantly, a couple of very cool trips. Elektra Records had their convention on a dude ranch outside of Phoenix, Arizona. On the flight to Phoenix, one of the stewardesses realized that a number of her passengers weren't "normal businessmen." She asked me what company we worked for and what our final destination was going to be. I told her, and she seemed excited. She said to me, "I have a three-day layover in Phoenix. Do you think one of you guys would let me stay in your hotel room for a few nights?" She was very cute! I said, "No problem. You can stay with me."

I hoped the stewardess, who seemed to be a small-town girl, would be cool about it. This was 1974, and any sexually-related diseases could be controlled with medication. I hoped that I would be in the position to find out if I was going to need medication, as I hoped to be having hot sex with this woman. My hope became reality. During the daytime at the convention, there were business meetings, some of which several of us didn't attend. We explored the area around the dude ranch, my first real experiences in the Southwest—cactus, rocky hills, and beautiful sunsets.

After three days, the stewardess had to fly on to catch her next work flight. She gave me her phone number and told me she lived in Tonawanda near Buffalo, New York. Over the next several months, she made sure she had flights to D.C. to visit me. We both knew that a long-distance relationship wouldn't work, and the visits stopped, and I never saw her again.

The other cool trip—and I mean very, very cool trip—was for Atlantic Records' twenty-fifth anniversary party in Paris. Atlantic chartered two 747s, one flying out of Los Angeles and the other out of New York. The plane flying out of New York was an Air India flight. A couple weeks before this trip, those of us going received letters from Atlantic Records with our itineraries and a stern warning not to bring drugs on the trip. At the least, most people in the music business at that time smoked marijuana. Cocaine was also becoming very fashionable. None of us wanted to lose our jobs, so most of us complied with the no-drug rule.

The Air India stewardesses (as they were known back then) were dressed in traditional Indian saris and seemed extremely straight-laced to most of us. Before meal service started, they passed around packages of betel nuts. Rumors started flying around the cabin that if you smoked these nuts, you could get high. Smoking was allowed on flights in those days, but the pungent odor of burning betel nuts might have aroused suspicion among the record company executives on the flight. People started streaming to the bathrooms, where someone had made a pipe out of a toilet paper roll and aluminum foil, and the smoking began.

Others of us began chewing the nuts hoping that we would get some kind of high from them. There seemed to be some truth to that. Historically, the chewing of betel nut quids (betel quid is a combination of betel leaf, areca nut, and slaked lime) has gone on for centuries. In many countries, tobacco is also added, and the product is known as gutka. In the first century AD, Sanskrit medical writings claimed that betel nut possessed thirteen qualities found in the region of heaven. It is pungent, bitter, spicy, sweet, salty, and astringent. It was said to expel wind, kill worms, remove phlegm, subdue bad odors, beautify the mouth, induce purification, and kindle passion. Because of its central nervous system–stimulating effects, betel nut is used in a manner similar to the Western use of tobacco or caffeine. Arecoline is responsible for some of the effects of betel quid chewing, such as alertness, increased stamina, a sense of well-being, euphoria, and salivation. Chewing the nut stimulates the flow of saliva to aid digestion. Betel nut also has been used to stimulate the appetite.

Our appetites were stimulated. Unfortunately, any high that anyone experienced was imagined. Dinner was served, and we were about to find out why Atlantic Records had told us to sit in the front of the plane if we were easily offended and in the rear of the plane if not. I sat in the rear of the plane. Since the plane was chartered by Atlantic Records, Atlantic brought two different movies on board, a PG-rated film for the front of the plane and, much to the surprise of everyone in the rear of the plane, *Deep Throat* for those of us not easily offended. *Deep Throat* was probably the first feature-length porno film with wide distribution. The stewardesses had trouble handing out coffee and tea to us while trying to cover their eyes and not look at Linda Lovelace discovering that her clitoris was in her throat.

The Atlantic Records anniversary party/convention in Paris was a great trip. Just as in the Arizona trip, several of us skipped the business meetings and went out on our own to explore Paris. Our hotel, Le Meridien Etoile, was almost brand new, as it opened in 1972. Each guest room had a machine that looked like a modern version of an old-time cigarette pack–dispensing machine. However, this machine dispensed miniature liquor bottles (all top shelf). Atlantic Records had made the mistake of telling us to not worry about anything that we charged to our rooms. Well, each time we inserted our room key into the liquor-dispensing machine, a charge of several dollars went on our room bill. On the day we were checking out of the hotel, I inserted my room key into the machine and emptied it of at least 100 miniature bottles of liquor. I realized the bottles wouldn't fit in my suitcase and if they did could break and wreak havoc on my clothing. I bought an inexpensive rucksack and filled it with the miniatures.

The flight back from Paris to New York City was uneventful—none of the shenanigans that went down a week earlier on the flight to Paris. Arriving at customs in New York, I wasn't sure how they would react to my rucksack loaded down with 100 miniatures of liquor, liqueurs, and wine. I figured the worst that could happen would be that they would confiscate the bottles or figure out some sum of money that I would owe for bringing that amount of spirits into the United States. When I reached the customs agent, he lifted the rucksack and said, "Oh, wow, what do you have in there?" I responded, "Spirits." He unzipped it, and a smile lit up his face. "How did you come by these?" He asked, and I explained. He laughed and said, "Just go on through. I'm not going to add up the amounts in each bottle and figure out a total, take too much time. Have fun and welcome back home." Well, all those miniatures made nice little birthday gifts, anniversary presents, table toppers at parties, and so on. I think it took more than two years to use them all up.

Time to go back to work and sell records. There was one main problem, and his name was Everett Smith. Everett was the Maryland branch manager and my direct boss. His idea of a workday was to come into the office around 11 a.m. and show those of us who worked there Polaroid photos he had taken of nude women. Everett liked to frequent massage parlors and photo studios where you paid to photograph women in the buff. It wasn't my thing, but I could live with it if that was all that was wrong with Everett. But that was the tip of the iceberg.

One of my accounts in Baltimore was a "mom and pop" record store, not part of a chain, in a shopping mall in Baltimore. When the Rolling Stones album *Goat's Head Soup* was announced, the store owner told me they wanted to order 1,000 copies of it. I asked them if they were certain, as there really wasn't room in the store for 1,000 copies of any one album. They said they were certain. They wanted to stack the albums all over the store. They wanted window displays. I think they were hoping to sell at least a couple of hundred of them, knowing at that point in time that Warner/Elektra/Atlantic accepted 100 percent returns on unsold goods. Okay, so this small store wanted to take a risk-free chance, and I was okay with that. After all, I would receive a commission on the sale.

Well, the albums shipped to the store, and six weeks later the store had sold only about seventy-five copies. No problem, I told them. I'll just write up a return authorization, Everett will sign it, and you can ship the albums back that didn't sell. I went to see Everett at the office and told him that the store was returning more than 900 albums. He hit the ceiling. Okay, so the branch manager wasn't happy, but he had to sign the return authorization as per how the company operated. A few weeks later, I went back to the store that had ordered the LPs, and the owner asked me when he would see the credit on his account. I was surprised it had not happened already, and I went back to the office to talk to Everett. He wasn't in and was probably taking care of his porno needs somewhere in Baltimore. I opened the desk drawer where he usually kept the return authorizations. I expected that he had sent the authorization to the main branch in Cherry Hill and that I would not find it sitting in his drawer. Was I ever wrong! There was a stack of unsigned return authorization in his desk. Besides mine, there were others dating back several months. There was nothing I could do except go over his head and talk to the branch manager in Cherry Hill and try to get the matter straightened out. I did. The store got the credit they were owed, but now I was on Everett's shit list.

The incident with the Rolling Stones LP gave me pause to think about whether I still wanted to work at this branch office. I decided that I was working for major record companies and that I should stick it out until a position with either Warner Brothers, Elektra, or Atlantic opened in one of their main offices. That decision didn't last long. On Christmas Day, I received a phone call from the buyer of one of my largest accounts.

"Michael, can you meet me at our Towson, Maryland, location?" I said, "It's Christmas Day. Is this urgent?" She responded, "Yes, or I wouldn't be calling you on Christmas." I told her I would meet her there in two hours, all the while wondering what could be so urgent that I would have to meet her in the parking lot of her Towson location. When I arrived, she was standing outside of her car with a package partially wrapped in Christmas wrapping. I thought, maybe she had a gift for me, but why couldn't it wait until after Christmas? But it's really me who should be giving her a gift.

As I approached her, she had a dour look on her face. "Michael, she said, "I want you to see the Christmas present that Everett Smith sent to me." I opened the box, and staring me in the face was a dildo. Yes, a sex toy—obviously not an expensive dildo because it had a hand crank on the end instead of being battery-operated. "Holy cow," I said to her, or some such words. "I can't believe this. Well, actually, I can believe this. It fits Everett's modus operandi." She asked what I meant, and I said I would rather not say at this moment. I apologized for the company and said, "If you will let me take this gift up to our Cherry Hill office and talk to them, I would appreciate it." Off I drove with the dildo. When the office in Cherry Hill reopened after the Christmas break, I took the train from Baltimore to Cherry Hill to see Marv Slaveter, the regional branch manager. I handed Marv the dildo and told him the story and explained that I could no longer work for Everett Smith. The guy did not sign return authorizations and sent a Christmas gift of a sex toy to the buyer of one of my largest accounts. Marvin asked me if that meant I was quitting. I said yes. Marvin asked if I would please stay with the company. They valued me as an employee. Would I like to move to the Atlanta branch, the Boston branch, or anywhere else in the country? I said, "No, I'm giving you my two-week notice. Two weeks later, I was no longer an employee of Warner/Elektra/Atlantic and was looking for another job in the music industry. A friend of mine who still worked at Warner/Elektra/Atlantic told me that a few weeks after my meeting in Cherry Hill, Everett was told to report to Cherry Hill. He was fired for his untoward digressions and not just the ones I had reported but apparently others that had poured into the office. I was told that Everett left quickly after being fired and that he forgot his briefcase at the office. Marv opened the briefcase and found rubber tongue extensions, another dildo, nude photos and 8-mm pornographic films.

Next stop for me was a new job search.

# Musings . . . Record Distribution and Geoff Edwards

I MET GEOFFREY EDWARDS IN LATE 1973 WHEN I WENT TO WORK AS HIS assistant at Warner/Elektra/Atlantic distribution in Maryland. We have remained friends since that time. Geoff and his partner, Harriet, spend winters in Florida. Lucky me: they have an extra condo that I often use for a week or two while they are in the Sunshine State.

I sat down with Geoff in 2019 and let him talk about his life in the music business and beyond. These are his words:

What was my first paying job in music? My first paying job, I was just a stock boy in RCA's warehouse. That was a long time ago, a long time ago. It was 1965 to be exact. As a stock boy, the only thing I learned was that I didn't want to be a stock boy. I wanted to be a sales guy because that is where I had come from. Previous to the stock boy job, I was selling "brown goods" (television sets, audio equipment, and similar household appliances) at the RCA distributorship. When the music end merged with the brown goods end, I ended up being demoted. So, I ended up pulling records and eight-track tapes, and that's not what I wanted to be doing. I was doing it for the stores in Washington, D.C. I got to know all the stores. I knew the buyers for the stores because they wanted RCA product. Like Elvis Presley. What was better than Elvis Presley at that time? The Beatles certainly happened in 1964, but Elvis's comeback was really a motivator for sales.

I was hired away from RCA by Steve Ross, who was at that time putting together a music conglomerate called WEA, which stood for Warner/Elektra/Atlantic Records. Ross found me because while

I was with RCA, a couple of records that I promoted broke out of the Washington area. Actually, I stopped being a stock boy and became a promotion guy because Joe Del Medico (a well-known promotion guy) fell in love with a woman while at a conference in Florida. He decided he didn't want to be a promotion guy anymore. I was right there at RCA, and they needed somebody to take his place. The first act I ever worked with at RCA was Lana Cantrell. I was successful in promotion. A lot of acts came through D.C. One thing led to another, and I made friendships like with you.

So, when I went over to Warner/Elektra/Atlantic, Eddie Kalicka (Warner Bros.' promo man) said, "I'd like to get Michael Oberman a job here." There was incredible financial growth in the music business from that time forward and for the next I don't know how many years. Before Warner/Elektra/Atlantic formed their distribution company, there were only three labels, RCA, Columbia, and Capitol, who distributed their own product to the stores. Most labels were distributed in the D.C./Maryland/Virginia area by independent distributors like Schwartz Brothers or Zamoiski. Eddie Kalicka came out of Schwartz Brothers. When Eddie left Schwartz Brothers, he had already been working for Warner Bros. So, when the Warner/Elektra/Atlantic company was founded, Eddie worked there for Warner Bros.

When I came on board at Warner/Elektra/Atlantic, I guess I was the de facto branch manager. Joe Del Medico replaced me, and I became a sales guy. Everything was exploding. The business was taking in so much money. I was let go from WEA after about eighteen months I think. Fired. Getting fired from there was the best thing that ever happened to me. I was twenty-three or twenty-four, had a couple of kids and a wife and a lot of responsibilities. Getting fired pushed me to the next stage of my life. I told my boss at the time, Marv Slaveter, as they say in the song, "Take This Job and Shove It." I said that in his ear, not out in public. It turned out it wasn't Marv who was responsible for me getting fired. I think he sort of respected my saying to shove the job. I was selling so much that I was making more money and commissions than the sales manager made in his salary.

The real reason I left WEA was because George Rossi terminated me. His reason for terminating me was my attitude. I enjoyed my job. The Elektra conference in Litchfield Park, Arizona, was exciting. I mean the Doors were there, Carly Simon. That was really exciting. Then Atlantic Records announces their twenty-fifth anniversary party is going to be a weeklong trip to Paris. It included everyone from the branches to the main office from high level down to inventory clerks. That Paris trip may have been part of my undoing. You know, we didn't attend meetings. We went out and saw Paris.

Going back to Warner Bros. for a minute, the death of Lowell George of Little Feat was like the death of John Lennon to me. I had long hair, a ponytail back in those days, but I wasn't a hippie. I mean I had two kids, and I wore Alligator shirts you know.

After leaving WEA, I went to work for ABC Records, but that imploded in a scandal that I don't want to talk about. Then I spent a short time at a local label, Adelphi Records. I really didn't like it there, but I got to promote and sell an album by a group you managed, the Rosslyn Mountain Boys.

After Adelphi, I never worked for another record company. I went to work for a company that manufactured plastic shopping carts for grocery stores. I remember the scene from the movie *The Graduate* where, "plastics my son, get into plastics." I did very, very well there. When I left that business, I simply retired.

# Musings . . . Some Things Geoff Didn't Say about Record Sales and Distribution

IN THE 1970S, A LOT OF ALBUMS SHIPPED GOLD, MEANING THAT 500,000 OF any one LP were shipped to stores. In essence, albums were being certified as "gold records" even before the public had purchased them. Why should this have mattered, and how was it happening? It mattered because when radio stations saw (mostly through the *Billboard* and *Cashbox* charts) that albums were "gold," stations that might not have been playing one of those albums didn't want to be left in the dust, so those stations started playing those albums. It was happening for several reasons, two of which I will elaborate on. First was the fact that record stores could return 100 percent of unsold goods. That meant that if a salesperson for a label went to a store and said, "Mr. Store Manager, order 100 copies of the new album by Atomic Rooster. Here's a box of twenty-five LPs for you to keep at no charge," the store would order 100 Atomic Rooster albums, sell only two, and return ninety-eight. They get to keep the twenty-five free albums, and the label reports sales figure of the 100 that were originally shipped to the store.

Because stores are reporting to *Billboard* and *Cashbox* on the numbers of albums ordered, suddenly Atomic Rooster is on the charts. Goal accomplished. The other thing that was going on was something called "store lists." Store lists were basically sheets of paper under the counter with numbers that might range from 1 to 100 in the left margin. A salesman for a label goes into a store and might say, "Mr. Store Manager, here's a box of LPs for you to keep at no charge. Can I see your store list?" The salesman takes the list and, not being greedy, writes next to the number 14 (pick any number that hasn't already been filled in) "Atomic Rooster." That signifies that the album by Atomic Rooster is the fourteenth best-selling LP in the store. Why does that matter? It matters because radio stations called a number of stores in their broadcast area to find out what was selling. So, WXXX calls a store and finds out that Atomic Rooster is selling (based on false information), and the music director of the station thinks, "We better start playing Atomic Rooster." Additionally, *Billboard* and *Cashbox* call stores around the country, and they are fed the same false information. Let me say, I witnessed this firsthand when I was a salesman at WEA.

A lot of artists who have gold or platinum albums framed, on the wall, and certified as gold or platinum by the Recording Industry Association of America either achieved those sales legitimately or their albums never should have been certified gold or platinum.

When the term "payola" is thrown around, what comes to mind is a disc jockey accepting money, drugs, prostitutes, trips to the Bahamas, or other things of value in return for playing a record. In my mind, payola should also refer to what was going on in record stores prior to 1991.

The "sea change" that brought some honesty to "sales numbers" occurred in 1991. That was the year that Nielsen SoundScan came out. SoundScan is a tracking system operated by the Nielsen Corporation that tracks sales of music and music video products throughout the United States and Canada. Any music product that carries a UPC or EAN bar code and ISRC code is eligible to be tracked by Nielsen SoundScan. According to their website, "Sales data from point-of-sale cash registers is collected weekly from over 14,000 retail, mass merchant and non-traditional (on-line stores, venues, etc.) outlets. Weekly data is compiled and made available every Wednesday. Nielsen SoundScan is the sales source for the Billboard music charts."

When SoundScan came into widespread use, groups like Fishbone that were charting in the top ten dropped off the charts. Artists like Garth Brooks were suddenly in the top ten when the week before they weren't even in the top 200. SoundScan proved that country and other genres that weren't represented on the charts were, in reality, selling.

Thank you, SoundScan!

# Musings . . . In the Cellar Door . . . Out the Cellar Door

After my departure from Warner/Elektra/Atlantic, my friend Eddie Kalicka asked me if I would like to talk to Jack Boyle about working for him at the Cellar Door nightclub. The Cellar Door was one of the premier clubs in the United States for musicians and comedians—Neil Young, Joni Mitchell, Buddy Rich, Steve Martin, Linda Ronstadt, James Taylor, Jackson Browne, Miles Davis, and John Denver—and had a seating capacity of around 250, squeezed into a space that was really meant for 125.

I was very familiar with the club. I did many interviews in the dressing room above the club. The club established its reputation under the ownership of Charles Fichman, who had worked his way up as waiter, bartender, cook, manager, part owner, and finally, in 1964, full owner. Most of my interviews at the club happened when Fichman owned the venue. Fichman was laid back and a guy who always made me feel comfortable.

I didn't know Jack Boyle when Eddie asked about my interest in working for him. Eddie arranged for me to meet Jack. At that time, Jack's staff consisted of people who worked in the club itself: bartenders, waiters, cooks, soundmen, and doormen. His office staff was basically Jack and a secretary who also took reservations for the club.

Jack was very different than Fichman. I couldn't really "read" him. He asked me what my salary was at WEA, and after a ten-minute interview, he offered me the job as his assistant at the same salary I made at WEA. I accepted, not knowing what really was in store for me.

Among my duties was doing all publicity for the club, buying newspaper and radio advertising for the club, and doing anything else that came to Jack's mind. At first, my hours were 10 a.m. to 6 p.m. Often, I wouldn't leave the club until late at night, usually when I wanted to stay and catch a set or two of whomever was performing.

It didn't take long before my duties included booking acts into the club. That was fairly easy, as Jack would tell me whom he wanted booked and the parameters of the money offer to the artist's agency. Jack always liked to tell people, "I don't know anything about music. I don't even have a record player." That was true. What Jack knew was how to make money, lots of money. Jack knew that Joni Mitchell or John Denver meant dollar signs. Major booking agencies loved the Cellar Door and would put the cream of the crop into the club knowing that Jack would take up-and-coming acts of theirs as openers for the headliners.

Jack had a large office above the club at 34th and M streets in Georgetown. Jack's office was beautiful and brick walled with a window overlooking M Street. My office was tiny but private. There was also a dressing room on the same floor and another office the same size as Jack's. When I started working at the Cellar Door, the office that wasn't used by Jack was empty save a desk and a couple of chairs.

The empty office became occupied about six weeks after I started working for Jack. When I accepted the job, Jack had not told me that he had a partner named Sam L'Hommedieu. Sam was the new occupant of the office. While Jack and Sam were partners, they were like oil and water. I soon became caught in the middle of partners who didn't really care for each other. Jack would buzz my office and say, "Mike, try to get Mary Travers [of Peter, Paul and Mary] booked into the club. Sam would then buzz my office and say, "Mike, don't book Mary Travers."

A few weeks after Sam moved into his office, I stayed late at the club to catch a performance. The bartender that night loaded my drinks. I knew I couldn't drive home. I went upstairs and decided to sleep it off on the couch in Jack's office. I woke up around 4 a.m. and realized my face had been laying in a pool of vomit (my own of course). I got up and went into Sam's office and went to sleep on his couch. At around 7:30 that morning, I felt someone shaking my shoulder. It was Sam. "Mike," he said. "Do you have any idea who threw up on Jack's couch?"

I knew I had been the culprit, but I replied, "No Sam." Sam never brought it up again.

As Cellar Door grew from the club to Cellar Door Productions, my job expanded, but my salary did not. Jack and Sam knew that acts like Gordon Lightfoot could sell out the Cellar Door for two weeks straight. Why not do Gordon in concert for one night and make as much or more money than having him at the club? Constitution Hall and the Kennedy Center were two of the concert venues that Cellar Door Productions began using. Now, I also had to do publicity and advertising for concerts in addition to the club. I was also asked to make certain that everything that was in the riders to artist contracts for concerts was taken care of, from food in the dressing room to number of stagehands to sound equipment.

One day, Jack called me into his office. He had a big grin on his face. "Mike, we just landed the contract to do all concerts at the Capital Centre." The Capital Centre had recently been built as a sports arena by Abe Pollin, owner of the National Basketball Association's Washington Bullets (now the Washington Wizards). Jack threw me the keys to his Mercedes and asked me to deliver the signed concert deal to Mr. Pollin. Now, we had a 19,000-seat arena to book. Any promoter who wanted to do a concert at the Capital Centre had to partner with Cellar Door or go elsewhere.

While I was learning a lot about concert promotion and production, my work hours had expanded from forty hours a week to more than seventy hours a week. I went to Jack and Sam and asked for a pay raise. They agreed to a $50 bump in pay. That just wasn't enough to justify getting home at 1 a.m. from a concert and having Sam call me at 7 a.m. to ask how the concert went.

Mentally, I was ready to resign. I needed to find another way to stay in the music business and make a living. That other way came in the form of a band called the Rosslyn Mountain Boys, who gave me the impetus to tell Jack I was resigning.

# Musings . . . Management . . .
# Part Two . . . The Rosslyn Mountain Boys

I HAD ALREADY MADE UP MIND TO LEAVE CELLAR DOOR. LIFE IS TOO short to be an employee of a company owned by two people who did not share the vision of where the company should be heading, Jack Boyle telling me to do one thing and Sam L'Hommedieu telling me to do the opposite. Add a pretty lousy salary and long working hours, and all I needed was to have some kind of sign that the time was right to say, "I quit!"

That sign came with four feet clomping up the stairs outside my office. Two feet belonged to Joe Triplett and two to Bob Berberich. I had managed Joe when he was in Claude Jones, and I had known Bob Berberich for years from his time playing drums for the Hangmen to his role as drummer in Nils Lofgren's great trio, Grin.

Joe and Bob came into my office, and after some small talk, Joe said to me, "Mike, you should come hear our band, the Rosslyn Mountain Boys." I knew that meant they were looking for management, or they wouldn't have driven to Georgetown just to invite me to hear their band. I told them I would come to their next gig.

I went to see the band at the Shamrock Tavern in Georgetown. The Shamrock was a real honky-tonk in a combination gentrified and hippie neighborhood. The crowd tended to be "working-class" lovers of country music. Much to my surprise, besides Joe and Bob, two other members of the band were guys I knew, Jay Sprague on bass and Happy Acosta on guitar. Jay and Happy had also been in Claude Jones. The fifth member of the band was Tommy Hannum on pedal steel guitar. After one set of music, I knew I wanted to manage the group. Although the name of the band evoked bluegrass, this wasn't a bluegrass band. Rather, they played some old-school country, rockabilly, and rock 'n' roll, a combination of original material written by both Joe and Tommy and cover songs made their own with a unique sound.

From a 2009 online blog by Rich McManus explaining the origins of the band:

Of course there's no such thing as the Rosslyn Mountains. The name poked fun at the ridiculous City-in-a-Box that Rosslyn, Virginia, just across the Potomac River from D.C., was becoming in the 1970s. Two young guys—Happy Acosta and Joe Triplett—were getting ready to perform as a freshly minted duo in front of a barroom audience. They needed a name in a hurry, so Acosta blurted it out, in tribute to the neighborhood where the two musicians shared what Triplett calls "a shack."

"I thought the name was kind of lame, but it was just for one night," said Triplett. "I mean, we weren't going to call ourselves 'Joe and Happy.'"

The year was 1973. The inaugural show was at a bar called the 21st Amendment, on Pennsylvania Ave. The two friends were already veterans of a host of bands whose names were never destined to appear on anyone's iPod playlist (ever hear of the Jackals or the Human Zeroes?). Joe had most recently spent 3 years as a member of Claude Jones, which was Warrenton, Virginia's answer to the Grateful Dead—a hippie band whose members all lived together at a rural outpost they called The Amoeba Farm. Acosta had been a guitarist in the band. A picture of the group, sprawled across a rustic hillside, had run in the Style section of the Washington Post. "We were the darlings of the Washington rock scene in 1970," notes Triplett wistfully.

Though a virtual unknown, Triplett had, even at this obscure junction of his life, already accomplished something the best bands in the world had not: he had knocked the Beatles out of the number 1 slot on Washington AM radio.

In 1966, while home on summer vacation from studies at Kentucky's Transylvania University, Triplett had been the lead singer in a band called The Reekers. The band, a bunch of suburban Maryland kids, had a hit on its hands called "What A Girl Can't Do."

"It was a concerted effort to sound like the Beatles," he remembers. But bandleader and guitarist Tom Guernsey felt stardom would be hampered by such a noxious name, so the musicians came up with something that sounded more radio-ready—The Hangmen.

Their high-energy hit, which featured Triplett growling "I don't wanna have to tell you what a girl can't do," bumped the Beatles' "We Can Work It Out" from the top of the charts, at least for a few weeks, Guernsey recalls in an online interview.

No one growing up in D.C. in the 1960s heard that song and said, "That's Joe Triplett." It was a Tom Guernsey and the Hangmen song. Yet in each of its 2 minutes, 27 seconds, the tune delivered exactly what Triplett has always delivered, and still delivers to this day—raw assurance that the singer believes his song.

"I always wanted to play country music, and became a convert to hard-core country—Merle Haggard, Hank Williams, George Jones," Triplett said. "I thought, God, that's what I want to do. That's what I really love."

Prior to the RMB's debut, the original two Mountain Boys, Triplett and Acosta, "sat around for months listening to Waylon Jennings, Willie Nelson, the Osborne Brothers, Jimmie Rodgers," Triplett recalls. "Hap turned me on to a lot of stuff I'd never heard of." The duo soon added drummer Bob Berberich, a fellow Washingtonian who had played with Grin, guitarist Nils Lofgren's (now of Bruce Springsteen's E St. Band) breakout band.

In June 1974, classic-era RMB blossomed when Bonta was lured away from the Nighthawks by Triplett and Acosta. "Happy and Joe came to see me playing with the Nighthawks at the [Washington nightclub] Reading Gaol, since the 'Hawks were really garnering a hot local rep," Bonta remembers. "They asked me to join and I was actually the band's first bass player because they couldn't afford to have me and a bass player. They asked if I played bass and I lied and said, 'Sure!' I bought a bass and played it for a few weeks until we had enough gigs to ask Claude Jones' bassist, Jay Sprague, to join.

"I was a huge fan of Joe's since the Hangmen and Claude Jones," Bonta recalls. "I couldn't believe the great Joe Triplett wanted me to join the band."

"Our first break came when we became the house band at the Shamrock Tavern in Georgetown," drummer Berberich recalls.

Soon after, the RMB earned a weekly engagement Wednesday nights at the now-venerable Birchmere nightclub, then located in a storefront off of I-395 in Virginia near Shirlington. Audiences grew by word of mouth—"Triplett had people in the audience crying last night"—and clubs were packed whenever they played.

"We had lines around the block to get in the Birchmere, [and other Washington clubs including] Desperado's and the Cellar Door," said Berberich. Adds Triplett, "We were drawin' pretty good back then. I remember seeing lines snaking out the door and thinking, 'Wow, they're lined up around the block to see us.'"

"If there's one thing that consistently sets the Rosslyn Mountain Boys apart from the pack of local bands who ply their trade nightly in the D.C. and suburban bars, it is the emotional credibility of their music," wrote Joe Sasfy, a music critic for Washington's alternative weekly, *The Unicorn Times*. Sasfy, now a consultant to Time-Life's music division, published perhaps the definitive review of the band in 1977. "With a stage presence and vocal style that are the most captivating of any performer in the D.C. area, Triplett acts out a nightly drama of cheatin' women, perplexed lovers, juiced rednecks, tired truckers and stifled lust," Sasfy continued. "Triplett is able to stand in the center of each song and claim it as his own."

"That was the high-water mark of the band," recalls Bonta. Their first self-titled record had come out on Adelphi Records in 1976 and was selling well regionally. He and Triplett fondly recall a weekend bill at the Stardust Inn in rural Waldorf, Maryland, where the RMB opened for Conway Twitty and Loretta Lynn.

"Conway was totally impressed that Joe sang 'I Didn't Lose Her, I Threw Her Away,'" said Bonta. "Conway was dumbstruck. He said, 'I never do that live because I can't hit the notes.'" Triplett remembers the frenzy that Twitty generated among the women—many of them in bee-hive hairdos—who had come to the show. "I thought the place was gonna melt."

By this time in the band's history, the lineup had changed to Joe Triplett, vocals and rhythm guitar; Peter Bonta, keyboards and guitar; Rico Petruccelli, bass; Tommy Hannum, pedal steel guitar and vocals; and Bob

Berberich, drums and vocals. While Triplett took most of the lead vocals, democracy in the band led to everyone doing lead vocals occasionally.

While the band's first album had done well in large part to heavy airplay on WHFS-FM, the band and I made the decision not to do another album for Adelphi Records. The songs on the first album have stood the test of time. I am biased to loving the cover art for that LP, partly because I did the front and back cover photographs, and graphic artist Dick Bangham did a fabulous job airbrushing color onto my black-and-white photos.

The follow-up album was titled *Lone Outsider*. Like the first album, it was recorded at Bias Studios in Falls Church, Virginia, with Bob Dawson engineering. Unlike the first album, we had Neil Young's producer, David Briggs, producing the sessions. David knew Bob Berberich from working on Grin album projects. The Internal Revenue Service had put a lien on David's income for failure to pay back taxes. David told us, "I'll produce the album. Just pay for me to get to the East Coast [from California], give me a place to sleep, enough tequila, and some other shit and we'll just do it."

It was pretty exciting and a bit scary to have Briggs in town for the recording project: exciting because of his credentials, scary because of his reputation as a barroom brawler. Mixing tequila with brawling kept me on the edge of my seat the entire time Briggs was in town. The closest he came to fisticuffs was a night when the band was playing at a D.C. club called Childe Harold. It was a small club but one with a great reputation with acts like Emmylou Harris and Bruce Springsteen gracing the venue. That night we had an A & R executive from Capitol Records at the club to hear the band. He was in the upstairs dressing room with the band when word came that someone from an independent label was going to come upstairs to the dressing room. That "someone" was a person no one in the band wanted to see, especially with a major label rep in the house. Briggs got out of his chair in the dressing room and walked out to the landing at the top of the stairs when that "someone" began to walk up the stairs. I remember saying to Briggs, "Just don't hurt the guy!" To this day, I'm sorry I said that. The independent label "someone" saw Briggs glaring at him and decided to turn around and leave.

By the time the band had finished laying all the tracks for the new album, everyone was pretty happy about the way things had gone in the studio. Now it was time to do final mixes on the tracks. Apparently, someone thought it would be a good idea for some of us, including Briggs, to take a dose of the drug MDMA. (From the National Institutes of Health website, "3,4-methylenedioxy-methamphetamine [MDMA] is a synthetic drug that alters mood and perception [awareness of surrounding objects and conditions]. It is chemically similar to both stimulants and hallucinogens, producing feelings of increased energy, pleasure, emotional warmth, and distorted sensory and time perception.") In today's parlance, MDMA is better known as Ecstasy or Molly.

In the studio control room, on the wall facing the mixing console, were four huge speaker cabinets. Actually, only two housed speakers. The other two were empty but had speaker grill cloths hiding the emptiness. Before Briggs entered the control room, we took the grill cloth off of one of the cabinets. Joe Triplett stood on a chair and managed to get inside the cabinet. We put the grill cloth back on the cabinet, and nothing looked amiss.

Now, the fun was about to begin. We were mixing the title track, "Lone Outsider," with Briggs and Bob Dawson at the controls. Beginning with a playback of the song before the mix was to start, ominous words could be heard coming from the speakers about midway through the song. "Briggs sucks," was being whispered by Triplett, secreted in the speaker cabinet.

"Okay, who was the asshole who said that while we were recording," a very stoned Briggs shouted. "Now I have to isolate which track that's on." Playing back just the bass track, "Briggs sucks" is heard at the same point in the song that it was heard on the initial playback. "Okay," Briggs says, "I guess we'll have to rerecord the bass." Then Briggs plays back the vocal track, and "Briggs sucks" is heard at the same point in the song. "Fuck," an agitated and stoned Briggs shouts. "That can't be on every track." Briggs plays the drum track, and there it is again. At that point, Triplett kicks out the grill cloth and jumps down from his hiding place—anger, then relief, then stoned laughter from Briggs—a classic prank pulled off seamlessly.

With the album finished and Briggs on his way back to California, I began making appointments to play the album for record companies in Los Angeles. Little did I know that John Travolta and the Bee Gees would be my biggest stumbling block in Los Angeles.

My first appointment was with Epic Records. I was sitting in a waiting area in the A & R department when Rick Nelson walked out of the office where I was about to have my appointment. Rick, to my surprise and delight, recognized me and asked what I was doing at Epic. I told him, and he replied, "I hope your album doesn't have pedal steel guitar on it." I said it did and asked him why that would be a problem. "Mike," he said, "Epic just dropped me and the Stone Canyon Band. They don't want anything that sounds country. 'Saturday Night Fever' has killed it for us." Truer words were never spoken.

With 15 million copies sold in the United States alone, *Saturday Night Fever* was the top-selling sound track album of all time before being supplanted by *The Bodyguard* some fifteen years later. It's also one of the only disco records to win the Grammy for Album of the Year.

Record companies, I have found, are usually not innovators. After disco hit, labels would say, "Bring me disco." After Springsteen hit, they would say "Bring me another Springsteen." Eventually, the cycle peters out, and you hear, "Don't bring me disco" or "Don't bring me anything that sounds like Springsteen."

Unfortunately, I was shopping a band to labels that were saying, "Bring me disco" and "No steel guitar." Our album had pedal steel guitar on every cut. When I struck out in Los Angeles, I knew the end was nearing for the Rosslyn Mountain Boys. I returned to D.C. with the bad news. We were all crestfallen, but I think Joe Triplett took it the hardest.

One night I suggested to Joe that we go see the movie *Payday*. I had already seen it and thought that Rip Torn deserved an Oscar for his starring role as a hardscrabble country singer. We went, and Joe loved the movie. We had always wrestled with the band's name. Record companies automatically thought the band was bluegrass without even hearing a single note. After all, how many bands with "Mountain Boys" in their names didn't kindle banjos, fiddles, and bluegrass?

Our final mistake wasn't changing the band's name. It was changing the name and the music. We decided to give "making the big time" one last chance. We changed the name of the band to Payday. The band worked up kind of a "soul medley" of "Stubborn Kind of Fella," "Devil with a Blue Dress," and "And I Thank You." I had set up a showcase gig in New York City and invited more than a dozen record company executives in addition to agents and publicists. I also chartered a bus to take sixty-five of our fervent fans from D.C. to New York and back to ensure that we had a cheering audience. While the gig was good, it didn't get the band a deal.

Joe decided to move to Los Angeles to woodshed and write songs. Payday continued to perform, but without Joe, it wasn't the same. The band broke up.

Postscript: Everyone in the band continued (and as I write this book continues) to play music. Among their accomplishments, Rico went on to be bass player for Mary Chapin Carpenter; Tommy moved to Nashville and became pedal steel player for Ricky Van Shelton and then for Wynonna Judd; Peter Bonta joined Artful Dodger before opening Wally Cleaver's Recording Studio in Fredericksburg, Virginia; and Bob married vocalist Martha Hull, and he and Martha continued performing in a number of bands before opening Vinyl Acres, a store specializing in good old twelve-inch vinyl LPs. Joe Triplett has a farm in the hinterlands of Virginia. He has continued to record both singles and albums as a solo artist.

Rosslyn Mountain Boys Album Cover
(COVER PHOTO TAKEN IN BLACK AND WHITE BY MICHAEL OBERMAN, AIRBRUSHED IN COLOR BY DICK BANGHAM)

# Musings . . . Management . . . Part Three . . . Gene Ryder . . . Beginning of the End

THE YEAR WAS 1985. I MET GENE RYDER WHEN MY LANDLADY HIRED HIM to paint the exterior of my house in D.C. He soon realized I was in the music business. One day, after he finished painting, he handed me a cassette recording and told me he was a musician and had a demo he recorded at Wally Cleaver's Studio in Fredericksburg. What a coincidence: the studio was owned and run by Peter Bonta, whom I managed when he was in the Rosslyn Mountain Boys. I listened to the tape and thought the songs were great and the playing stellar. Steuart Smith was lead guitarist on the demos and has now been a lead guitarist with the Eagles for years.

I had a trip to Los Angeles planned for about a month after Gene finished painting the house. I didn't tell Gene I was taking his demo with me. I had been working on another project that was good (I'll call that Project X) but not as good as Gene's demo. I was obligated to shop Project X, with Gene's demo in my briefcase as a back-up. I had always made it my business to be in an A & R rep's office when he or she played a demo I had brought with me. I could judge their enthusiasm (or lack thereof) by the looks on their faces and whether they were taking phone calls while a demo was playing or whether they were hitting "Fast Forward" a lot. Project X elicited a lot of fast-forwards and everyone saying, "Good, but I'll pass." Passing meant no. One step above passing would have been, "Good, but I'd like to hear more." The best answer would be, "Good, when can I see the act onstage?"

If an artist wasn't located in Los Angeles, New York, or Nashville, that usually meant the artist would need to play in one of those cities. That way, a number of record companies could see the act at one time. Otherwise, if an act was showcasing in their hometown, it would be difficult to even get one record company to fly into town, much less several.

So, each time Project X got a thumbs-down, I would say, "Do you have time to listen to something else?" Almost everyone said yes. I could tell by the reactions on their faces when I played Gene's demo that everyone liked it. And, yes, almost everyone asked, "When can I see him live?"

I phoned Gene back on the East Coast. He had no idea that I had been playing his demo for record companies. He seemed surprised and delighted. Now, he needed to put together a band. The musicians on the demo weren't a band per se. A band was now necessary for any showcase gigs for record companies.

When I returned home to D.C., there were two priorities. The first and most obvious was in Gene's hands: getting a band together. The second priority was mine: figuring out where the money would come from for me to manage Gene Ryder full-time. I had been living off of rapidly dwindling savings and some money I made by teaching a class called "The Music Business Course."

I knew that musicians, songwriters, booking agents, and even other managers probably did not know all of the ins and outs of an industry that I had two decades of experience working in. I decided to put together classes in management, booking, publishing, marketing, and all other aspects of the music business and advertise "The Music Business Course" in the *Washington City Paper*. I could fit eight to ten people in my living room and figured the "course" could be taught for three hours a night on six consecutive Monday nights (Monday was chosen, as it was the least likely night that musicians would have gigs). The response from my first classified ad in the *City Paper* was tremendous. Ten people signed up, and I had a waiting list for a second six–Monday night class.

One of my students in the first class was an attorney named Patrick Clancy. Pat and I had a lot in common. We both attended the University of Maryland, and Pat had represented a number of artists in his capacity as an attorney. One night after class, Pat asked me about Gene Ryder. I had mentioned Gene to my students and had played one of his songs in class. Pat said, "Gene sounded great. What's happening with him?"

I explained that I thought Gene would be signed by a major label but that, to make that happen, I needed to work on it full-time, and I needed money to do that. A few weeks later, Pat phoned me and said, "I think I might have an investor for you." I asked who it was and when I could meet the person. I wasn't thrilled about having someone own part of my management company, but it was a move I needed to make.

A meeting was set up. The amount of money I asked for was nixed by the investor. He offered me one-third of what I asked for, but it was enough money that I could spread it out over a couple of years and survive while taking on management of Gene and looking for other artists to manage. It turned out that having a "partner" in a personal services company was a mistake. While the money invested allowed me to build my company, partnership was still a mistake. Enough said.

Gene put together a band—a very good band. We decided to call the band the Lifters. Now the band had a new identity as Gene Ryder and the Lifters. Our goal was to showcase for record companies in Los Angeles. I already knew that Gene had spent more than a year in Los Angeles and had some very bad experiences out there that left him "depleted." This, hopefully, would be a better experience. After some trials and tribulations during rehearsals in a rented space in Kensington, Maryland, the band was ready for the trip to the West Coast. I had set up three gigs in three different clubs in Los Angeles. The first club was really just a place for the band to get acclimated in the city without record company reps being invited. The next two gigs were the make-or-break gigs: label reps, booking agencies, and publishers were invited, and most showed up. It went well. We had the label interest we came for.

When we returned to Maryland, to say things went haywire would be an understatement. Our drummer, Alan Cornett, was paralyzed when a speeding car ran a stop sign. Our guitarist, Steuart Smith, didn't want to wait too long for the band to be signed. The emotional impact of Alan's injuries took its toll on all of us, but emotional impact was nothing compared to Alan's physical and emotional injuries. We had a solid core of Gene, Peter Bonta, Brian Goddard, and (temporarily) Steuart Smith.

We needed to find a solid drummer, and we did: Chris Salamone. Our temporary agreement with Steuart was running short on time. We were building a sizable fan base, particularly in Northern Virginia, where we had a weekly gig at a club called Quincy's. Interest from record companies hadn't dwindled, but the strongest interest was coming from PolyGram. I was beginning to worry about Gene's temperament. It wasn't as though I had never dealt with a temperamental musician before. It seemed to me to be more than temperament. An attitude had surfaced in Gene that had probably been simmering for years.

Shortly after our agreement with Steuart ran out and he left the band, our bass player, Brian Goddard, also left. As a parent of a five-year-old, Brian felt (justifiably) that his family responsibilities took precedence over being in the band. Brian was replaced by Pete Fields on bass, but Gene had a tougher time auditioning potential lead guitar players.

After auditioning a number of guitarists and not being satisfied by any of them, Gene asked if I knew of anyone who was stellar and had not yet auditioned. I told him about a guitar player I knew named Gantt Kushner. I said I would try to reach him—and I did. He was playing in a club in Ocean City, Maryland, which was about a three-hour drive from where the band was rehearsing in Kensington, Maryland. I was able to reach Gantt, and he told me he would love a shot at playing guitar in Gene's band. Arrangements were made for Gantt to come audition and still have time to make it back to Ocean City for his club gig.

The day of Gantt's audition, he arrived on time. I greeted him in the hallway of Rehearsal Spaces in Kensington. The door to the rehearsal room was open, and Gene peered out and saw Gantt. Gene called out to me to please come speak with him. I excused myself and left Gantt in the hallway. "Tell him to go back to Ocean City," Gene said to me. I responded, "Why, he just drove three hours for a scheduled audition?" Gene said, "He has a beard!" I tried to control my temper. "Gene," I said, "at least audition him. You can always say his playing style wasn't right for you." Gene responded, "No!" That was the first time I felt like saying to Gene, "Take this job and shove it!" It wouldn't be the last time.

I went back out to the hallway and made up an excuse. I might have said to Gantt that Gene was exhausted or that Gene had just auditioned someone else who fit the bill. I didn't tell him that it was "the beard."

PolyGram's interest was peaking. An A & R rep, Jim Lewis, was making regular trips to town to see and hear Gene at Quincy's. By this time, Steuart had been replaced, and the band was in a groove.

Fast-forwarding a bit, Gene was signed to Mercury Records (a PolyGram label). The Lifters were not signed but remained Gene's band. None of the producers Gene requested for the album were available. PolyGram told us that legendary producer/engineer Tom Dowd (Aretha Franklin, Eric Clapton, and dozens of others) was available. Tom lived in Florida. He flew to Maryland for two weeks of rehearsals with Gene. The only thing that foreshadowed Tom not being the right guy to produce Gene was what I call the "metronome syndrome." Tom was a stopwatch-and-metronome guy. Everything needed to be "right on." That's not necessarily the right recipe for rock 'n' roll.

A decision was made to record the album in North Miami, Florida, at the legendary Criteria Recording Studios. The band lineup to begin the recording was Gene, John Jennings on guitar, Pete Fields on bass, Chris Salamone on drums, and Peter Bonta on keyboards and some guitar. Much to Gene's dismay, Tom Dowd was going to not only produce the album but also engineer the sessions. We had what's called a "lockout" on one of Criteria's studios. It was ours 24/7. That assured that all instruments could remain in place, drum mics stayed in position, etc. The folks who ran Criteria were wonderful. Every morning when we arrived, there was a basket of fresh fruit waiting for us. We also had a separate room with a regulation-size pool table for relaxation. Unfortunately, there wasn't much relaxation for us.

After the first day, Gene's attitude was not conducive to any relaxation. I was there for the first two weeks, and those two weeks felt more like I was in no man's land between northern Israel and Hezbollah in southern Lebanon. Tension, tension, tension. I called Jim Lewis at the PolyGram office in New York and told him he needed to come to Florida and talk to Gene. Jim did fly down. I believe he ended up taking Gene fishing. Tom Dowd wasn't working out, and Gene was changing around some of his material. What I was hearing in the studio wasn't as good as the original demos.

After the basic tracks were done, Pete Fields flew home to Virginia. I was already back in D.C. Meanwhile, back in Florida, it was decided that Gene should finish up the album elsewhere. PolyGram told Tom Dowd it wasn't working, and they ended up paying him $25,000 instead of his $50,000 fee. Gene called me from Florida and told me he no longer wanted Pete Fields in the band. He told me to fire Pete. I had already shoveled enough shit for Gene, but now I had to fire Pete.

Gene finished the album in Austin, Texas, with producer Jeff Glixman (Kansas, Gary Moore, Yngwie Malmsteen, the Georgia Satellites, and Black Sabbath) at the helm. When the album was finished, it was decided that the album release party would be at the Bayou in Georgetown. PolyGram would pick up the tab. New players were now on board, including Indiana guitarist

Marc Rogers, keyboard player Patti Clements, and the original bass player, Brian Goddard, along with Gene and Chris.

The album was titled *Last Cigarette and a Blindfold*. If I had been a smoker, all I would have needed was the blindfold. The single released from the album was "Feels Like a Gun." The single was getting some airplay and decent reaction from radio station tip sheets. PolyGram was not very enthusiastic. Although MTV could have been a big help, PolyGram wouldn't pay for a video. The company did put up enough money for tour support for a very short tour. I hired Tim Foster (Neil Young's road manager) and an old friend of mine to go on that tour and keep things under control.

Word filtered back to me that when the band played a club in Philadelphia, the local Philly PolyGram promo person wanted to say hello to Gene in the dressing room. Gene did not allow that to happen. For me, that was the last straw. Gene was now biting the hand that might have fed him. His digressions weren't just hurting him; they were hurting the band, me, and his record company. If Gene's album had been a success and he was a multiplatinum performer, perhaps some of his ego and transgressions could have been forgiven (though not by me). The album was not selling very well. I told the investor in my management company that I was planning to drop Gene. The investor had been privy to the high level of stress caused in no small part by the artist I wanted to drop. By this time, I had signed an act in Detroit, the Shy, and another D.C. act called radioblue (yes, small "r"). All of my eggs weren't in one basket, though Gene was the biggest egg, and I had worked for years to get him signed.

I called Gene and told him I needed to talk with him. I drove to his townhouse in Falls Church. I'm sure Gene thought this was just going to be Oberman telling him that his attitude was destructive and needed to change. I knocked on his door. The door opened, and Gene told me to come in. "You want a beer," he declared more than asked. I said no. "I quit," I said emphatically. "What do you mean, you can't quit. We have a contract," Gene said. I responded, "There's no more indentured servitude in this country," and I walked out the door. I haven't seen or spoken with Gene since that night in 1989.

Fast-forwarding thirty years to September 2019, I asked Brian Goddard to write his thoughts on Gene and what went down. Brian was an original Lifter, quit, and then returned to the band after the album was released.

This is what Brian wrote:

We came close. For a while I thought it was going to happen. Then someone ran a stop sign, and Alan Cornett was in an ambulance on the way to intensive care. Steuart Smith left to produce artists in Nashville. At that point I felt I had to leave too. I was a single dad and my five-year-old son took precedence. By the time I rejoined the band to tour the album in 1988, it was over. The thunder was gone.

Now, thirty-one years later, Michael graciously asked that I share my thoughts about Gene Ryder and the Lifters. It started as a simple thing. Gene wrote great songs and the band recorded great demos. Several major labels were interested. We went to L.A. and crushed a live showcase. We were on track. Then we lost Alan and Steuart, but there was a deeper problem. It was Gene. A great songwriter and lead vocalist, not a great bandleader.

Years later, Gene and I sat on his porch next to Shenandoah National Park. We talked about fishing and baseball and Bob Dylan. We talked about what happened. He knew, and that's all I needed to know.

I find resolution when I think of everything that's happened since. Latest word is Gene is well. Michael is a world-class photographer and has nearly finished this memoir. For twenty years the Eagles have counted on the brilliant guitar work of Steuart Smith. Peter Bonta and his wife built a great life in Italy. And Alan Cornett. After the accident, it took him six years to be able to hit a drum without the stick flying out of his hand. He didn't quit. He's still playing. and his groove is still there. That alone speaks volumes about the man and the true spirit of rock 'n' roll.

In 1985 six lives intersected. We created thunder and took it to L.A. We delivered a knockout punch. Then life interceded.

In the mid-1990s, Gene Ryder surfaced in my life again in a way I never expected. I had been hired to shop a demo of a female singer. She was good but a little too "straight pop" for me to want to manage her. The demo sounded very good, so I was happy to take it to record companies in New

York. Additionally, the singer's father was paying me to try to get her signed to a record deal.

I had an appointment with the senior vice president of A & R for a company that had a great track record with female vocalists. As I was waiting to go into his office, his door opened, and blaring through his speakers was the original Gene Ryder demo I had given him almost a decade earlier. I was floored. "Michael," he says, "I'll be happy to listen to what you've brought me, but first I need to tell you why I'm playing Gene Ryder. I love his songs, and I'm sorry I didn't sign him."

Then he said, "I'd like to get two or three of his songs for one of our acts whose last album sold over 7 million copies." He told me the name of the act, and I knew that Gene's songs would work and that having songs on a multiplatinum album would mean lots of dollars. I am not writing the name of the record company or the name of the act for reasons that will become clear in the next couple of paragraphs.

I told him that PolyGram Music Publishing was Gene's publisher and that they had between sixty and seventy of his songs. "No," he said, "I want brand new material so that we can publish it." I told him I would see what I could do. I played the demo of the female vocalist, and while he thought it was good, it wasn't good enough. I'm sure part of it was because he had Gene Ryder on his mind.

When I returned to D.C., I called Gene's former attorney and asked if he was still in touch with Gene. He asked me why I wanted to know, and I told him the story of what happened in New York. I also told him that I would not reveal the name of the record company or the group. I explained that I had put in years of work with Gene and really had nothing but aggravation to show for it. If Gene had new material, I would get it to the label. But I wanted to be compensated if things went well. I told him that I did not want Gene doing an "end around" and going directly to the label or the group.

Gene's lawyer told Gene the story, and about six weeks later, I received a five- or six-song demo from Gene. I listened to it, and it had none of the magic that Gene's older material had. I made the decision to follow up with the record company and send them Gene's new material while also letting them know my feelings about the songs. The label listened to the demo and agreed with my assessment, and that was the end of the story.

One can't live on "what could have been."

# Musings . . . Jimmy Arnold
# and Southern Soul

IN THE MID-1980S, I MET JIMMY ARNOLD. PETER BONTA INTRODUCED ME to him while I was working with Peter and Gene Ryder on demos in Peter's studio in Fredericksburg, Virginia. Peter gave me a copy of Jimmy's album *Southern Soul*, and I was blown away. I knew of Jimmy's first two albums and what a great banjo player he was. Until I heard *Southern Soul*, I hadn't realized he was also a great fiddler, guitarist, songwriter, and singer.

My first in-person meeting with Jimmy was at the tattoo parlor he owned in Falmouth, Virginia. Jimmy was a rebel. With a teardrop tattooed under one eye, I wondered what his prison connection was (popular belief is that there is a prison connection to that tattoo). Jimmy wanted to know if I wanted to help promote his music career. Although *Southern Soul* struck me as an important album and I saw incredible possibilities for Jimmy and his playing and songwriting, I knew he was a rebel—and rebels tend to be difficult to work with. I told him I would think about it.

A few weeks later, I received a phone call from Jimmy asking if he could pay me a visit at my home in D.C. and play me some more tunes. I was open to that, so I said yes. A few days later, Jimmy and six other guys roared onto Rodman Street (where I lived) on their chopped Harleys. They looked like they had just come off the set of *Hell's Angels on Wheels*. It took only a few minutes for me to feel like the conversation coming from these guys was probably fueled by methamphetamines. I was happy that Ramona, my German shepherd, was by my side.

At one point, Jimmy (whose tattoos were visible running up his neck) said to me, "Hey Mike, wanna see my favorite tattoo?" I wasn't about to say no. Jimmy dropped his pants, and his favorite tattoo was the rear half of a mouse, the front half not visible, as it was going into Jimmy's anus. That pretty much clinched it for me. My rule of thumb was never to work with musicians whom I wouldn't feel comfortable introducing to my mother.

I never saw Jimmy again. Continued severe alcohol abuse weakened him fatally, and at age forty, he was dead. *Southern Soul* was and is among the finest examples of Americana music I've ever heard. Although it's a concept album about the American Civil War told from the viewpoint of Rebel soldiers, it isn't about the causes of the war—it is just one of the finest albums of its genre. If you like Americana music, it was reissued on CD in 1994 and should be heard.

# Musings . . . Richard Harrington . . .
## The *Washington Post*

RICHARD AND I GO WAY BACK IN TERMS OF KNOWING ONE ANOTHER AND being involved with and in the D.C. music scene. When I left music journalism to manage artists, produce concerts, and otherwise be a music business guy, I recommended that Richard take over my weekly music column in the *Washington Star*. I knew his writing style from various "underground" publications he wrote for, and I knew he was a good interviewer. Richard accepted the position at the *Star* and eventually moved over to the *Washington Post* as that paper's pop music critic.

Another thing Richard and I have in common is kind of a warped sense of humor. I think it was in December 1973 when I pulled off a prank on Richard that he and I still laugh about to this day. I was in the lobby of Constitution Hall in D.C., taking a break between afternoon and evening concerts by John McLaughlin and the Mahavishnu orchestra, Richard arrived after the first show had finished, clearly anticipating an evening of sonic fireworks.

Richard approached me and said, "Hey Mike, how is McLaughlin?" I responded, "The concert is over. He poured gasoline on himself and self-immolated onstage as a protest against the war in Vietnam." Richard ran over to a pay phone and called in a story to the paper, saying, "Run this. McLaughlin set himself on fire at Constitution Hall. He's dead. More details to come." I knew that Richard believed me. Buddhist monks were protesting in Vietnam and at times setting themselves ablaze. Richard didn't ask details, nor did I tell him that McLaughlin was a devotee of Chinmoy Kumar Ghose, better known as Sri Chinmoy—not a Buddhist but rather a follower of Hinduism.

After finishing his brief phone call, Richard walked back over to me and asked for more details. I said, "Richard, I was just kidding. It's intermission. He'll be back on in a few minutes." At first, Richard looked angry, but his anger quickly subsided, and a sly grin appeared on his face. "You got me," he chortled. Then he went back to the pay phone, called the newspaper, and told them to "kill" what he had called in a few minutes earlier. That was probably the cruelest prank I ever played on him. I kind of regret what I told him—but not really.

I sat down with Richard in August 2019 and asked to interview him on tape for this book. As pop music writer at the *Washington Post*, Harrington was and is an important figure in the music scene. I have condensed that interview to what you will read below:

Yeah I was in boarding school in New York at the Harvey School during the folk revival, the folk scare of the late 1950s and early 1960s. I actually formed a trio up there when I was in the eighth grade, and one of the other people in the trio was Loudon Wainwright. We were a Kingston Trio type of group, as embarrassing as that might be, but they were very popular. For an eighth grader, I did a very sincere version of "Scotch & Soda." Now imagine that song coming out of an eighth-grade voice. I was also playing guitar in the group. After I graduated, from there I went to a school called the Hotchkiss School. Hotchkiss was a feeder for Yale, Princeton, and Harvard. My father had done that whole process of Hotchkiss to Yale, and I would have done that as well except that I ended up going to jail instead.

I sold a nickel of weed to an undercover agent in 1968. Coincidentally, my very first appearance in the *Washington Post* was in a story about that drug bust. In D.C., I was living above what later became Desperados nightclub. At the time, it was called Groovy's. So, after I sold to the undercover agent, I went before Judge Gerhard A. Gesell, a federal judge who presided over momentous cases in the Watergate scandals, the release of the secret Pentagon Papers, the Iran-Contra affair, and the legalization of abortion. He was not in a good mood and sentenced me to twenty months to five years for possession and sale of a nickel of grass. I pleaded guilty to possession, and they dropped the sale charge. However, the judge was still in a bad mood, and he sent me to Lorton. My lawyer got me out after a little less than six months. Then I spent the next six months on parole. At Lorton, there was medium security and heavy security. I was in medium security. I knew enough people in prison from the street, and they told me the best thing you can do since you already look like Charles Manson is to act like you're crazy. Prisoners know that a crazy person will kill you without looking. I never even had a fight when I was in Lorton because I looked really crazy. Also, I don't think I was a good fantasy fuck. I'm not the kind of guy that anyone would fantasize as a girlfriend so to speak.

So, it's still on the records as a felony, and I'm not allowed to vote. I never looked into getting it expunged. To me it was always a badge to have had that experience. The experience was important to me because when I got out, I never wanted to be in a situation where I wasted time again. I became a workaholic. I knew that I never again wanted to be in a situation where I was locked up and couldn't do anything. When I got out of jail, I had no idea what I wanted to do. That same year, when I got out, I did a little bit of answering phones at the *Washington Free Press*, but I never wrote or did anything like that. Then, somehow or other, I became part of the original staff at *Quicksilver Times*. Famously, one of the writers who wrote there under the name Sal Torre was actually Sal Ferrara, undercover agent with the Central Intelligence Agency.

He wrote some of the more controversial stories in the paper as part of the COINTELPRO (derived from COunter INTELligence PROgram) (1956–1971), a series of covert and, at times, illegal projects conducted by the U.S. Federal Bureau of Investigation (FBI) aimed at surveilling, infiltrating, discrediting, and disrupting domestic political organizations. Later we found out that probably two or three other people who were on the staff (and it was not a big staff) were from the Metropolitan Police Department and the FBI. I've been trying to get the *Washington Post* for years to do a story about it. Sal was a very smart guy, a very smart political operative, and definitely a rabble-rouser. That's why he was there—not only to observe but to incite. I think it's a great story. I'd love to see that story told someplace. In the history of the underground press and Washington, there's very little information about this. Quicksilver is where I first started writing. The first review I ever did was the *Boys in the Band* play at the National Theater, then I did a bunch of music reviews, not very distinguished, I must say.

Then I got tired of the politics at *Quicksilver*, so I decided I wanted to do my own paper and just have it be about the arts. That's when I started *Woodwind*. *Woodwind* was meant to be arts, poetry, graphics, short stories, etcetera. It wasn't a very good paper. It became a good paper when I left and Mike Schreibman took over. I used to do the paper from Mike Schreibman's apartment. Mike was a salesman for the paper at the time, and I did the layout, which is why those early issues look really terrible. After hearing Buzzy Linhart at the Cellar Door, I decided I needed to get out of Washington, so I moved to Boston. I was in Boston for about seven or eight months and really didn't get anything together up there, so I came back to D.C. That's when I started writing for the *Star* when you had left the paper.

At a Who concert at Georgetown University, I actually followed the group Love, Cry, Want and performed before the Who came on. Mike Schreibman, my pal, was the promoter of the show. This was in 1968. There was dickering going on backstage for more money; otherwise, the Who was going to refuse to go on because the Who knew that a lot of people crashed the gates. So, while they were dickering, Mike said, "Can you go out there and grab a guitar?" Of course, I hadn't brought a guitar, so I must have gotten one of Pete Townsend's. I went out there and did about five numbers. I was not well received. I don't even know if the microphone was on. There was no spotlight on me. I think I was just sort of a weird little distraction. Many years later, the first time I interviewed Pete, I said, "Listen Pete, we've had two previous encounters; one was at Georgetown, and the other time was when you played Merriweather Post Pavilion in 1970 and there was traffic going up Route

29 five miles in each direction and somehow or the other I ended up being the emcee of that concert." So, I said to Pete, "You guys were dickering backstage about all the people who had crashed the concert. Thirty-five thousand people showed up, and the venue only held 19,000." Pete said, "We used to do that all the time." He was laughing out loud and said, "We were highway robbers." He was laughing so hard, and from his point, I could see it was pretty funny. They had me go up onstage because they knew me from *Woodwind* magazine and thought I looked like the kind of person who could go up onstage and calm the masses. So, with the Who concert at Georgetown, my career ended fifty years ago because that was the last time I ever played live.

I left the *Star* around the time I met my first wife, Carolyn. On a whim, we moved up near Woodstock. I was freelancing, a few stories for the *Star*, a few stories for the *Chicago Sun-Times*, some stuff for the *New York Times*, but there was just not enough work up there. Now I have no idea why we moved there. There's a lot of things in my life that I have no idea how I ended up in these situations. We had a nice little house in the Catskills, in the mountains. To make enough money to live up there, I sold off a lot of my records, and Carolyn made quilts and pillows and stuff like that. That's one reason we moved back: there just wasn't enough work up there. When I came back to D.C., the first thing I ever wrote for the *Post* was in 1976. My memories of the first thing I wrote for the post was a review of the Osmonds at the Capital Centre. So, I was mostly writing concert reviews. I was also writing freelance features in the "Style" section. Then I became the editor of *Unicorn Times* in 1976 while I was still writing for the *Post*.

I had met Elliott Ryan that year at the Unicorn Coffee House in D.C. I occasionally performed there as a folkie. I had no illusions about the quality of my work. Tom Zito (a *Washington Post* music journalist at the time) always thought for some reason that I was a very good guitar player, but I wasn't. I knew how to play about three or four different things really well. I was not a jammer, I was not a virtuoso. So, I was doing *Unicorn*, selling advertising, doing the designing and layout, and that was my main thing. I had been freelancing on a number of stories for the *Washington Post*. So, in 1982 or 1983, the Newspaper Guild thought that I had been working there for a number of years and found out that I hadn't. Though I had a desk at the *Post* and made a number of assignments, I wasn't a member of the Guild. But they thought that I was a staff writer because I wrote more than many people on the staff. The Guild filed a grievance on my behalf and went before the National Labor Relations Board. The *Post* didn't want to set precedence, so they settled and created a position for me, which was fine. My title became pop music critic. They had never had an official pop music critic at that point. That took me from about 1982 or 1983 to 2008. During that time, I did long-form interviews and reviews and made assignments for others.

Before me, usually no one got hired at the *Post* without having an interview with Ben Bradlee. I never had an interview with Ben Bradlee.

By 2008, the *Post* had already had two major buyouts. There was a third one, and they made it pretty clear that it was time for me to move on and also made it clear that this was going to be the last generous buyout. Depending on how many years you were there, the terms of the buyout were really, really good—plus you could access your pension right away. So, it kind of made sense. So, in 2008, I took the buyout. Since that time, I've done some liner notes for people, and I've done some program notes, like for the Woodstock fiftieth anniversary show at the Warner Theater. Then I started to work on this history of controversial album covers. I did about 300 interviews for that and wrote most of the stuff for a book on those album covers. Then, a little more than five years ago, my sister came down with dementia. I had a book contract, and Dick Bangham had done some fantastic layouts, but when my sister became ill, I became her guardian and conservator. Basically, those first two years were insane adjusting and being her main supervising caregiver and stuff. By the time I was ready to come out of that, the publishing industry had changed, and what was to have been a forty-five to fifty-dollar coffee-table book, about 300 pages or so, suddenly was not in the realm of possibilities. There were controversial aspects of it which two years earlier had been one of its charms and now less so. So, I put it aside, and the last couple of years, until my sister died in May, she needed to have round-the-clock care. Plus, I was helping my friend Mike Schreibman, who was in a difficult situation. So now I'm thinking, the book is already done; I may just put it up online for free because I don't really need the money. I never was going to make a lot of money off it. I was going to make two or three dollars per book. That's not really good for the amount of work I put into it. So, I'd rather put it out for free and have lots of people see it.

Richard lives in Takoma Park, Maryland. He continues to take part in music-related seminars and he (along with me) can be seen in the documentary *Led Zeppelin Played Here*.

# Musings . . . 1998 . . . Floating Dollar . . . Banning Landmines . . . Harris, Earle, Crow, and Carpenter

WAS IT FATE? WAS IT MAGIC? WAS IT TIMING? WAS IT SOMETHING THAT just happened, no rhyme or reason? I walked a few blocks from my house in D.C. to Connecticut Avenue in the Cleveland Park neighborhood. It was a walk I had taken a few times every week for more than twenty years. There were more than a dozen restaurants to choose from, and I made the right choice that night.

When I walked into the door of the restaurant, I immediately spotted a table occupied by several friends. They asked if I would like to join them. I said yes, ordered a drink, and looked at the menu. Before I had a chance to order dinner, one of my friends said, "Michael, will you do some levitation?"—a strange question for most people to hear and answer. My friend knew I was an amateur close-up magician and that one of my best illusions was "floating a dollar bill." I said, "Sure. Will someone lend me a dollar bill or any denomination of paper money?" A friend at the table handed me a bill; I crumpled it up and made it float about a foot off the table—oohs and ahs from those at the table that had never seen me do any magic.

I thought, "Okay, now I can order dinner." Then someone came up from behind me and tapped me on the shoulder. I turned around, and the person who tapped me said, "Unbelievable! Will you come over to my table and make something float?" I said, "No, once is entertainment, twice is education" (a standard line when I didn't want to repeat an illusion). The woman said, "Please, we're celebrating. We just won the Nobel Peace Prize." I thought the woman was crazy, but I was curious.

The woman pointed to the table where she had been sitting. There were several people sitting at the table, including a man in a wheelchair. I asked, in a sarcastic tone, what they had won the Nobel Prize for. She responded, "We're with the International Campaign to Ban Landmines." Now, I was beginning to believe her.

I walked over to her table, and she introduced me to everyone. The man in the wheelchair was Bobby Muller. He had been a combat lieutenant leading a marine infantry platoon. In April 1969, while leading an assault in Vietnam, a bullet entered his chest and severed his spinal cord, leaving him paralyzed from the chest down. From Wikipedia: After returning from Vietnam, Muller became a staunch advocate for veterans' rights and a peace activist. In 1974, he earned his law degree from the Hofstra University School of Law. In the same year, he appeared in the antiwar documentary film *Hearts and Minds*, speaking about his life before, during, and after the Vietnam War. He founded Vietnam Veterans of America (VVA) in 1978 and the Vietnam Veterans of America Foundation (VVAF) in 1980. The VVAF cofounded the International Campaign to Ban Landmines, which won a 1997 Nobel Peace Prize.

So, I floated a dollar bill for them. "How did you do that," seemed to come from all at the table. I just smiled. Someone at the table asked what else I did besides float things. I explained the variety of things I did in the music business.

Bobby Muller began chatting with me. We had some mutual friends in the music field. I'm not certain whether it was Bobby or someone else at the table who said, "We need someone like you to help us produce a benefit concert." That led to further discussions, and I came on board as a consultant for one month.

We set up a meeting at their offices to discuss what they expected me to do and what I needed as compensation for fulfilling their expectations. The concert was to take place at the National Building Museum in D.C. The National Building Museum is housed in the former Pension Bureau building, a brick structure completed in 1887. The vast interior, measuring 316 by 116 feet, has been used to hold inauguration balls; a Presidential Seal is set into the floor near the south entrance. It was to be a $500-per-ticket dinner and concert honoring Senator Patrick Leahy of Vermont.

The lineup for the concert was going to be Emmylou Harris, Steve Earle, Sheryl Crow, Mary Chapin Carpenter, and one or two lesser-known acts. I was excited, as I loved the music of all of the artists. My preproduction duties included arranging for a stage manager and seeing what each of the acts needed in terms of equipment and any other requests they might have. All of the artists were donating their time, but their expenses needed to be taken care of. Mary Chapin Carpenter was no problem, as she lived in the D.C. area. All of the other artists were coming from elsewhere. Air travel needed to be arranged.

Emmylou would have Buddy Miller from her Spyboy band on guitar. She also asked if it was okay and if we would pay for her mother to fly in with her. The organization said yes. There were only a couple of hitches that needed solving. Sheryl Crow's road manger said that we needed to rent "Jerry Jones" guitars for her band. I had never heard of a Jerry Jones guitar. I called music equipment rental facilities from D.C. to New York City, and no place had Jerry Jones guitars to rent. I called the road manager back and said, "I'm sorry, I can get Fender, Gibson, and various other makes of guitars but not what you want." After some hesitation, he agreed to have the band bring their own Jerry Jones guitars.

When my friends found out I was helping to produce the benefit concert, they began calling and typically would say, "Michael, can you get me a guest pass?" My answer was, "If you have $500 and a tuxedo." It was going to be a beautiful black-tie-and-gown evening.

I had recently begun dating a woman named Gwen Hammer. She was finishing up her PhD in Baltimore and when done was going to take a three-month scuba diving trip in the waters off Africa and elsewhere. Gwen also played the bass guitar and loved music. She asked if she could accompany me to the concert. I explained that I was going to be very busy at the event, but I would ask if she could attend. She said to me, "I don't think I ever told you this story about how I kept Steve Earle from being arrested in New York." Gwen proceeded to tell me that Steve was playing a club in Manhattan. Gwen was standing outside the club, and Steve was in the doorway of his tour bus smoking a joint. A New York City policeman saw Steve with the joint and began to approach the bus. Gwen stepped between the cop and the bus and said, "Do you have a search warrant?", to which the cop replied, "I don't need a search warrant." Gwen told the cop that the tour bus was Steve Earle's home and that to enter it, he needed a search warrant. Gwen was making things up as she went along. The cop seemed to believe her and continued walking down the street.

I brought Gwen with me to the event, and she and Steve Earle had a reunion in the dressing room. The only thing that gave me pause the evening of the concert was that the person I was reporting to at the VVAF said that Mary Chapin Carpenter had to be the opening act. I said that wasn't right—there was another artist on the bill other than the headliners who should open. I was told to tell Chapin she was opening. I told her. She wasn't happy about it, but she did open, and the entire show was like being in Americana music heaven.

The last part of my contract with the VVAF was to write a report and give my recommendations as to whether the organization should spend funds to produce a benefit album. I wrote the report, and my recommendation was to nix the album idea. Most benefit compilation albums don't even return the expenses of their production.

When my contract was up with the VVAF, I moved on.

Steve Earle and Gwen Hammer, Dressing Room, International Campaign to Ban Landmines Concert and Dinner in Washington, D.C. (1998)

OBERMAN FAMILY ARCHIVES

# Musings . . . 2011 . . . Smithsonian Folklife Festival Brings Soul to the Washington Mall

RHYTHM-AND-BLUES MUSIC IS A MAJOR PORTION OF THE SOUNDTRACK TO my life. The yearly Smithsonian Folklife Festival is presented on the National Mall in Washington, D.C., by the Smithsonian Center for Folklife and Cultural Heritage and co-sponsored by the National Park Service. Admission is always free. It is always a great multiday event. For me, the 2011 folklife festival was special. One of the themes was rhythm and blues. Many of the artists I grew up listening to would be performing at the festival.

I knew that unlike concerts where you had to buy tickets and there would be security guards keeping you away from the stage, at this festival, I could bring my Nikon and get up close and personal with the artists. Not only would it be ear candy for me, it would also be eye candy.

I was most looking forward to seeing and hearing the Funk Brothers, the Motown Records studio musicians who helped define the sound of some of the best-known rhythm-and-blues recordings between 1959 and 1972. They were like the unsung heroes of Motown music. The core group and a cast of others helped to catapult countless artists to the top of the charts, including the Supremes, the Four Tops, Gladys Knight and the Pips, the Temptations, and Stevie Wonder. They were not credited on an album until Marvin Gaye's 1971 masterpiece *What's Going On*.

With the release of Allan Slutsky's book *Standing in the Shadows of Motown* (1989) and Paul Justman's 2002 documentary film of the same name, the Funk Brothers' definitive contributions to rhythm and blues were finally being recognized. At the festival, I couldn't take my eyes off of Funk Brother Eddie Willis, whose guitar riffs brought chills to my spine. Onstage, his playing looked effortless. It was as if his guitar was a natural extension of his body and soul.

Guest vocalist with the Funk Brothers at the festival was Kim Weston. Weston had a number of high-charting hits with Motown in the 1960s, including "Take Me in Your Arms (Rock Me a Little While)" and "It Takes Two," a duet with Marvin Gaye.

Among the other artists I was drawn to at the festival was Mabel John. In 1959, she began her recording career in Detroit, becoming the first female vocalist signed to Berry Gordy's Tamla label. Her 1960 release "Who Wouldn't Love a Man Like That" was her most successful release with the label. Beginning in 1962, she spent several years backing Ray Charles as a Raelette and also working with her brother, the famous rhythm-and-blues singer "Little Willie" John.

In 1993, Mabel John had become Dr. Mabel John when she received a doctorate in divinity. In 1994, she received a Pioneer Award from the Rhythm & Blues Foundation.

I was in soul heaven—Martha Reeves (without the Vandellas), the Dixie Cups ("Chapel of Love"), and so many other Motown and Stax-Volt artists—and I felt like I was at the Apollo Theater in the 1960s, except it was 2011, and a number of the artists I was seeing and hearing were now in their seventies and eighties. Not one of them sounded like they had lost an octave since the height of their careers.

Eddie Willis, Motown Funk Brother at Smithsonian Folklife Festival, 2011, Washington, D.C.
PHOTO BY MICHAEL OBERMAN

Kim Weston at Smithsonian Folklife Festival, 2011, Washington, D.C.
PHOTO BY MICHAEL OBERMAN

Mabel John at Smithsonian Folklife Festival, 2011, Washington, D.C.
PHOTO BY MICHAEL OBERMAN

Martha Reeves (of Martha and the Vandellas) at Smithsonian Folklife Festival, 2011, Washington, D.C.
PHOTO BY MICHAEL OBERMAN

# Musings ... My Current
# Life as a Photographer

AROUND 2001, I MOVED FROM WASHINGTON, D.C., TO COLUMBIA, Maryland. Shortly after the move, I was walking around one of the lakes in Columbia when a great blue heron landed nearby. I had seen only photos of herons before. Seeing one land close to me was an epiphany. I always had an interest in photography, dating back to my time as a copyboy at the *Evening Star.* The darkroom at the newspaper was a great place to get away from my boss and the sometimes harried life in the newsroom. I became friends with some of the staff photographers and sometimes wished I knew more about photography.

In the mid-1970s, I was given a Nikon film camera and began to photograph people, places, and things. When I was managing the Rosslyn Mountain Boys, a photographer was hired to shoot our first album cover. The photos she took bordered between bad and terrible. I took the proverbial "bull by the horns" and set up my own shoot with the group. I shot black-and-white film and was happily surprised at how good the photos came out. They were good enough that the front and back covers of the LP were my shots. Dick Bangham, an artist for Adelphi Records (our label for that first LP), took my photos and airbrushed them into stylized color shots, and the album was released looking very nice.

By the time I had moved to Columbia, digital photography was beginning to take off. I decided to make the switch and bought my first digital camera, a Fujifilm FinePix S602 Zoom. It was a very good camera for landscapes and portraits but not for action shots. I wanted to capture birds in flight. The Fuji, being a high-end point-and-shoot, suffered from shutter lag. I needed a digital single-lens reflex camera. I decided on Nikon, as I still had some Nikon lenses from my "film camera days." My first Nikon was the D70. In the years since, I have had a Nikon D200, D300, D7100, and D600 and my two current Nikons: the D500 for nature and wildlife and the mirrorless Z6 for landscapes and portraits.

In 2007, a photo I had taken of a dragonfly on a water lily was named one of the top photos of the year by The Nature Conservancy and *Parade* magazine. The photo appeared in *Parade* that year. I decided to make a go of nature and wildlife photography. It has been very fulfilling. There are no temptations when I'm in the field photographing wildlife. No woodpecker or eagle is going to offer me drugs. No groupie is going to knock on the dressing room door (there don't tend to be any dressing rooms in a wetland or wildlife refuge).

My photos have appeared in books, magazines, and galleries and on websites and have been displayed in numerous museums in the United States, Canada, and elsewhere. Some of my photos grace kiosks in U.S. national parks. Nature photography gives me as many thrills as I had in the music business. I also began teaching my craft fifteen years ago. Cameras and smartphones have become so good that almost anyone can take a good photo. There is still a line between taking a good photo and knowing how to take a great photo. Ego notwithstanding, I have crossed that line.

My photography website is www.MichaelObermanPhotography.com.

# Musings . . . Ending This Memoir

I KNEW WHEN I BEGAN WRITING THIS BOOK HOW I WOULD END IT. EDDIE Kalicka, my friend and mentor, passed away in October 2016. I was asked by his family to write and read a eulogy at his funeral. This is the eulogy:

> I met Eddie Kalicka in December of 1967. I was twenty years old and a music columnist for the *Evening Star* newspaper. Eddie was a record promotion man at Schwartz Brothers Distributors and almost two decades older than me. That was around the time of the Berkeley Free Speech movement when Mario Savio said, "Never trust anyone over thirty." I trusted Eddie the moment I met him.
>
> Eddie was a promotion man without any hype. He promoted artists and records he believed in, from Rod Stewart to Bonnie Raitt. From Randy Newman to Little Feat. It certainly helped that Eddie was promoting Warner Bros. Records, as they were a company that signed a lot of quality acts.
>
> Eddie and I became close friends. We each had a dog from the same litter. He had Leroy, and I had Jason. Let me digress for a moment. My friendship with Eddie was a package deal; his package was his wife Betty and his five children: Paul (only a year younger than me), Linda, Renee, Faye, and Danny.
>
> Eddie and Betty's house in Silver Spring became a meeting place on Fridays for a bunch of us in the music business. It was a good thing that Betty was working on Fridays. She would come home from work and find that most of her tuna salad, deviled eggs, and other food was gone. Part of the Friday ritual was smoking a little reefer, getting the munchies, and, well, eating everything we could find. It helped that Betty was and still is a great cook.

When Eddie left the music business and moved to Los Angeles to work in and learn the T-shirt business, I was upset, but at that time my brother was living in L.A. and I was managing musical artists, so I found myself in Los Angeles quite a bit. Whenever I saw Eddie in California, I knew that he longed to be back in Maryland—and he did move back to Maryland. Eddie opened Tasty Shirts, a company now run by his son Danny Kalicka.

Over the years, Eddie and Betty and I had some great trips together, traveling kinds of trips I mean—twice to Mexico, once to Margarita Island off the coast of Venezuela.

During all that time, I never met anyone who didn't like or love Eddie. As we grew older, I began to feel that Eddie was immortal. We hiked part of the Everglades when he was eighty and I was sixty-one. His stamina was unending. I had to occasionally say, "Eddie let's sit down and just look at the alligators." Florida was special to Eddie and Betty. Eddie in particular loved the Wakodahatchee Wetlands, home to many species of birds and some huge alligators.

Eddie also loved the American Southwest, from Chaco Canyon in New Mexico to the Grand Canyon.

When I found out that Eddie had cancer, I was certain that if anyone could kick that disease to the curb, it would be Eddie. During his treatment and after he decided on home hospice care, Eddie was never alone, Betty was always there, and Eddie's five children rotated staying with Eddie and Betty at their condo. Of course, his grandchildren were there whenever they could be, and friends like Geoff Edwards, myself, and others came to be with him: make him smile, get him stoned, and hope for the best.

I last saw Eddie Sunday night. I went into his bedroom, and Paul woke him; he opened his eyes, and we held hands. His hands were warm and felt good. I knew it would be the last time I would see him. Eddie passed peacefully. He left his mark on so many people. In the Washington-area music scene, Eddie was and still is a legend. Legends never die. Eddie is still with all of us who knew and loved him and even with people who never met him but still knew of him. Eddie is gone but will never be forgotten.

Eddie Kalicka at age 80, Loxahatchee (North Everglades, Florida)
PHOTO BY MICHAEL OBERMAN

# INDEX

# Text Permissions

Grateful acknowledgment is made to the following for permission to use previously published and unpublished material:

*Claire M.:* E-mail correspondence.

*Brian Goddard:* Essay on Gene Ryder.

*Mark C. Nelson, Kevin Avery, and Gary Groth at Fantagraphics Books:* Excerpt from *Everything Is an Afterthought: The Life and Writings of Paul Nelson* by Kevin Avery. (Avery, Kevin, *Everything Is an Afterthought: The Life and Writings of Paul Nelson*, published by Fantagraphics Books, 2011. Reprinted with the permission of Mark C. Nelson, Kevin Avery, and Fantagraphics Books.)

*Rich McManus:* Blog entry on the Rosslyn Mountain Boys: http://furious.com/perfect/rosslyn mountainboys.html

*Gene Wishnia:* Interview with Michael Oberman.

*While every reasonable effort has been made to secure permission for materials reproduced in this work, we offer apologies for any instances in which this was not possible and for any inadvertent omissions.*